SAN DIEGO PUBLIC LIBRARY

LIBRARY RULES

TIME: — Books may be kept 14 days, unless dated otherwise.

RENEWALS: — Books may be renewed once at the agency where borrowed, unless on reserve. Bring book with you.

FINES: — Five cents a day will be charged for each book kept overtime.

DAMAGES: — *Injury to the book from tearing, penciling, unusual soiling or other ill-usage, will be charged to the card owner. Please report to us when a mutilated book is issued to you.*

CARDS — ALWAYS BRING YOUR CARD WITH YOU.

SUTTER'S FORT: GATEWAY TO THE GOLD FIELDS

THE AMERICAN FORTS SERIES
as planned by Stewart H. Holbrook

GUNS AT THE FORKS
(Forts Duquesne and Pitt)
by Walter O'Meara

LOUISBOURG: KEY TO A CONTINENT
by Fairfax Downey

SUTTER'S FORT: GATEWAY TO THE GOLD FIELDS
by Oscar Lewis

★   ★   ★

Other Subjects in Preparation

FORT LARAMIE
Remi Nadeau

VINCENNES
August Derleth

FORT NIAGARA
Robert West Howard

THE FORTS OF MACKINAC
Walter Havighurst

FORTS OF THE UPPER MISSOURI
Robert G. Athearn

Books by Oscar Lewis

★

SUTTER'S

Gateway to the Gold Fields

FORT

By Oscar Lewis

PRENTICE-HALL, INC. *Englewood Cliffs, N.J.*

Sutter's Fort: Gateway to the Gold Fields
by Oscar Lewis

Library of Congress Catalog Card Number: 66-12566

Printed in the United States of America

T 87920

PRENTICE-HALL INTERNATIONAL, INC., *London*
PRENTICE-HALL OF AUSTRALIA, PTY., LTD., *Sydney*
PRENTICE-HALL OF CANADA, LTD., *Toronto*
PRENTICE-HALL OF INDIA (PRIVATE) LTD., *New Delhi*
PRENTICE-HALL OF JAPAN, INC., *Tokyo*

PREFACE

In the story of the evolution of the Far West, Sutter's Fort occupied a position of importance for only a scant ten years. But the decade during which it flourished—that is, from 1839 to 1849—chanced to be the most active and the most decisive in shaping the future course of events in the history of the entire western third of the nation. Little of consequence took place during that period that was not in some degree influenced by happenings at the fort.

On the day in 1839 when thirty-six-year-old John Augustus Sutter first reached California, there was almost nothing to indicate that this remote and neglected Mexican possession was about to awaken from its long sleep. To all outward appearances the province was little changed from what it had been when the first missions and presidios were established there nearly seventy years earlier. By far the greater part of its area was still an unexplored wilderness, sparsely populated by bands of unenterprising native Indians and with members of the ruling race occupying a series of tiny coastal settlements spaced a day's travel apart, from the vicinity of San Francisco Bay to San Diego.

California's chief industry was cattle-raising. Until quite recently its contacts with the outside world had been confined almost entirely to the Boston trading ships that from time to time dropped anchor in one or another of the few harbors to barter manufactured goods for hides and tallow produced by the local rancheros. The inhabitants were ruled over by officials appointed by the central government at Mexico City where a few squads of ill paid and badly equipped soldiers provided their only protection against hostile Indians or foreign aggressors.

From 1769, when Father Junípero Serra founded the first California mission, until fifty-three years later (when Mexico gained its independence from Spain), the friars of the Franciscan order had played the leading part in the development of the new land. At each of the missions—which eventually reached a total of twenty-one—the natives were given religious training and taught to till the soil, tend the mission herds and perform other useful tasks. But, with the passage of the secularization act by the Congress of Mexico in 1833, that era had gradually drawn to a close. The mission lands were thrown open to settlement and the neophytes were turned loose to shift for themselves, many of them returning to their ancestral hunting grounds and resuming their old way of life.

At the time of Sutter's arrival, the secularization of the missions, which had long been the mainstay of the economy of the province, had been completed. The coastal hills and valleys from San Diego north to Sonoma were occupied by huge cattle ranches, most of them many thousands of acres in extent. The chief towns were Monterey, the capital; Yerba Buena, on San Francisco Bay; Santa Barbara, and the pueblos of Los Angeles and San Diego; the majority were small clusters of adobe buildings with whitewashed walls and tile roofs huddled about a central plaza.

There arose among the Californians a growing dissatisfaction for what they regarded an indifference and neglect by the home government: they were given no proper voice in the management of their own affairs; burdensome restrictions were placed on their dealings with foreigners; both the number and quality of soldiers sent to protect them were woefully inadequate. This situation was further complicated by dissension among the Californians themselves which had resulted in frequent (but, fortunately, nearly always bloodless) revolutions and counter-revolutions, as first one faction and then another sought to seize control of the government.

Meanwhile a new group had begun to play an increasingly important role in the affairs of the province. These were the foreign-born merchants, most of whom were Americans or Englishmen who had established trading posts at the seaport towns and provided the ranch owners and others with needed goods from abroad in exchange for the products of the country. In a number of instances these traders had taken out Mexican citizenship, married the daughters of leading local families and become influential members of their communities.

The middle and late 1830's had seen still another development, one that was causing growing concern to the authorities at Monterey and Mexico City. This latest problem was caused by the Yankee hunters and trappers who were beginning to journey over the newly opened overland trails. The newcomers were typical products of the frontier, accustomed to come and go as they pleased and resentful of any attempt to restrict their freedom of movement. Hence, they showed no inclination to obey the laws barring foreigners from the province, and the California officials lacked means of expelling them by force.

Such was the uneasy situation in California at the time of Sutter's arrival. But there were indications, too, that events of much broader significance were likely to take place in the near future. Few believed that Mexico's hold on its remote and weakly controlled province could be maintained indefinitely and the much debated question there, and elsewhere, was into whose hands the prize would fall. A number of nations were openly or covertly laying plans toward that end. Among them were England and France, both of whom were ambitious to extend their holdings in the New World; Russia, who for several decades had maintained a settlement on California's northern coast; and, finally, the United States, whose leaders made no secret of their desire to push the country's borders to the shore of the Pacific.

On the day when John Sutter first set foot on California soil, all was outwardly calm. The Swiss adventurer had no fore-knowledge of the series of dramatic happenings that, during the next decade, would completely change this former Mexican province and focus on it the wondering attention of the rest of the world. Nor did he foresee the part he was to play in bringing such changes about.

Oscar Lewis

San Francisco

1966

CONTENTS

SUTTER'S FORT: GATEWAY TO THE GOLD FIELDS

one

A Young Man from Burgdorf

1 GUNFIRE IN THE WILDERNESS

As the ships of the little armada left the shelter of Yerba Buena Cove and met the roll and pitch of the open bay, they could hardly have presented an impressive sight to the group that had gathered on the beach to witness their departure.

There were three vessels in all, the *Isabella* and *Nicholas,* both small open-deck schooners normally used to transport hides and other goods between the village and the ranchos on the lower bay, and, drawing up in the rear, a sixteen-foot ship's pinnace manned by four Hawaiian oarsmen.

The errand on which the ships were setting out was looked on by the spectators as a harebrained scheme; it is only in retrospect that it takes on significance as a major step in the evolution of the Far West. For that August morning in 1839 saw the beginning of a movement that was to open to settlement California's interior valley, and to build there a frontier outpost around which during the next dozen years events—first of local, then of national, and finally of world-wide import—would revolve.

In charge of the expedition was hustling, talkative, thirty-seven-year-old John Augustus Sutter, German-born of Swiss parents, who had arrived in San Francisco bay less than a month earlier.

He had had his seemingly foolhardy project approved by the authorities at Monterey, and was now setting forth to establish the first outpost of civilization in the interior of the remote Mexican province of California.

1

The two sailing ships had been chartered from Yerba Buena's pioneer trading firm of Spear and Hinckley. They had been loaded with provisions, tools, weapons and other materials, and carried as passengers a number of Swiss and German artisans and about a dozen Kanakas. The men had all been recruited in the Sandwich Islands and brought to California to help found the projected colony.

The small fleet made its way up the San Francisco and San Pablo bays, passed through the Carquinez Strait into Suisun bay and, after several days of searching through the maze of estuaries in the Sacramento-San Joaquin delta, finally located and entered the channel of the Sacramento. Then for eight days the party, one of the first to navigate the waters of the river, pushed up-stream against the sluggish current. Sutter and his four Kanakas led the little procession in the pinnace, exploring the many sloughs and inlets and tying bits of colored cloth to the over-hanging boughs of trees to mark the channel for those who followed.

Each evening after the party had gone ashore to spend the night Sutter explored the surrounding countryside, observing the contour of the land and examining soil and vegetation and wild-life, searching for an ideal spot for his future colony.

Toward the end of the second week the expedition had reached the mouth of the Feather River, a day's travel upstream from present-day Sacramento. There the crews of the chartered ships, along with some of Sutter's own men, grew alarmed at the thought of venturing farther into the wilderness and demanded that they be allowed to turn back. Sutter was anxious to continue the exploration; however, faced by an incipient mutiny, he re-luctantly gave the order to head downstream again. At the junc-tion of the Sacramento and American rivers, which was reached the next day, the party turned into the last-named stream and after proceeding up the channel for a little distance Sutter or-dered that the boats be landed and their cargoes discharged. Of the places he had seen on the journey up from the bay this was the one that had pleased him most.

The intrusion of this numerous group of white men into their ancestral hunting grounds had not gone unobserved by the Indians of the valley. At one of the party's overnight stopping places a crowd of more than a hundred warriors, decked out in feathered headdresses and with their bodies daubed with brilliant colored paints, had gathered about the campsite. At their approach the men of the Sutter party, alarmed at the shouting, gesticulating throng, had hurriedly taken up their weapons and prepared to defend themselves. Sutter, however, bruskly ordered them to withhold their fire. Then, himself unarmed, he approached the nearest of the Indians, calling a friendly greeting. He addressed them in Spanish, knowing that among their number were likely to be some who had been wards of the padres at one or another of the California missions and so would understand that language.

In response to his greeting, several warriors stepped forward. To them Sutter explained that he and his party's presence in the valley was a peaceful one, that they planned to settle there permanently, and that once the colony had been established, the Indians would be welcome to visit them. The Spanish-speaking braves passed that reassuring message on to the others, whereupon their hostile demonstration ended. The Indians presently withdrew and, according to one account of the episode, the night passed without further incident, except for the discomfort caused by swarms of ravenous mosquitos.

On the day Sutter's party made its final stop another numerous band of natives gathered on the river bank and looked on while the supplies in the boats were unloaded and taken ashore. Among the material Sutter had brought with him were several small brass cannon. Before the party retired for the night he had these, along with the other weapons, placed in a conspicuous spot in front of the tents. The night passed without incident. Next morning as the *Isabella* and *Nicholas* were preparing to leave on the return trip to the bay, Sutter (who all his life had a liking for military display) ordered a nine-gun salute fired in honor of those aboard the departing ships.

This was the first time the sound of cannon fire had been heard in the valley, and as the explosions reverberated across the countryside their effect was startling. Many years later, William Heath Davis, then the youthful captain of the *Isabella*, described the scene:

> As the heavy report of the guns and the echoes died away, the camp of the little party was surrounded by hundreds of Indians, who were excited and astonished at the unusual sound. A large number of deer, elk, and other animals on the plains were startled, running to and fro, stopping to listen, their heads raised, full of curiosity and wonder, seemingly attracted and fascinated to the spot, while from the interior of the adjacent wood the howls of wolves and coyotes filled the air, and immense flocks of water fowl flew wildly about the camp.
>
> Standing on the deck of the "Isabel" . . . this remarkable sight . . . made an indelible impression on my mind. This salute was the first echo of civilization in the primitive wilderness soon to become . . . a great agricultural and commercial center.

2   FAILURE AND FLIGHT

John Sutter's presence at the confluence of the Sacramento and American rivers on that August morning in 1839 was the culmination of a plan that had taken definite shape only two or three years earlier, but the origin of which, and the influences and pressures that had brought it about, dated from a much earlier period.

In order to make clear the nature of these influences and pressures it is necessary to go back and sketch some of the circumstances that played a part in shaping Sutter's life up to the time he reached California.

He was born of Swiss parents in the German village of Kandern, a few miles beyond the Swiss border, on February 15, 1803. His grandfather, Johann Jakob Sutter, had been a foreman at a Kandern papermill, and his father, Johann Jakob, Jr., had succeeded to that position. The grandson was the eldest child and so might logically have inherited both the family name and the family occupation. He did neither. Instead, he was christened Johann August and, after brief schooling at his native village and a year at an academy in Neuchâtel, was apprenticed to a firm of printers and publishers in the city of Basel.

Evidently young Johann found neither the work nor the city to his liking, for after serving out his apprenticeship he left both. We next hear of him working as a clerk in a draper's shop in the town of Aarburg, some forty miles south of Basel. There he met his future wife, Annette Dübeld, and followed her to the neighboring town of Burgdorf, where the pair were married on October 24, 1826. The ceremony was performed none too soon, for on the day following the wedding the bride presented him with a child, a son, whom they named Johann August, Jr.

Having become a husband and a father all within the space of a few hours, Sutter, who was then twenty-three, seems to have made a conscientious effort to discharge his newfound obligations. For a time he worked as a clerk in the shop of a Burgdorf grocer. Then, with the backing of his widowed mother-in-law, who was evidently a woman of some means, he set up in business on his own, becoming chief owner of the Johann August Sutter Company, dealers in drygoods.

That venture proved unfortunate. So little did it prosper that at the end of four years its manager and principal owner found himself heavily in debt and facing bankruptcy. This had been brought about by a number of circumstances: by depressed economic conditions in the Burgdorf district at that time, by the peculations of one of his partners, and the refusal of Mrs. Dübeld to continue giving financial support to her son-in-law. These all played a part in the outcome, yet there can be little doubt that the primary cause of the debacle lay in the character and temperament of Sutter himself. For in this, his first serious tussle with the realities of commercial life, he exhibited precisely those qualities that in later years were time and again to carry him to and beyond the brink of disaster.

In all matters where his personal fortunes were involved, Sutter was an unswerving optimist. Because of his conviction that whatever he put his hand to was sure to be a shining success, he could never abide the period of waiting that more patient men took as a matter of course; with him, the benefits that might reasonably be expected in the future must be enjoyed today. Under prudent management the Burgdorf shop might have survived and even have prospered moderately. But that was never Sutter's way; whatever he undertook must be carried out on a grand scale, preferably with a touch of the dramatic. Thus the young man's expansive nature, his personal extravagancies—fine clothes and food and, for the time and place, lavish entertaining—plus his habit of granting over-liberal credit on the one hand and incurring recklessly large debts on the other, all contributed to the inevitable collapse. In the spring of 1834, Johann August Sutter & Company, which had been in serious difficulties for some time, was forced to close its doors. The firm's liabilities were listed at more than 50,000 francs and its assets at only about 15,000 francs.

When that blow fell, Sutter faced the alternatives of arrest and trial, with a strong likelihood of being sentenced to a prison term as a debtor, or of putting himself beyond the reach of the law. He chose the latter course. Working rapidly and in secret, he gathered up whatever cash could be salvaged from his disintegrating business, applied for and was granted a passport from the district court at Burgdorf, said a hasty good-bye to his wife and children (who by then numbered four), and slipped unobtrusively out of town.

He made his way across France to Le Havre, intent on putting the width of the Atlantic Ocean between himself and his creditors.

3 ST. CHARLES, SANTA FE, WESTPORT

On his travels from Switzerland to California Sutter followed a roundabout route.

He reached New York in the summer of 1834 and, perhaps fearing that he might not yet be beyond reach of the stringent Swiss laws, set off at once for the western frontier. His destination was the Missouri country, then a land of bright promise to thousands of young men all over central Europe. This had come about because of a widely read book by one Gottfried Duden, which pictured the region as a sort of latter-day Eden. Duden's romantic exaggerations had been avidly read in Teutonic countries and were credited with having helped set off a migration that by the mid-1830's had led to the establishment of a number of populous German-speaking colonies in the upper Mississippi Valley.

It was with one or another of such immigrant groups that Sutter was associated during the nearly four years he spent in the Middle West. Although in the several autobiographical passages he wrote or dictated during his later years he passed over that period with a few noncommittal sentences, there is evidence that it played a by no means negligible part in setting the pattern for his future life. For one thing, it was there that the thought first took shape in his mind of someday founding a colony over which he himself would have complete control. And, while there must have been times when the likelihood of his ever realizing that ambition seemed remote indeed, he never completely abandoned the idea.

Such funds as the free-spending young man carried with him to the frontier were soon exhausted, and in order to support himself he tried his hand at a number of ventures. For a time he operated a farm in the St. Charles area outside St. Louis. When that experiment failed to yield a livelihood, he joined a group of German emigrants on a trading expedition to Santa Fe. His stock-in-trade, which he hoped to sell at a profit to the Mexicans and Indians of the Southwest, consisted of "old pistols, cheap trinkets and old German student jackets," which he had bought—with borrowed money—in St. Louis pawnshops.

This 1835 expedition to Santa Fe, together with a second more elaborate trip he made the following year, form one of the most controversial chapters of Sutter's uncommonly contentious career. In his garrulous later years he pointedly steered clear of the subject—a sure indication that the role he had played reflected no credit on himself. Others who, either as participants or observers, had firsthand knowledge of what had transpired were not so reticent. However, because in most cases their own interests were involved, the testimony of such witnesses is open to the suspicion of having been warped by personal spite or malice.

In any event, Sutter's first trading venture seems to have been
a success. Life on the trail was varied and interesting, his traveling companions were congenial, and after his party reached Santa
Fe his dubious merchandise found a ready market at high prices.
He returned to Missouri full of enthusiasm for this lucrative new
way of life and at once began laying plans for another expedition
the following year, this time with himself as its leader. He appears to have had no trouble enlisting recruits from among acquaintances in and about St. Charles, for by mid-April of 1836
he was again en route to Santa Fe.

This time the party numbered fifteen, most of whom were German youths recently arrived from the fatherland. The members
were joint owners of merchandise valued at $14,000, nearly all
of which, including Sutter's share, had been bought on credit.
With their goods loaded on four ox-drawn carts and themselves
mounted on horses or mules, the little group traveled first to Independence, then to Council Grove. There they joined a caravan
of about eighty wagons and began the long trek toward the
Southwest.

Again Sutter found the weeks on the trail a pleasant experience. However, on reaching Santa Fe he and his companions
learned that conditions there were no longer what they had been
a year earlier. Goods that had been in brisk demand were now
almost impossible to sell at any price. One reason for the slack
times was that Indian uprisings had caused many of the mines
in the region to shut down, sharply reducing the flow of gold
into the town. Another reason was that by then traders from the
Missouri frontier had discovered that competition from the newly
formed Republic of Texas had broken their monopoly on the
Santa Fe trade.

The Missouri group found business so bad that on August 22
they dispatched a courier back to St. Louis telling of the "de-
lapidated state" of the Santa Fe economy and urging that plans
to send another party into the region the following year be abandoned. The letter was published in the *Missouri Republican* for
October 22; one of its twenty-six signers was "J. A. Sutter."

Up to that point the record is fairly clear; it is on the question of what happened next that the testimony differs. Did Sutter, as he himself claimed, share the losses sustained by other members of the St. Charles group? Or did he, as some of their number have charged, secretly sell their joint property, pocket the proceeds, and return posthaste to Missouri, leaving his former partners marooned and all but penniless at Santa Fe? The question remains unanswered, and at this late date it seems unlikely that the truth will ever be known.

What is known is that soon after his return from Santa Fe, Sutter left St. Charles and moved to Westport, a frontier settlement on the site of present-day Kansas City. His stay there was brief. By the spring of 1838 he was again on the move; this time he headed due west.

4 BY LAND AND SEA

During the time that elapsed between Sutter's landing at New York in 1834 and his departure for the Pacific Coast nearly four years later, a number of important changes took place in the young man's attitude toward himself and the world about him.

He had entered the country furtively, a bankrupt ex-shopkeeper who was fleeing from the wrath of his creditors, leaving a wife and four young children behind. The man who was leaving Westport and pushing farther into the wilderness was known to acquaintances there as "Captain" John A. Sutter, a seasoned frontiersman who, before migrating to America, had been an officer in the service of Charles X of France, and who was on his way to establish a colony in the Mexican province of California, over which he intended to rule as a benevolent despot.

The new role he had assumed was not entirely because of Sutter's personal vanity. Circumstances had made it necessary, or at any rate highly desirable, that on reaching the United States he assume a new identity. He had arrived in a strange country, among people who knew nothing of his background, and it was natural that he would wish to keep them in ignorance of certain phases of his recent past. To one of his self-dramatizing nature, moreover, what others might have looked on merely as a prudent

move, became to him a challenging opportunity. Since it was desirable that he invent a fictitious past, why not make it one of
which a man could be proud? Perhaps one reason for his decision
to raise himself several notches on the social scale was that during his stay at St. Charles he had associated with a group of
young German emigrants of education and established family
backgrounds. In their presence he could scarcely have been expected to play the part of a social inferior.

Sutter's fanciful past was hardly the invention of a moment;
in all likelihood it was a matter of slow growth. Having once
embarked on a course of deception, there could be no turning
back; each false claim had to be supported and bolstered by
others. Thus his father, Johann Jakob Sutter, Jr., the hard-working foreman at the Kandern papermill, became, in the son's
romanticized version, "a clergyman of the Lutheran faith." He
himself, so his story ran, had been educated at a military academy
at Thun—where one of his fellow students was Louis Napoleon,
the future emperor of France—and on completing his training
there he had "entered as a cadet at Berne, Switzerland, and
served in the army until I went to America." Playing his new
role to the hilt and daily finding it more to his taste, Sutter conferred on himself the rank of captain, and along with it cultivated
the military bearing appropriate to one who had been an officer
of King Charles' elite Swiss Guard.

The Missouri-Santa Fe period marked another important turning point in Sutter's career; that is, his decision to locate in California the colony he planned someday to establish. By his own
account, the person from whom he first learned of the attractions
of that then little-known land was Charles Beaubien, whom he
had met during the second of his trading expeditions to Santa
Fe. Beaubien was a French-Canadian and former priest who was
then serving as *alcalde* of the town of Taos. He had earlier spent
several years at the West Coast Mexican province, and his praise
of its beauty, fertility and matchless climate qualifies him as one
of the earliest and most persuasive of California's boosters.

Sutter's decision to make his way to the new Utopia was hastened by the failure of the general merchandise store he had

purchased (some said with funds that rightfully belonged to his partners in the Santa Fe trading venture) soon after his arrival in Westport. It was following this, his second business failure in less than six years, that he embarked on the next stage of his long journey westward. He rode out of Westport early in April, 1838, accompanied by a single companion, a fellow Swiss named Wetler. Both men were mounted on the small but sturdy Indian ponies of the region and carried their joint belongings on the back of a pack-horse.

In 1838 one did not lightly undertake a trip across the nearly two thousand miles of uninhabited and largely unexplored country that lay between the Mississippi Valley and the Pacific. Individuals and small groups who embarked on that journey usually attached themselves to one of the parties sent out each spring by the fur traders, carrying supplies to the hunters and trappers in the Rocky Mountain area and bringing back furs that had been gathered since the previous trip.

Sutter and his companion followed this practice by joining the expedition of John Jacob Astor's old firm, the American Fur Company, which left Independence on April 22. It was a large train, numbering seventeen loaded carts, about two hundred horses and mules, and upwards of sixty men. The slow-moving caravan arrived at Fort Laramie on June 2 and continued on to the point of rendezvous near the headwaters of the Wind River in western Wyoming, which was reached some three weeks later.

Beyond that point lay the hunting grounds of the American firm's chief competitor, the Hudson's Bay Company, and it was mainly with the help of officers of the last-named organization that Sutter was able to accomplish the second and most difficult part of his long trip. This time he was accompanied only by an Indian youth who served as companion and guide. "Under a good many dangers and other troubles," he wrote nearly two decades later, "I . . . passed the Different forts or trading posts of the Hudsons Bay Compy. and arrived at the Mission at the Dalls [Dalles] on Columbia River." From The Dalles he, with several others, continued on to the Willamette Mission. There he spent several weeks resting from his exertions, then made a leisurely trip by canoe down the river to the Company's headquarters at Fort Vancouver.

Visitors were then a rarity at that remote outpost, and the newcomer's high spirits and genial disposition, backed by his by then well-rehearsed story of social and military triumphs at home, made him a favored guest at the fort. So agreeable did he make himself that the commander at the post, James Douglas, urged him to remain with them until spring. Sutter, however, had other plans. The California colony had come to occupy all his thoughts, and he was impatient of anything that might delay putting it into effect. It had been his hope that on reaching Fort Vancouver he could find a ship on which he could travel down the coast to San Francisco bay. But no such vessel was then in port nor was one likely to appear for some time. However, the Company's bark, the *Columbia,* was about to sail for the Hawaiian Islands, and Sutter took passage on her, believing that at Honolulu he would have no trouble finding a ship that would carry him to California.

In that expectation he was again disappointed. No California-bound ship was in the Honolulu harbor when the *Columbia* arrived on December 8, nor did one appear for many weeks thereafter. His enforced delay on the Pacific island could not have been an altogether unpleasant experience for Sutter. Before leaving Fort Vancouver he had had the foresight to provide himself with letters of introduction from James Douglas and other newly-made friends there. These he presented on his arrival at Honolulu to government officials, foreign consuls, leading merchants and traders, and other dignitaries. The result was that the affable stranger was received with respect everywhere. During his stay he seems to have made himself a particular favorite of the royal family. By Sutter's own account, the ruling monarch, King Kamehameha III, urged him to remain in the Islands and "take charge of his military establishment"—which assignment Sutter, who of course had no practical knowledge of soldiering, prudently turned down.

Not only was his five-month stay on the Islands gratifying to Sutter's expanding ego—he was able to put it to practical use

by assembling supplies and enlisting recruits for his California
venture. Thus by the time the long-awaited sailing day arrived,
he had acquired—largely on credit—an assortment of tools and
agricultural implements, an arsenal of weapons (including two
small brass cannon), plus a company of followers that, in his
words, numbered "5 White Men and 8 Kanacas." He went on
to explain that three of the white men were trained mechanics,
possessed of skills that he foresaw would be useful in establishing an outpost of civilization in the California wilderness.

The ship on which the little party sailed was the British brig
Clementine which had been chartered by a Honolulu merchant
and dispatched on a trading mission to Russian settlements on
the coast of Alaska. In return for free passage for himself and
his group, Sutter served as supercargo throughout the voyage.
The *Clementine* spent a month at Sitka, where the major part
of her cargo was sold. Then, in the supercargo's words, she
"sailed down the Coast in heavy Gales, and entered in Distress
the Port of San Francisco, on the 2d of July 1839."

5 "I WANTED TO GET AWAY . . ."

As far as his own plans were concerned, Sutter arrived
in California at a particularly auspicious time.

Among residents of this, the northernmost and most remote of
the Mexican provinces, resentment at the neglect of the home
government had been building up for several decades. Moreover,
most of the grievances of which the Californians never tired of
complaining were well-founded. That the overlords at Mexico
City had little interest in, and less understanding of, the needs
of the Alta Californians, was shown in many ways: by the type
of men sent to rule over them, by a failure to provide them with
means of protecting themselves against foreign aggression, by
stringent laws designed to prevent their trading with other nations, and perhaps most of all, by a refusal to give them a larger
voice in how and by whom they were governed.

The result of these and other restrictive measures was that
California, for all the advantages of its location and its abundant

natural resources, was a long time emerging from its age-long isolation. Although the Spanish had founded the first missions and pueblos there a full seventy years earlier, by 1839 the white inhabitants—who numbered only a few thousand—were still concentrated on a narrow strip of coastal plains and valleys from San Diego north to San Francisco bay. The rest of the province, except for two small Russian settlements at Fort Ross and Bodega, was still a primitive wilderness, the greater part of it occupied only by bands of roving Indians.

At the time Sutter appeared on the scene California had at last begun to arouse itself from its long sleep. The secularization of the missions—which had got under way six years earlier and which had shifted the economic control of the province from the padres to the rancheros—had been completed. All but a few of the mission Indians had either returned to the ways of their ancestors or else had attached themselves to one of the cattle ranches, where they were held in a state of virtual serfdom.

The movement on the part of the Californians for a greater degree of self-government had by then partially succeeded, although it had taken a number of revolts—most of them bloodless—and the forcible expulsion of several governors to bring that about. And though the laws forbidding trade with foreign nations were still on the books, progressively less attempt was being made to enforce them. Both smuggling and the bribery of custom officials had become commonplace, and all up and down the coast trading ships were operating more or less openly.

There were still other evidences that Mexico's attempt to isolate its northern province from the rest of the world was failing. Despite strict measures designed to discourage immigration, the number of foreign-born residents had been growing year by year. During the 1820's and early 1830's many of the newcomers had circumvented the law limiting the ownership of land to Mexican nationals by marrying into the local families and taking out Mexican citizenship. These Californians-by-adoption had gradually become important factors in the business life of the province.

During the same period emigrants of another sort had begun to make an appearance—men who had reached the province by breaking new trails over the mountain passes to the east and north, drawn by the prospect of gathering the pelts of beaver and land otter along the course of the interior streams. These newcomers had nothing in common with the foreign-born merchants, importers, shipping agents and others who lived in the coastal settlements and had close business and social relations with the native Californians. The hunters and trappers were another breed entirely, an independent, self-assertive group, impatient of restraints of any kind. Their presence in increasing numbers, and their open defiance of laws barring them from the country, added a new complication to the already difficult situation facing the authorities at Monterey.

At the time Sutter reached California the man whose responsibility it was to cope with such problems was thirty-year-old Juan Bautista Alvarado, the provincial governor. Three years earlier Governor Alvarado—who was the first native-born Californian to hold that office—had organized several hundred of his discontented countrymen, attacked and captured Monterey, deported the regularly appointed governor, and himself assumed the post. By 1839, however, although the central government at Mexico City had officially confirmed his title to the office, Alvarado's position was none too secure. All during that period the political life of the province was notably unstable, and by the time Sutter appeared on the scene new dissentions had broken out. One of the points at issue was the insistence of those living in the southern part of the province that the capital be moved to the pueblo of Los Angeles.

When Sutter reached Monterey on July 3 and made known his plan of founding a colony somewhere in the interior, the Governor lent a sympathetic ear. There were several reasons for that. For one thing, such a colony would be well beyond all the existing settlements and, provided it could be maintained, would have the effect of extending governmental authority into areas where it had never before existed. Also, such an establishment, if strongly held and ably administered, could be useful to the government in still other ways. First, it might be a means of discouraging the influx of Yankee hunters and trappers from beyond the mountains, and, second, it could serve to prevent the Russians at Fort Ross from extending their holdings farther inland. Finally, it could hardly fail to be useful in deterring bands of Indians from raiding the outlying ranchos and driving off herds of horses and cattle.

Moreover, the manner in which the stranger presented his application left no doubt in Alvarado's mind that he was quite capable of carrying out his ambitious project. For the resourceful Sutter had seen to it that he did not arrive in California unknown or unheralded. During his stay in the Islands, and while the *Clementine* was at Sitka, he had made a number of additions to the sheaf of letters he had begun to assemble at Fort Vancouver. It was, in fact, one of that collection—a letter from the United States Consul at Honolulu to David Spence, a leading Monterey merchant—that had gained him an audience with the Governor and so enabled him to show that official his other flattering testimonials. "He had never seen a man with so many letters of introduction," Sutter recalled him saying.

The result of his well-prepared campaign was that after a stay of only two or three days at Monterey the triumphant Sutter was again aboard the *Clementine* heading back to Yerba Buena, his mission accomplished. Nearly twenty years later he thus summed up the result of his appeal to the Governor: "I got a General passport for my small Colony and permission to select a Territory wherever I would find it convenient, and to come in one Years time in Monterey to get my Citizenship and title of the land . . ."

The *Clementine* was back in San Francisco bay on August 7. There Sutter, his party, and his belongings were put ashore at the edge of Yerba Buena Cove, and soon thereafter, the ship sailed on her return voyage to Honolulu. Thereupon, Sutter prepared to set off on what he termed "my Exploring Journey to the inland Rivers, and particularly to find the Mouth of the River Sacramento, as I could find Nobody who could give me information, only that they Knew that some very large Rivers were in the interior." Nearly three weeks were spent procuring, outfitting, and loading the ships that would carry the party up the Sacramento. Meanwhile, Sutter had been showing his letters of introduction to merchants and traders of that bleak little settlement and laying the groundwork for future business relations with them.

During that period, the energetic stranger also found time to call on two of the most influential men in the northern part of the province. These were Governor Alvarado's uncle, General Mariano G. Vallejo, who from his headquarters at Sonoma commanded the military forces of the province, and Alexander Rotscheff, commandant of the Russian outposts at Fort Ross and Bodega. In each instance the caller's genial and confidence-inspiring manner, aided no doubt by his potent letters (one of those he showed Rotscheff bore the signature of the latter's superior officer at Sitka), assured him a cordial welcome and paved the way for helpful trade relations in the future.

Almost to a man, the Californians to whom Sutter made known his plan of establishing his colony in the remote interior of the province pronounced it a harebrained idea and predicted that it would end in failure. General Vallejo tried hard to dissuade him from embarking on so reckless an enterprise, pointing out that any amount of land suited to his purpose was to be had without venturing so far beyond the populated areas. Another of his new-found friends, Captain John Wilson, who had accompanied him from Yerba Buena to Vallejo's home, volunteered to sell him, on extremely liberal terms, a large ranch in the fertile Sonoma Valley. When Sutter declined his offer, Wilson demanded in a puzzled tone: "Well, by God, I would like to know what you do want!"

Sutter had his own sufficient reason for rejecting such well-meant advice and generous offers. He had not traveled halfway around the world in order to begin life anew at a spot where his activities would be under the close supervision and control of government officials, however lenient they might prove to be. "I wanted to get away from the Spaniards," he later wrote. "I wanted to be my own master . . ."

That to his mind was worth any discomfort or hardship or danger he might meet with in the wilderness.

two

Empire in the Making

---

1 PUTTING DOWN ROOTS

When on the morning of August 14, 1839, the ships that had brought Sutter and his party up the river turned about and returned to San Francisco bay, the group that remained behind consisted of Sutter himself, three white men he had recruited at Honolulu and Yerba Buena, the Indian youth who had joined him at the Rocky Mountain rendezvous more than a year earlier, and ten Kanakas, two of whom were women. A German, a Belgian, an Irishman, an Indian, and ten Sandwich Islanders—such was the party with which Sutter set about establishing the first outpost of civilization in California's remote central valley.

At first glance this seemed an insecure foundation on which to build his projected empire. Yet if Sutter had any doubts on that score he managed to conceal them. He later recalled that his first move after the boats had disappeared downstream was to dispatch the Indian youth and one of the white men on a hunting trip to replenish the party's scanty food supply. The pair returned after only a short time carrying the carcass of an elk. "After that, there was never any lack of meat."

Sutter's account continues [The excerpts quoted here and later are from a manuscript called *Personal Reminiscences* dictated in 1876 to the California historian, Hubert H. Bancroft. In setting down the speaker's words, Bancroft corrected his faulty English.]:

> From the landing place I went back about a quarter of a mile to the spot where the Fort subsequently stood . . . The Kanakas

19

first erected two grass houses after the manner of their houses on the Hawaiian Islands; the frames were made by white men and covered with grass by the Kanakas. The houses were very comfortable. Next I built a one story building of adobe. This house was about forty feet long and contained a blacksmith shop, a kitchen, and a room for myself. It was covered with tule and was completed just before the winter rains set in . . . In the spring, I had my men make a large quantity of adobe bricks for the walls of the Fort and for the other buildings. I also had a quantity of lumber cut and sawed up into boards. The white men taught the Indians to use the whipsaw and the other implements.

Sutter's Indian helpers were members of a Sacramento Valley tribe then called the Ochecamnes. Their leader, Chief Narciso, had been a ward of the padres at the San Jose Mission and so had some knowledge of the Spanish language. It was during this period that Sutter demonstrated qualities that proved highly useful to him then and later; namely, an understanding of the temperament of the natives and the ability to direct their activities into channels useful to himself. Thus, having gained Narciso's confidence and friendship, he was able, with gifts of beads, bits of colored cloth and like trinkets, to put crews of Indians to work building houses, clearing the fields in preparation for the first plantings, and performing other needed tasks.

But useful as they were, a large force of native workers was not enough. Sutter was almost without funds when he reached California, and he well knew that if his enterprise were to succeed, he must find means of financing it during the critical years until it could be put on a self-sustaining basis. With that in mind, he had stopped on his way up from Yerba Buena at the rancho of Ygnacio Martinez, which fronted on the Carquinez Strait, and persuaded the owner to supply him—on credit—with the horses, oxen, and other livestock he would need.

One of his first acts, accordingly, was to dispatch two Indians to the Martinez rancho with a letter asking that the animals be sent him "so quick as possible," and adding that the Indians would "show you the Road to my place." Then followed a passage that was to become an almost invariable part of Sutter's correspondence with the California rancheros and merchants during the next several years; that is, a plea for a further extension of his credit. Would his friend Martinez be so kind as to send him also a second yoke of oxen? And two additional milk cows? And ten or twelve bullocks? And several horses and mares? And some good young cows? All of which he promised to pay for promptly with goods he planned to raise—"goods with which you will be very much pleased."

But even that did not exhaust the list of his needs. The next paragraph read:

"Please send me also 2 or 3 Sadles [saddles] which I need very bad, the two Indians have no sadles; please to give them some old Sadles . . ." And a few lines farther: "please to send me 6 fanegas de Trigo and 6 fanegas Beans, 1 bag Mantego, 8 arobas dried meat and some Indian corn seed if you please . . ."

To this letter, which was dated August 14, no answer was forthcoming, either in the form of the goods ordered or in explanation of its nonappearance. Haste in such matters, and indeed in all things else, was not a characteristic of California life in the 1830's. Sutter, who was understandably impatient at the delay—for without the livestock, planting seeds, and other goods nothing could be accomplished—waited a full month, then sent a second message, and two weeks later, a third. It was not until October 23, nearly two months after the one-sided correspondence began, that he received an answer: a small herd of horses and cattle, far fewer than he had expected, and all in bad condition.

Of the other goods he had ordered with so lavish a hand only a few token items eventually arrived: a tub of tallow, some dried beef, small quantities of beans and wheat. When he discovered that these too were of poor quality, Sutter wrote Martinez an indignant letter complaining that the wheat was full of weevils and unfit for making flour. The rancher, moreover, had put his two Indians to work during their stay and had failed to offer them anything in the way of compensation. He ended by reminding his correspondent severely that such behavior was not usual among gentlemen. It does not appear, however, that Martinez was seriously disturbed at this charge of ungentlemanly conduct; in his reply he asked only that his bill be paid promptly and in full.

But despite the disappointing outcome of his dealings with the rancher, and the consequent shortage of many things he desperately needed, Sutter managed to make progress. Throughout the winter of 1839–40 the work of putting up temporary shelters and clearing land for the first crops continued. To care for his few cattle, two half-breed *vaqueros* were hired; in their spare time they set about building one of the clumsy, solid-wheeled *carretas*, then the only type of vehicle known in California. There was progress, too, in other directions. In later years Sutter recalled that "during the winter we cut a road through the woods and fixed up a landing place, the new embarcadero [on the bank of the Sacramento River, about two miles distant]. Soon it was time to make a garden and to sow some wheat after the soil had been broken with the poor California plows . . ."

It was still too early to know for sure if his bold plan for a wilderness colony was going to succeed. But a beginning had been made, and the outlook presently began to look brighter.

2   CHILDREN OF THE VALLEY

Throughout the first four decades of the nineteenth century, the cornerstones of California's economy, and the basis of such commercial relations as it had with the rest of the world, were its three chief products: hides, tallow, and furs. Accordingly, during his first years in the valley much of Sutter's time and effort were directed toward increasing the size of his herds on the one hand, and, on the other, organizing his Indians into hunting parties and sending them into the back country to trap beaver, land otter, and other fur-bearing animals.

Because he realized that some time must elapse before he could hope for any large return from his cattle-raising activities, it was mainly to his bands of native trappers that he looked for the revenue needed to tide him over the critical beginning years.

Thus his letters ordering supplies of various kinds from the merchants at Yerba Buena and Monterey usually ended with a promise that the goods sent him would be paid for with "furs of excellent quality." This was sound strategy on Sutter's part, for such skins were then in brisk demand on the world markets and hence were a favorite medium of barter between the merchants of the coastal towns and the visiting trading ships. In such exchanges beaver pelts commonly had a value of $4 each and those of the sea otter $3 per pound.

Unluckily for Sutter, however, such parties of Indian trappers as he was able to train and put in the field showed little aptitude for the work, and the consequence was that the number of furs they gathered was disappointingly small. Moreover, the Hudson's Bay Company trappers who, notwithstanding Mexican laws barring them from the province, frequently operated in California. Sometimes they came upon one of Sutter's Indian parties and persuaded it to part with its season's catch in return for a bottle or two of whiskey. As a result, in spite of his best efforts, Sutter's trade in furs became and remained a minor source of revenue.

His cattle-raising operations were more successful. But here too he had to start from the beginning and, handicapped as he was by lack of capital, building up the size of his herds to the point where they would become commercially profitable was a tedious and time-consuming process. Nonetheless, by persistent effort and in the face of frequent rebuffs, he was able to make progress. The nucleus of his holdings in livestock—which eventually came to be counted in the tens of thousands—was, as we have seen, the small number of indifferent animals he had bought on credit from Ygnacio Martinez. That was in early August of 1839. Something more than a year later he was able to buy, again on credit, a second and larger herd. The seller this time was Antonio Suñol, whose Rancho San José del Valle included the site of present-day San Jose.

Meanwhile the population of his little community had been growing moderately. The newcomers, like the original party, were an oddly assorted lot: sailors who had deserted their ships at Yerba Buena or Monterey and fled to this inland haven to avoid recapture; wide-ranging frontiersmen from beyond the Rockies or an occasional trapper who had wandered down from the Oregon country; now and then a Mexican-Indian *vaquero* or sheepherder from one of the outlying ranchos to the south and southwest.

But regardless of who they were and where they came from, all received a warm welcome, for Sutter was never so content as when he was playing the part of a gracious host. That had been true all his life; now, however, there was an added reason for his openhanded hospitality. He had need of whatever skills the strangers might possess, whether as hunters, trappers, farmers, carpenters, blacksmiths, boatmen or any of a dozen other crafts. No one was turned away; one and all they were urged to stay on and become permanent members of his entourage. To be sure, Sutter rarely had funds to pay his employees, but that was a lightly regarded detail. He was usually able to convince them—and his other creditors as well—that one of his impending deals was about to be consummated, and if only they would wait a few days (or at the most, a few weeks) longer, they would be liberally rewarded for their patience. By such means his staff grew from month to month. In the fall of 1840 he had, in his own words, "about twenty white men working for me in addition to a large number of natives."

It was, of course, the California Indians who then and later made up the greater part of Sutter's labor force, and it was clear from the beginning that the success or failure of his venture depended in large measure on the skill with which he handled his unpredictable charges. Fortunately, he was well qualified for that task. Unlike most Californians of his day, he had had considerable experience with the Indian tribes of the West prior to his arrival in the province. He had been in close contact with them both during his trading expeditions to Santa Fe and in the course of his travels through the Rocky Mountains and in the Northwest, all of which proved helpful in his dealings with the Sacramento Valley tribes.

His attitude toward his native workers might be likened to that of a kindly though strict parent toward a well-intentioned but headstrong and irresponsible child. So long as his Indian charges remained docile and acceptably carried out the simple tasks assigned them they were fairly treated. Their white master provided them with food and shelter—although the huts they occupied and the method of feeding them sometimes shocked visitors—and whenever he was able to do so, he paid them "wages" consisting of cotton shirts, lengths of cloth, glass beads or other bright-colored ornaments which they wore about their necks. "The Indians were sometimes troublesome," Sutter once remarked, "but on the whole I got along very nicely with them."

Perhaps the chief reason why they rarely gave him serious trouble was that whenever they showed a tendency toward wrong-doing he saw to it that their punishment was both prompt and severe. He realized that not only was such treatment necessary in order to maintain discipline, it was also a safety measure. For his little company of white men were outnumbered many times over and in the event the Indians rose in revolt, their plight, separated as they were by many miles from the nearest settlements, might well have been a desperate one.

During his first winter in the valley Sutter had an experience that taught him the need to be constantly vigilant. One night while he and one of his assistants—a young Frenchman named Octave Custot, whom he had met at the Martinez rancho—were talking in Sutter's quarters they heard a sharp outcry. On investigating, they discovered an Indian just outside the door who was being attacked by a bulldog Sutter had brought with him from Hawaii. Sutter's account of the incident continues:

> The Indian had hardly been brought into the house when a similar cry was heard and a second fellow was caught in the same manner. It appeared that a whole band of Indians had come to kill all of us and seize my settlement. . . I sewed up the wounds of the savages and told them I would forgive them this time but that further attempts would be met with severe punishment.

Not long thereafter he learned that other native workers had been smuggling weapons into their quarters and secreting them beneath their blankets with the evident intention of launching a new attack. "When I asked them why they wanted to kill me, who had treated them well, they answered that they simply wanted to plunder."

The result of Sutter's efforts to domesticate the natives and instruct them in the ways of civilization closely paralleled that of the priests at the California missions a generation earlier. In both instances the tribesmen, for a time, contentedly performed the tasks their white overseers set for them. Eventually, however, the novelty of making adobe bricks, tilling and planting the soil or tending cattle wore off, and they found themselves looking back with regret to the unfettered life they had known prior to the coming of the white man.

By the spring of 1840 that feeling of unrest had become evident among many of Sutter's native workers. Next came the theft of his horses and cattle and other ominous signs of revolt against his authority. Finally, he discovered one day that his entire force of Indian laborers had left their quarters and withdrawn to a point beyond the Cosumnes River, some twenty miles to the southeast. Fearing that this presaged an attack on his settlement, he decided to forestall such a move by staging one of his own. Gathering a small force of armed and mounted men, he led them to the Indians' hideaway, launched an attack at dawn, and having taken the natives by surprise, succeeded in routing them.

"After we had killed six of their number," he wrote, "they ceased their resistance and asked for mercy. None of my men had been killed or wounded. I told them that everything would be forgotten if they would come back to the village and attend to their work as before."

Thereafter, by adhering to his policy of ruthlessness on the one hand and fair dealing on the other, Sutter managed to avoid further serious trouble with his Indian charges. Another reason for the amiable employer-employee relations that usually existed at the fort was that Sutter never failed to make some token payment, however insignificant, in return for whatever work was done. During the first several years the laborers were, as stated earlier, paid with glass beads or other articles of trifling value. Later he introduced a sort of private coinage system. This consisted of small pieces of tin, circular in shape and stamped with a star, which were passed out to the workers at the end of each day and could be exchanged for merchandise at the store that was soon established at the fort. Still another of Sutter's innovations, one that pleased the young braves mightily, was to form them into a military company, provide them with uniforms and firearms, and teach them drills and other simple maneuvers.

On the whole, Sutter and his Indians lived together in comparative peace and harmony. Had his relations with his neighbors of Spanish-Mexican origin been equally friendly, his stay in the valley would have been far less contentious.

3 SEÑOR JUAN AUGUSTO

On his first visit to Monterey in the summer of 1839, Sutter learned that the ownership of land in Alta California was restricted to Mexican citizens, and that to be eligible for citizenship a foreigner must have lived in the province a full year.

To Governor Alvarado he made known his intention of taking out citizenship and becoming a permanent California resident. He also explained his plan of founding a colony somewhere in the interior, and asked the Governor's permission to organize an exploring expedition and lead it up the Sacramento River to locate a suitable site. The Governor listened with interest while the persuasive Swiss outlined his plans. At the end, he warmly approved the other's project and advised him to return to Monterey at the end of a year, at which time his citizenship papers would be forthcoming.

Accordingly, as the twelve-month waiting period drew toward an end, Sutter prepared to pay a second visit to the provincial capital. All his life he had had a flair for the dramatic, a liking for doing things on a scale a bit more elaborate than the occasion called for. This time he was able to indulge his taste for display by traveling in style; his party, he once wrote, consisted of "two

vaqueros and two armed men as an escort, and . . . thirty
horses." The picturesque cavalcade reached Monterey toward
the end of August 1840, and its leader was cordially received by
the Governor and other high officials. A few days later, in ac-
cordance with Alvarado's promise, he officially became Juan
Augusto Sutter, citizen of the Republic of Mexico.

But the newly naturalized Don Juan was to receive further
evidence on the confidence reposed in him by the Mexican authorities. On September 1 he was given a document, signed by
Secretary of State Jimeno Casarin, naming him the official representative of the provincial government in the Sacramento River
region. To one who had been a citizen of the country less than
a week, this must be counted an unusual mark of esteem. For
the office to which he had been appointed was no empty honor;
it gave him sole authority to interpret and enforce the law over
a very large expanse of territory. As Sutter himself correctly
stated, "From that time on I had the power of life and death
both over Indians and whites in my district."

But substantial as these honors were, Sutter was not altogether
satisfied. One of his fondest hopes had been that Alvarado would
make him a captain in the Mexican army. Such a move would
have fulfilled his lifelong ambition to shine as a military figure;
besides, it would in a sense have legalized the title by which
he preferred to be addressed—that is, as "Captain" Sutter.

His explanation of why the Governor failed to grant him the
coveted commission was that he feared that by doing so he
would offend his uncle, General Mariano G. Vallejo, who was
commander-in-chief of the Mexican forces in California and
whose duties included the defense of the northern frontier. Moreover, the Governor's fears on that score seem to have been well
founded. For although the two men eventually became friends,
during Sutter's first years in the valley Vallejo looked on him as
a presumptuous intruder and treated him accordingly.

Notwithstanding the failure of his hopes for a military title,
Sutter returned to his colony in high spirits and full of bright
plans for the future. He had every reason to be content. For his
probationary period was now over; he was no longer a stranger

in a foreign country but a full-fledged citizen of his adopted land, a duly appointed government official, and in another year he would be eligible to receive title to an expanse of fertile land exceeding in size that of many of the Old World principalities.

Now that he had successfully accomplished the preliminary phases of his plan he set about with renewed energy to carry out the next steps. During his stay at Monterey and at points where he had stopped during his travels to and from the capital, he had been at pains to establish friendly relations with a number of merchants and ranch owners, and so had laid the groundwork for a new series of purchases. (Incidentally, this set off yet another round of letters to creditors explaining his inability to pay for goods they had already furnished him.)

By the fall of 1840 Sutter had come to realize that the time was at hand for a bold move forward. His little community had more than doubled in size during its first year. Besides the natives, his employees now numbered well over twenty and with winter approaching, there was need for better housing than the temporary huts they had been occupying. In addition, the fields about the fort needed to be laid out and cleared and made ready for the planting of spring crops; the number of horses, oxen, and other draft animals were too few to perform the many tasks that needed to be done, and of the thousands of head of cattle he would require in the future he had been able to assemble only a few score. It was the same all down the line. The time had come when a new and more vigorous attempt must be made to break up the log-jam of scarcities that was threatening the success of his enterprise and to start it moving ahead on all fronts.

A reading of the dozens of letters Sutter wrote during that period—most of them laboriously composed in his unfamiliar English and Spanish—makes clear just how many and how urgent were his needs. In the letters we find repeated requests that he be sent seed for planting wheat, corn, potatoes and other crops, for milch cows, domestic fowl, and for cuttings of fruit trees and grape and berry vines. Other items that were always in short supply were beads, cloth, and like objects for his Indian workers, and clothing, food and drugs for himself and staff. And always, most desperately needed of all, were such manufactured goods as plows, hoes, rakes and other farming implements; also wagons, saddles, harnesses, hammers, saws, axes, nails, fishhooks, files, knives, guns, ammunition—the list is endless.

In the fall of 1840 Sutter had the good fortune to add a blacksmith to his staff. Thereafter, it became possible to produce in his own shop some of the articles he had formerly had to buy at Monterey or Yerba Buena, or if they were not to be had there—which was usually the case—to do without. From then on, his most pressing need was for iron, any sort of iron that could be made to serve any purpose. His unremitting search for that metal runs like a sort of refrain through his correspondence during the early and middle 1840's.

Typical of his letters of that period is one written on July 22, 1845, addressed to the pioneer Monterey merchant, Thomas O. Larkin, who was also the United States Consul there. Having led off with the flattering comment that "I look upon you as the only person in this country who assists and encourages enterprise," he appended a "List of Articles wanted." This runs to close to one hundred separate items. At its head is a request for "irons for a saw Mill, Saws and files," followed by "Iron of all Description, particular heavy iron for making Ploughs and Wagons; Cast steel, likewise good engl. Blister-steel; Blacksmith files of all sizes (a good Supply); one good Anvil, & 1 good Vice; Some Screwplates & 5 lb. of Borax."

Other items include "Shoemakers Rasps and Shoemaker thread; 12 American Axes & 2 good large Broadaxes; 2 kegs of Shingling & 2 Kegs of flooring Nails; American Ploughs of the heavier kind, so many as you can get; 2 dozen of Shovels & 1 Dozen of Spates; 2 Crosscut Saws, 3 Handsaws & 2 Shingling hatchets; 12 Gimlets, Chissel and Gautches assortet; 6 House Door locks; 12 Chest and 12 Padlocks; 6 dozen of good Butcherknives [and] 1000 fishhooks of different sizes." A bit farther down the lengthy list are "200 lb of fine Rifle Powder; 100 lb of Musket Do; 300 lb of Lead & 400 lb of Beaver or Duck Shot; 10,000 Precusion Caps, [plus] 5,000 flints for Shotguns & Muskets."

With the needs of his Indian workers in mind he asked that he be furnished with "200 lb of white and red Beads of the right kind, like I had from you a few lb when at Monterey the last time; 2 bales of good brown Manta; 20 dozen of good Cotton Hdkfs; 20 pieces of dark colored good Callico; [and] 10 pieces of Stripe Cotton for strong Shirts." The pages-long list ends with requests for six dozen "Jackets and Pantalons of blue Nankin & Duck," assorted paint brushes, one keg each of black and green paint, a "beril" of paint oil, 1,000 to 2,000 needles of assorted sizes, and "2 flour sifts."

4 "THE KING'S ORPHAN"

In his *Personal Reminiscences,* which he dictated to Hubert H. Bancroft in the mid-1870's, Sutter stated:

> After my return from Monterey . . . [in September, 1840] I built a large house near the first adobe building . . . This I surrounded with walls eighteen feet high, enclosing altogether 75,000 square feet. The walls were made of adobe bricks and were two and a half feet thick. At two corners I built bastions; under these bastions were the prisons. Within the enclosure I erected other buildings; barracks for the soldiers, workshops and dwellings, a bakery, a mill and blanket factory . . . There were several outhouses for vaqueros and other employees.

Months of preparation were required before the building of the colony's permanent headquarters could get under way. During the first half of 1840 gangs of natives were kept busy mixing straw with the native soil and making thousands of sun-dried adobe bricks. At the same time other crews were cutting down the large oaks and other trees that grew in the vicinity and sawing them into timbers for use as floors, doors, window frames, and roof supports of the buildings.

The new headquarters was on a far more extensive scale than the old. Not only must living quarters be provided for his growing staff; there must also be shops where his mechanics and other craftsmen could work, plus space for the storage of home-grown crops and other supplies. In addition, the Captain himself must have suitable quarters from which to direct his large enterprise and where his visitors could be properly entertained. Finally, strong outer walls must be built to convert the little settlement into a fort and so make it safe from attack by Indians or other enemies.

Not all the buildings Sutter mentioned in his dictation to Bancroft were put up in 1840; a number date from a later period of the fort's evolution. Shortages of essential materials, plus a lack of qualified workers, caused frequent delays, and after three years had passed, the fort was still uncompleted. But even in its unfinished state it impressed visitors to the valley, many of whom expressed their astonishment at coming on so substantial a group of buildings in the midst of many miles of uninhabited wilderness.

Among those who visited the spot in the early 1840's was G. M. Waseurtz of Sandels, a Swedish naturalist and artist who spent several months in California in 1842–43 and who left a record of his impression in both words and drawings. In the fall of 1842 the genial Swede—who, because he had been educated in a government school, called himself "The King's Orphan"—set out from Yerba Buena aboard a schooner carrying supplies to Sutters' colony. The party spent a night at the Ygnacio Martinez rancho near the present-day town of Martinez, then continued on to the mouth of the Sacramento.

Of their passage up the river he wrote:

> Occasionally a deer would betray itself among the tangled ruins that hung in profusion from the larger trees, or cattle almost as wild as the deer themselves, would rush along crashing the undergrowth with heavy tread. No signs of civilization were to be seen save a deserted hut. Several times we landed to pick blackberries along the banks.
>
> Although not very distant from the mouth of the river in a straight line, the settlement of Captain Sutter was reached only after many turns of the river. So we arrived at the embarcadero

late in the evening, having seen only one hut and some sheep
pens on the right side of the river all the passage up. At the
embarcadero, or port, were some huts situated under the shade
of lofty sycamores and oaks . . . New Helvetia [which was the
name Sutter had given the settlement] lay two and a half miles
from this landing. The road, over a level and well-timbered
ground, led to a higher ground, clothed with timber, where the
fort and habitations were located.

On learning of the arrival of the schooner, Sutter dispatched
a horse to the embarcadero to carry the visitor to the fort.

"I arrived very early in the morning," his account continues,
"just as the discordant notes of the Mexican drum were calling
the people to assemble for labor. I alighted and proceeded immediately to pay my compliments to the Captain. Although he
was very busily employed distributing orders for the day, he most
hospitably received and made me at home under his roof."

Wheat was being harvested in the nearby fields and before
being sent out with their sickles, rakes, and other tools, the Indian crews were brought inside the enclosure and given their
morning meal. The method of feeding the natives shocked the
visitor. "I must confess," he wrote, "I could not reconcile my
feelings to see these fellows being driven, as it were, around some
narrow troughs of hollow tree trunks, out of which, crouched
on their haunches, they fed more like beasts than human beings,
using their hands in hurried manner to convey to their mouths
the thin porrage which was served to them. Soon they . . . filed
off to the fields after having, I fancy, half satisfied their physical
wants."

Sutter and his guest then sat down to their own breakfast,
which was served "in a small building detached from the dwelling house, and under the same roof as the kitchen." Their meal
bore no likeness to that served the Indians. It consisted of "excellent beefsteak, tea, butter with coarse bread, eggs, beans, etc.,
etc."

At the time of the visit of the King's Orphan, industrial activity
at the fort, though less diversified than it later became, was al-

ready well advanced. In the sheds ranged about the inner sides of the walls the visitor saw the distillery, where a fiery native brandy, *aguardiente*, was being made from home-grown wheat and wild grapes that grew along the river banks; he was also shown the shops where a carpenter, a blacksmith, a cooper, and a saddler were at work. Outside the walls were corrals where the domestic animals were kept, and an adobe building used to store wheat, corn, and other farm products. A little distance away was an assemblage of huts where the native workers lived, and, to the rear of the fort, "a large pond bordered with fine willows and other trees."

While the visitor made clear his admiration for how much Sutter had accomplished in the face of so many difficulties, some aspects of the settlement he viewed with a critical eye. Not only had his sensibilities been shocked at the method of feeding the Indian workers; in addition, the place had a dirty, unkempt appearance that offended his sense of neatness and order. Of the pond behind the fort he remarked that it "could have been a most valuable asset, ornamental and useful, providing water for both domestic use and for irrigating the newly laid out kitchen garden. However, it had been unpardonably neglected, and had thus become a source of colds and fever."

5 NEW HELVETIA

In the summer of 1841 Sutter made another trip to Monterey. On this occasion, too, his errand was an important one; he went to claim title to the Sacramento Valley lands he had applied for a year earlier when he was granted Mexican citizenship.

By the standards of today, the tract of land he sought was of generous size. But it must be remembered that in the early 1840's California's population was still extremely small, and land was so abundant that it had almost no value. Hence, during a period when grants of 20,000 to 30,000 acres in return for some trifling service to the government (or for none at all) were by no means uncommon, Sutter's request, while it could hardly be termed modest, was not entirely out of line.

The New Helvetia grant—as it came to be called—consisted of two parcels having a combined area of eleven square leagues—just short of 50,000 acres. The first, comprising about 9,000 acres, was at the junction of the American and Sacramento rivers and included the site of the fort and most of present-day Sacramento. The second was farther to the north and bordered on both sides of a tributary of the Sacramento, the Feather. It was on this tract that Sutter a few years later established a second home, which he called Hock Farm.

Because he had complied with the regulations governing the ownership of land in the province—and because he had been at pains to keep on friendly terms with the authorities at the capital—his application for land was speedily approved. The property was awarded him on June 18, 1841, and a map of the grant, based on a survey made the previous December by his fellow Swiss, Jean Jacques Vioget, was filed in the provincial archives. Once these formalities were over, Governor Alvarado, according to Sutter's later account, complimented him on the manner in which he had discharged his official duties as the government's agent in the valley, as well as on his success at holding the natives in check and training them in the ways of civilization.

But the friendship that existed between Sutter and the officials at Monterey cooled rapidly. Not long after his return to the valley rumblings of discontent began to be heard from both sides. Sutter's dissatisfaction was due in large part to the Governor's failure to make good his promise that the Hudson's Bay Company trappers would be barred from the valley. This was a matter of much importance to Sutter because, as noted earlier, he had looked on the furs gathered by his own trappers as a prime source of revenue. However, in the absence of strong protests from Monterey, the managers of the British concern continued to send their crews into what Sutter believed was rightfully his own exclusive hunting grounds. As the months passed, his protests at the Governor's inaction grew more frequent and heated.

Meanwhile Sutter's Sacramento Valley colony had begun to arouse uneasiness among influential Californians at Monterey and elsewhere. The fact that, notwithstanding his protestations of friendship and support of the government, he had built his head-

quarters in the form of a fort and mounted cannon on its outer
walls was looked on as a suspicious circumstance. But equally
disturbing in the opinion of many was the knowledge that he
had gathered at the fort a large number of foreigners, all of
whom were illegally in the country and if permitted to remain
might well endanger its security.

On that score the concern of the Californians is understandable. For by all accounts Sutter's white employees during the
first years were an unprepossessing lot. For the most part they
were made up of deserters from the whalers or merchant or navy
ships that visited coastal towns, of Yankee hunters or trappers
who had drifted into the valley from beyond the mountains, or
of renegade Mexicans anxious to keep beyond reach of the law
in more settled parts of the province. In other words, they were
a cross section of the restless, footloose and rebellious of half
the world.

Sutter was himself well aware that the quality of the staff he
had been able to recruit left much to be desired. But California
was then a sparsely populated land, and his needs were too many
and too urgent to permit him to pick and choose. Later, recalling
his visit to the capital in June, 1841, when he had received title
to his New Helvetia grant, he stated:

> In Monterey I hired some new recruits, about half a dozen
> men, mostly mechanics. Among them was a Negro, a good
> cooper and the first darkey ever to come to the valley. When
> I was ready to return, I gathered my people in front of Mr.
> Spence's house [David Spence, a Scotch trader who had married
> into one of the local families and was then serving as justice
> of the peace at Monterey]. When several ship captains, who hap-
> pened to be present, saw my motley crew, they exclaimed: "My
> God! How can you manage such vagabonds!" I told them I got
> along well with them, because I gave them nothing to drink
> but water.

When his critics charged that he had assembled a large and
potentially dangerous group of foreigners at the fort, Sutter re-
minded them that one of the conditions under which he had been

granted his land was that he encourage others to settle in the area and thereby lessen the threat of Indian attacks on the settlements to the south and west. His expectation was that large numbers of Europeans would eventually migrate to the valley and take up land there. Meanwhile, it was his belief that by fostering the beginnings of agriculture and industry there he was paving the way for those who would follow.

While he professed to resent the suspicion with which many Californians had come to regard him and his activities, he could not have found this altogether displeasing. For it was an admission on their part that the little colony he had founded on a shoelace only two or three years earlier had grown to the point where they looked on it as a threat to the security of all California.

That knowledge was heady medicine to the former Burgdorf shopkeeper.

three

The Russians Find a Buyer

1 FORT ROSS AND BODEGA

Soon after he reached California in 1839, and before he and his party set out to explore the Sacramento River, Sutter paid a brief visit to the Russian settlements on the rugged coast some eighty miles north of San Francisco Bay.

On his way to the Russian-American Company outposts he made a courtesy call on General Mariano Vallejo at the latter's home at Sonoma. Vallejo received the stranger with the hospitality characteristic of the early California dons. Although he, like the other Mexican officials, strongly resented the Russians' presence in the province, he made no attempt to dissuade Sutter from continuing on to Fort Ross; in fact, when it came time for his guest to leave, Vallejo detailed one of his *vaqueros* to accompany him and show him the way.

In preparation for his meeting with the local Russian commander, Alexander Rotscheff, Sutter had followed his usual custom of providing himself with letters of introduction, a procedure that in the past had assured him of a cordial welcome and gained support for whatever enterprises he had in mind. The letter he presented to Rotscheff was a potent one, for it had been written by Rotscheff's superior, the head of the Russian company's operations in Alaska; Sutter had added it to his collection during his stay at Sitka some weeks earlier. The result was as he had anticipated: he was warmly welcomed at Fort Ross and accorded all the attentions due an honored guest.

Even without benefit of the letter from Alaska, however, it is likely that he and Rotscheff would have struck it off well, for the two had a great deal in common. Both were men of European background whose restless natures had rebelled against the humdrum life at home and sent them ranging over the globe, eventually to find their way to this remote frontier. Of the two, Rotscheff's presence at this bleak coastal settlement was the more incongruous. For he was a man of scholarly bent, a writer and linguist who was later to publish a number of books of travel and world politics as well as translations into Russian of numerous English classics. Sutter on his part, while he lacked the Russian's learning and polished urbanity, was a born raconteur; moreover, by long practice he had learned to conduct himself as one accustomed to move in the polite military and social circles of Europe.

In any event, the young host—Rotscheff was then but twenty-six—and his gracious wife, the former Princess Helena Gargarin, said to be a member of a noble St. Petersburg family, made Sutter's stay a memorable one. His "Reminiscences" make clear that the main purpose of his visit was accomplished, for his account of his stay ends with these words: "I told the Governor of my intention to settle in the Sacramento Valley, and he asked me to call on him if he could be of any service to me."

At the time of Sutter's arrival, the Russian company's occupation of its California outposts was already drawing to a close. They had been founded more than a quarter-century earlier to serve as a base for its fur-gathering operations off the California coast and, incidentally, as a source of food for the Russian settlements in Alaska and on the Kamchatka Peninsula. They were the most remote of the outposts of the far-flung Russian-American Fur Company, an organization sponsored by the Imperial Russian government which since the late eighteenth century had enjoyed a monopoly on trade in the far northern waters of the Pacific. It might well have been that still another reason for the California settlements was that Russia hoped thereby to strengthen its claim to the coastal area north of San Francisco Bay.

The site of Fort Ross, the earliest and largest of the two settlements, was ill-adapted to its intended uses, for it lacked both
a safe harbor and sufficient land for large-scale agriculture or
stock-raising. It stood at the edge of high sea cliffs with the ocean
on one side and the wooded slopes of the Coast Range Mountains
on the other. Between the two was a strip of comparatively level
ground about half a mile wide and several miles long, with an
area of approximately a thousand acres. Although an
uncommonly wide variety of crops were planted by the colonists,
in only a few cases did soil and climate prove cooperative. Barley,
rye, buckwheat, and other cereals were produced in some quantity, as were certain fruits and vegetables, but the growing of
the latter was hampered by the difficulty of protecting the young
plants from gophers, rabbits, and other small animals. At the settlement of Bodega, a few miles down the coast near the bay of
that name, farming and cattle-raising were more successful. All
in all, however, as a means of providing food for the far northern
settlements, the California colonies fell short of expectations.

On the other hand, as a base for the seal and sea-otter hunters
Fort Ross was, during the early years, all that could be desired.
The party sent down from Sitka in 1812 to found the colony included a group of eighty natives of the Aleutian Islands. The
Aleuts were seasoned hunters who, skillfully plying their frail
kayaks sought out their quarry in the waters off the Farallon
Islands and elsewhere along the coast. During the first several
seasons they gathered large quantities of furs. So thoroughly did
they do their work that in less than a decade the herds were
all but exterminated. The number of skins taken fell from forty
thousand in 1812 to less than one per cent of that number in
1819.

At the time Fort Ross was founded, however, it is doubtful
if anyone foresaw that the fur hunts would end so soon. Indeed,
there seemed every likelihood that the Russians expected this
highly profitable phase of the operation would continue indefinitely. This is evidenced by the construction of the fort itself,
which was built of permanent materials and clearly intended to
last a long time.

The central part of the colony was laid out in the form of a rectangle, measuring some 280 by 300 feet and enclosed in a stockade 12 feet high. This wall was made of eight-inch-thick slabs split from the logs of the large redwood trees that grew in the nearby mountain canyons. The bases of the slabs were sunk several feet into the ground, and their crests were topped with iron spikes. At the southeast and northwest corners of the stockade stood massive bastions, one with eight sides, the other with seven. Each was two stories high and was built of logs mortised at the corners and pierced by portholes through which in the event of an attack the defenders could fire on the approaching enemy. (Incidentally, it might well be that these impressive-looking bastions were responsible for the fact that Sutter later incorporated somewhat similar structures into the design of his own fort at New Helvetia.)

All but one of the buildings within the enclosure followed the same general plan. Their walls were made of logs laid horizontally and bound together by mortar; the walls and partitions were of redwood slabs, and the roofs of shakes. The one building that did not conform to that pattern—and the most interesting of the group architecturally—was the chapel. This quaint little structure, which stood at the southwest corner of the compound, had walls and floors of split redwood, narrow Gothic windows, and a high-pitched wooden roof surmounted by two miniature towers. (The chapel that now stands on the site is a restoration; however, it closely follows the lines of the original and contains some of the original timbers.)

Other buildings inside the stockade were the commandant's house, a soldiers' barracks, officers' quarters, a warehouse, a kitchen, and a jail. All were grouped close to the stockade wall, leaving the center of the enclosure clear.

Although by the time of Sutter's visit fur hunting had long since ceased to be of any consequence, the fort was still an active place. The number of buildings then totaled more than fifty, all but a few of which were outside the stockade. Among them were a blacksmith shop, carpenter and cooper shops, a tannery, bakery, flourmill, a dairy house, barns, storehouses, and quarters for the

Aleut fishermen and their families. Nearby, too, were stables, corrals and pens for the cattle and domestic animals, and, on the beach at the foot of the cliffs, a landing pier, a boathouse, and a shipbuilding ways.

While the Russians were looked on as trespassers by the Mexicans and all trade with them was officially interdicted, there had always been an exchange of goods and services between the two. From the rancheros and mission fathers the Russians had bought quantities of grain, dried beef, and other foodstuffs to forward to their outposts in Alaska. On the other hand, the tools, kitchen utensils, and other appliances of wood and iron turned out by the Russian craftsmen were in demand by the Californians, who found them superior to those made by their own workers. The shipyard at Fort Ross was the first such plant of any size in California. During the 1820's several schooners and barges were built there for the missions at San Francisco and San José, where they were used to transport goods to and from the trading ships that by then were making regular visits to the coast.

When Sutter arrived in 1839 Fort Ross had been in existence nearly thirty years, and although the fact was still a closely guarded secret, the Russians had already reached a decision to abandon their settlements and withdraw from California. That decision was not made hastily; for some years it had been obvious to the company's managers that the colonies were not fulfilling their intended purposes. The hunt for seals and sea otter in the nearby waters had long since ended. Besides, the quantity of food produced on the farms and orchards and cattle ranges had fallen far short of expectations. The failure in that respect was due in large measure to a lack of practical farming experience on the part of the workers and their overseers. Another reason was the limited amount of land in the vicinity that was adapted to the large-scale raising of crops and running of cattle. Yet other factors were unfavorable climatic conditions and the damage done to both crops and livestock by predatory animals.

As early as 1830 it had come to be recognized that if the California outposts were to serve a useful purpose, the farming and stock-raising phases of the operation would have to be moved inland where there was ample level land and where soil and climate were more cooperative. For a time the possibility of relocating in one or another of the fertile valleys north of San Francisco was considered. In 1833 Baron Ferdinand Wrangell, head of the fur company's operations in the New World, came down from Sitka and conferred with Governor Figueroa of California, seeking means of establishing closer trade relations with his people. Their discussions were conducted in an amiable spirit, and for a while it appeared that a mutually satisfactory agreement would be reached. However, it was necessary that their recommendations be submitted to their home governments, and once that was done the matter became a pawn in an international chess game. Mexico City insisted that its approval of the Wrangell-Figueroa covenant must be made contingent on Russia's recognition of Mexico's independence from Spain—an independence that had been gained as a result of the revolution of 1822. Baron Wrangell forwarded word of that condition to his superiors at St. Petersburg, by whom it was submitted to the Czar. Communications between the West Coast and the capitals of Europe was then a tediously slow process. More than a year passed before word of the Czar's decision reached California; when it arrived, it proved to be a flat rejection of the condition laid down by the Mexicans.

The breakdown of these negotiations marked the beginning of the end of the Russians' California adventure. Not long thereafter the company's managers asked permission of the Imperial Government to abandon their unprofitable southern settlements and withdraw to Alaska. On April 15, 1839—less than three months before Sutter first appeared at Fort Ross—the decision to withdraw was officially approved by the Russian emperor.

2   A COSTLY BARGAIN

Early in 1840, as a prelude to the liquidation of its California holdings, the Russian American Fur Company entered into an agreement with the Hudson's Bay Company by which that firm undertook to supply the Russian settlements in Alaska with fixed amounts of foodstuffs each year.

Once that matter was settled, the Russians' next step was to arrange for the sale of the properties at Fort Ross and Bodega. Peter Kostromitinoff, the company's agent at Yerba Buena, was put in charge of the sale. Kostromitinoff's first move was to offer the property, including the land (to which the company's title was highly doubtful), livestock, buildings, and equipment, to General Vallejo, whose holdings at Sonoma were the northernmost of the large Mexican ranchos. The price asked was $30,000, one-half of which was to be paid in drafts drawn on the Hudson's Bay Company and the balance in the products of the country. The agreement provided that each year for three years the buyer deliver to the company's representative at Yerba Buena the following products: 6,000 *fanegas* of wheat (one *fanega* equalled 1.6 bushels), 300 *fanegas* of peas, 400 *arrobas* of soap (one *arroba* equalled 25 pounds), 700 *arrobas* of tallow, and 400 *arrobas* of suet. Credit for the goods received was to be at the rate of 2 pesos per *fanega* for the wheat and peas, 3½ pesos per *arroba* for the soap, 1½ pesos for the tallow, and 2 pesos for the suet. It was specified too that the products delivered be of good quality, the wheat and peas newly harvested, the soap dry, and the tallow and suet clean.

The negotiations continued for some time. In the end, Vallejo rejected the proposal and offered instead to pay $9,000 for the company's livestock, which consisted of 1,700 oxen and cows, 940 horses and mules, and 900 sheep. This was unacceptable to the agent, who was under orders to dispose of all the company's holdings in California. He next sought to interest other possible buyers, including Vallejo's brother-in-law, Jacob P. Leese. Leese reportedly made an unsuccessful offer of $20,000 for the property, to be paid in four annual installments of $5,000. There is evidence, too, that Kostromitinoff invited the Mexican government to enter a bid, an invitation that Governor Alvarado rejected on the ground that Mexico already owned the land and that the lumber used in the buildings and other improvements had been cut from government-owned trees.

In his search for buyers Kostromitinoff did not fail to get in touch with the owner of the newly established colony in the Sacramento Valley. At the time he was first approached, however,

Sutter—like Vallejo—was interested only in the livestock, and he therefore refused to bid on the other property. In his later account of the episode he states that the company officials at Sitka—with whom he had become acquainted during his visit in 1838—would have much preferred to sell to him rather than to the Mexicans. He accordingly found the agent's long-drawn-out negotiations with Vallejo, Alvarado, and others a source of irritation. His temper was not improved when toward the end of July, 1841, his friend Rotscheff wrote him from Fort Ross:

> the decision of the Governor of the Russian colonies in America had not been in your favor, since you have not the intention of buying the real estate . . . but merely the cattle, whilst the agent for the Company . . . has found wholesale purchasers, that is to say, for the houses, ranches, and the cattle.

Two weeks later, a rumor having reached him that the pending sale to Vallejo had been consummated, he wrote an indignant letter to Antonio Suñol at San José:

> The Russian gentlemen have found buyers for all their houses and ranches, a fact that pleases me not at all. In the meantime you can get some insight into the character of the Russians. They spoke very loud of preferring to burn all the houses before selling them to a local man, especially to Mr. Vallejo, who had insulted the Russian flag, etc., etc., and now, just to make a few thousands of piastres more, they are not ashamed to make arrangements like this one. I would much rather they did not make any deals with me . . .

In a second letter to Suñol, this one dated September 1, he wrote: "It seems that the Russian gentlemen cannot come to an agreement with Mr. Vallejo; they are renewing negotiations with me, but I shall be a little more exacting now."

But Sutter's resentment was short lived. Four days after his September 1 letter to Suñol he had an unexpected visitor: His friend Alexander Rotscheff, the agent in charge at Fort Ross, arrived at New Helvetia aboard the Russian schooner *Constantine*.

In Sutter's later account of the visit he stated that Rotscheff "offered me the whole establishment at Bodega and Ross for sale, and invited me to come right of [f] with him, as there was a vessel at Bodega, and some Officers with plein power to transact this business with me, and particularly they would give me the preference, as they became well acquainted with me during my months stay at Sitka . . ."

The two proceeded down the river on the *Constantine,* to a landing place on the bay near the San Rafael Mission, where horses were waiting to take them to Bodega. There they were received by Kostromitinoff—who had recently returned from conferring with his superiors at Sitka—aboard the ship *Helena.* After a convivial dinner, which put the guest in a receptive mood, Kostromitinoff got down to business.

In his *Reminiscences* Sutter gives this account of what followed:

> He offered me the Russian establishment at Bodega and Fort Ross, together with the farms and the stores, as well as all the cattle and implements, and the schooner, aboard which the Governor [Rotscheff] had come to my Fort. The price for all this was extremely low—thirty thousand dollars, with a down payment of two thousand dollars. The rest I was to pay in produce, chiefly wheat at two dollars per fanega. No time was specified; every year the Russians would send down a vessel from Alaska and receive from me whatever quantity of wheat I could give them . . .
>
> I did not hesitate to accept this favorable offer. The deed was drawn up immediately, written in French and containing the sentence, 'With the consent of the Emperor of all the Russias!' Since the document had to be witnessed before an *alcalde,* we intended to go to Yerba Buena. Before starting on our trip across the Golden Gate, however, we had a grand dinner on board the *Helena.* Champaigne flowed freely; we drank to the health of the Russian Emperor, and I was toasted as the new owner of Ross and Bodega.

The contract signed under these festive circumstances differs in certain important respects from Sutter's version given above.

The $2,000 down payment was in addition to the original asking price of $30,000, hence the total amount he agreed to pay was $32,000. His statement that no time limit for making payments was specified is also in error; the document stated that the balance was to be paid in four yearly installments. During each of the first and second years Sutter agreed to deliver produce to the value of $5,000. The quota for the third year was to be $10,000, also in wheat and other products, and the final $10,000, due at the end of the fourth year, was to be paid in cash.

The businesslike document contained these further provisions: that all goods must be delivered each September at a designated embarkation point on San Francisco bay and loaded without cost to the company aboard the ships sent to receive it; that the seller must pay such duties or port charges as were levied against the ships during the loading, and that in the event Russia became involved in a war that prevented picking up the produce within the specified time, then "the sanctity of this agreement shall remain inviolable, and as soon as peace is restored, it shall resume its full force." Finally, it was provided that should the buyer fail to meet the terms of the agreement, then his establishment at New Helvetia, "together with all his movable and fixed property, which is in that place, shall serve as a guarantee."

What did Sutter receive in return for shouldering so large a debt and putting all he possessed in jeopardy in the event he was unable to meet his obligations when they fell due? Then and later, the general opinion was that he had made a bad bargain. In the California of the early 1840's $32,000 was no inconsequential sum of money. How much it represented in terms of the products of the country may be seen from the fact that to make up his first two annual payments, which had a value of $5,000 each, he was required to furnish 1,600 bushels of wheat, 160 bushels of peas, 40 bushels of beans, 5,000 pounds each of soap and suet, and 6,250 pounds of tallow.

At the time he assumed his heavy obligation Sutter was aware that the existing facilities at the fort were much too small to produce such quantities of food and other products as the agreement called for, and at the same time provide for the needs of his own numerous staff. On the other hand, his letters make clear that the one thing above all others that was holding back the development of his colony was a lack of just such materials as the Russian purchase would make available. Among these were lumber for houses, workshops, and other buildings; agricultural implements, including plows, rakes, and hoes; horses and mules, harnesses, carts and wagons, a forge, a gristmill, the equipment for cooperage and tanning shops, plus the twenty-ton schooner *Constantine* and several other seagoing ships.

Moreover, his purchase of the Russian properties would, he foresaw, open up a dependable new source of merchandise he would need in the future. "With every vessel that came down the coast to fetch my installment," he later wrote, "they sent supplies which were very necessary to me: iron, steel, ammunition, etc."

Then followed this sentence, which in the light of subsequent happenings takes on an added significance:

"At times I had more ammunition stored up than the whole California Government possessed."

3 THE "FORTRESS"

The deed by which Sutter acquired title to the Fort Ross and Bodega properties was dated December 13, 1841. The document was attested by Francisco Guerrero, the *alcalde* at Yerba Buena, and the signatures were witnessed by Jean Jacques Vioget and Jacob P. Leese.

But Sutter was so proud of his new acquisition and of the added prestige he felt it would give him throughout California that he could not await the formal signing of the agreement before announcing the news to the world. Several weeks earlier he dispatched this curt message to his Sonoma neighbor, General Vallejo:

Esteemed and Honored Sir:

Notice to you that I have bought all the movable and fixed property of the Honorable Russian American Company at Ross and that I am going to send a party of men by land to that place for embarking of the above mentioned furniture, etc. Please be kind enough to allow them to pass the frontier toward Ross and not put any obstacle in their way.

Both the contents of this letter and its tone reflect a marked change that had taken place in Sutter's attitude toward those in authority. In his earlier dealings with them his role had been that of a stranger in a new land asking permission to remain and take out citizenship in order that he might eventually become eligible to receive a grant of land. Less than three years had passed since then, but in the interval his status had changed enormously. He was no longer a suppliant humbly asking favors from the rulers of the province. Such a role had ever been distasteful to him, and now that he felt he could safely do so he lost no time shunting it off. His immense holdings in the Sacramento Valley, the fast-growing community he had created there, and his latest exploit of buying out the Russians—all these had made him a force to be reckoned with. His position now was such that when he wished to ask a favor of a public official—as in the case of his letter to General Vallejo, the commander-in-chief of the military forces in the province—he felt free to so phrase it that it sounded as much like a command as a request.

The California leaders, no less than Sutter himself, were aware of his growing power. Belatedly they had came to realize that one of the chief results of having permitted the persuasive stranger to settle in the interior was that it had attracted to the province the type of emigrants they were most anxious to exclude; namely, the Yankee hunters, trappers, and other veterans of the western trails. By the early 1840's the influx from beyond the mountains was just getting under way. As yet it was only a thin trickle, but the knowledge that Sutter was making the newcomers welcome and was actively encouraging others to follow them was already arousing concern both at Monterey and Mexico City.

The nature of the stronghold the Captain was building in the valley did nothing to allay the misgivings of the Californians.

The fact that he had mounted cannon on its walls, together with the widely held belief that he had formerly been a professional soldier, convinced many that Sutter and his colony were a threat to the security of the province. That feeling was strengthened when it was learned that the goods he had bought from the Russians included a brass fieldpiece and several scores of French flintlock muskets. (Incidentally, the latter were said to have been abandoned by Napaleon's troops during their retreat from Moscow in 1812.)

Relations between Sutter and the California authorities were further strained as the result af a visit in the fall of 1841 of Eugène Duflot de Mofras, a youthful attaché of the French embassy at Mexico City. On his arrival at New Helvetia de Mofras was warmly greeted by Sutter, whereas his reception at Monterey and elsewhere—where he was suspected of having come to spy out the state of the country's defenses—had been much less effusive.

The close friendship that developed between the two was probably based in part on the fact that both felt they had just grievances against the Californians—Sutter because of what he regarded as their hostile attitude toward him and his activities, and de Mofras because af the coolness of his official welcome. But they had other interests in common. One opinion they shared was that Mexico's hold on California was yearly becoming less secure and that it could not be much longer maintained. There is evidence that in the Captain's room at the fort the two discussed the pros and cons of a bold move: no less than a plot by which Sutter would renounce all ties with Mexico and declare New Helvetia an independent state under the protection of France. At the same time, according to the scheme, France was to dispatch a warship to California to aid him in carrying out his coup.

The belief that this picturesque plot was seriously discussed between the two is strengthened by the fact that in his report to his home government de Mofras emphasized what he termed Sutter's long-time admiration for and loyalty to the French. Had he not served as a captain in Charles Tenth's elite Home Guard?

And did not the group he had assembled at New Helvetia include a number of Frenchmen and French Canadians? Finally, the young diplomat was of the opinion that any nation that would support Sutter's bid for independence with a single gunboat and as few as two hundred men could gain control not only of Sutter's Fort but of all California.

Talk of that sort was strong medicine indeed to the impressionable Sutter, and it is not surprising that it caused him to ignore the hard realities of his situation. Moreover, there was basis for his belief that the Californians looked on him as a threat to the security of the province. His taking over of the Russian properties had surprised and disconcerted them. That exploit, plus his intimacy with the visiting French diplomat, had increased the suspicion already aroused by building and arming his massive fort. He was accused of harboring foreigners who were in the country illegally, and of offering asylum to runaway sailors and other fugitives from the coastal towns—both of which charges were true. He was accused too of maintaining a private army by arming his Indian charges and putting them through daily drills, and of failing to return to their owners livestock he had recovered from Indian cattle thieves, and finally, of refusing to make good on promises to pay ranchers and merchants for the large quantities of goods he had bought from them.

Among the Californians who now turned against him were several who had once been helpful. The two rancheros, Ygancio Martinez and Antonio Suñol, were loudly demanding payment for the cattle and other supplies furnished him during his first year in the valley. General Vallejo, who had himself been hopeful of buying out the Russians, wrote the Minister of War and Marine at Mexico City accusing Sutter of holding land at Bodega and Fort Ross "in violation of the rights of the legitimate owners." Even Governor Alvarado, who had been his chief benefactor, was so far disillusioned with the former protégé as to refer to him as "an ungrateful villain."

Suttter's response to such attacks was prompt and emphatic. Writing from what he termed the "Fortress of New Helvetia," on November 8, 1841, he directed a veritable broadside at his critics. His letter was addressed to the Yerba Buena merchant, Jacob P. Leese, but his real targets were Vallejo, Alvarado, and other high government officials.

He began by stating that he had been faithful to the best interests of his adopted country and that he proposed to remain so—but only so long as he was permitted to live in peace and security. He went on to state that "very curious Rapports" had reached him concerning threats of his enemies to drive him from the country, and he assured Leese that should the "poor wretches" attempt to carry out their threats they would meet with "a very warm and hearty reception." He next hinted broadly that should the attacks on him continue he was prepared to "proclaim California for a Republique independent of Mexico" —with, presumably, himself at its head. "The people don't know me yet, but soon they will find out what I am able to do. It is too late now to drive me out of the country."

To back up that boast he listed the weapons then held in readiness at the fort, an arsenal that included ten "well mounted" guns as well as "two field-pieces." At his command too was an army of "about 50 faithful Indians which shot their musquet very quick." (It will be observed that in the Captain's correspondence the more deeply his emotions were involved, the less secure became his command of the language.)

His onslaught continued. The new fort, he boasted, was strong enough to repel any force the Californians might be able to send against it. Moreover, he had powerful allies among the Indians of the Rocky Mountains and the Northwest, whose friendship he had gained during his journey to the coast in 1838; he had but to send a courier telling of how he was being mistreated and they would come rushing to his aid. Nor did he forget his talks with his French friend and the latter's promise of help from that quarter. "The first french fregate to come here will do me justice!" he thundered.

Sutter's blasts were answered by the Californians with salvos of abuse and bombast fully equal to his own. The battle of words continued for some months. No violence ensued, however, and when more pressing concerns came to engage the time and attention of both sides, the old enmities gradually subsided, though they were never entirely forgotten.

4 THE NEW OWNER TAKES CHARGE

> In purchasing the Ross property Sutter had not deliberately intended to swindle the sellers. He had, as was usual with him, assumed a heavy obligation without considering his prospective ability to meet it. That he could make no payments within the time assigned to paying the whole sum did not seem to him an alarming state of affairs.

This comment by Hubert H. Bancroft seems an accurate appraisal of Sutter's intentions on taking over the Russian settlements. He well knew that in order to meet the large debt he had contracted, the yield from his wheat fields and cattle and fur-gathering operations would have to be increased many times over. To produce and deliver 1,600 bushels of wheat and from two-and-a-half to three tons of soap and suet during the first two years, and double that amount during the third, would have been a formidable task even during the period, five or six years in the future, when his colony would reach its fullest development. To one who as yet owned only a few hundred head of cattle, and who lacked both the implements needed to plant and harvest his crops and the workmen trained to use them—to one so situated the outlook seemed hopeless.

But Sutter was never one to take a gloomy view of his own prospects. In his opinion, his deal with the Russians, instead of saddling him with a debt that would take many years to pay off, would be the means of solving all his problems, large and small. The opportunity, by a stroke of the pen, to acquire 3,500 head of cattle, a seagoing launch, several vehicles, a large supply of lumber, tools, and other implements—of all of which he was in dire need—as well as enough guns and ammunition to make his colony secure against any attack by the jealous Californians—that to him would have seemed a bargain at any price. Years later he was so much of the same opinion that he wrote: "I did not hesitate to take their favorable offer."

Once the papers were signed, the Russians, who were anxious to reach Sitka before winter closed down, withdrew to their waiting ship. The new owner's first act, accordingly, was to dispatch a party, headed by a young ex-sailor named Robert Ridley, to arrange for driving the livestock to New Helvetia. It was in preparation for that move that Sutter wrote his curt note to Vallejo asking him not to interfere with the transfer.

A second letter to the Mexican general, written several weeks later, makes clear that not only did Vallejo place no obstacles in the way of the cattle drive but on the contrary did all he could to assist it. "I am very much obliged to you," Sutter wrote him on December 8, "for the help and good advice you gave my men when they passed by Sonoma with the animals, and if I can serve you in any way, please use freely."

That this lengthy drive from Fort Ross to New Helvetia—more than 125 miles separated the two points, without roads of any sort save occasional Indian trails—was successfully accomplished was mainly due to the California *vaqueros*, that proficient breed of Mexican-Indian horsemen who spent virtually their entire adult lives in the saddle. It was not until the drive was nearly over that serious trouble developed. While the animals were being made to ford the Sacramento River about one hundred head, out of a total of nearly two thousand, were swept downstream and drowned. This, however, was not a total loss for, in Sutter's words, "Most of them we could save the hides, our Cal. Bank-notes of the time."

It was at this point that John Bidwell, a twenty-three-year-old youth who had arrived in California with the pioneer Bartleson party a few weeks earlier, reached the fort. He was promptly hired by Sutter and for a number of years remained perhaps the ablest and most loyal of his employees. In his reminiscences written in the late 1880's Bidwell recalled:

He [Sutter] engaged me in January, 1842, to go to Bodega and Fort Ross and to stay there until he could finish removing the property which he had bought from the Russians. At that time the Russians had an orchard of two or three acres of peaches and apples at Fort Ross. I dried the peaches and some of the apples and made cider of the remainder. A small vineyard of white grapes had also been planted . . . I remained at Bodega and Fort Ross fourteen months until everything was removed . . .

During Bidwell's stay the Russian schooner *Constantine*, which Sutter had renamed the *Sacramento*, made frequent trips between Bodega Bay and New Helvetia, carrying whatever materials Sutter thought might be useful to him at the fort: lumber from the dismantled buildings at Fort Ross, farming implements, tools and equipment from the shops and workrooms, household furniture, glass from the windows of the commandant's house, the bell of the Greek chapel, and much else.

Sutter later recalled a picturesque incident in connection with the dismantling af the commandant's house at Ross. When Governor Rotscheff's wife, the former Princess Gargaren, learned of the plan to demolish the building, she urged Sutter to preserve its small glass-walled sunroom, where she and the governor had, she said, spent many pleasant hours. Sutter accordingly had the little room carefully taken apart and taken to New Helvetia. However, his workmen there were unable to fit the parts together again and his plan of reassembling it had to be abandoned.

Within two years after the purchase of the Russian outposts everything Sutter considered salvageable had been removed and transfered to his valley headquarters. Then, in 1844 or 1845, he leased the land, together with such materials as remained, to one of his former employees, William Benitz. That transaction again brought into question the validity of Sutter's title to the property. The position of the Mexican authorities had all along been that neither land nor improvements had ever belonged to the Russians and hence they could not legally be transferred to anyone else. Acting on that assumption Pío Pico, then the governor, in 1845 granted the Rancho Muniz—which consisted of 18,000 acres of heavily wooded land extending from the mouth of the Russian

River to four miles north of Fort Ross—to one Manuel Torres. Most accounts state that William Benitz later bought part of the rancho from Torres, and at about the same time paid Sutter $6,000 to relinquish whatever claims he might have on the property.

This, however, does not agree with Sutter's version. In his dictation to Bancroft, made in 1876, he charged that the Mexican officials "not only refused to give me a title, but sold titles to other settlers who went to Ross and Bodega and took possession of my property." He hinted that this had come about because he had refused to pay a bribe to the provincial Secretary of State, Jimeno Casarin, "who was not very friendly toward me." The upshot, according to his statement, was that "I never received a cent for all the property I was obliged to leave there . . . Yet I had made a good bargain, especially since the payments were easy . . ."

Just how "easy" the payments proved to be and what effect they had on Sutter's future prospects will presently be made clear.

four

Trailbreakers

---

1 THE SUPPLICANT

Sutter was well aware that if the annual installments of his debt to the Russians were to be met, his farming, stock-raising, and other revenue-producing activities would have to be greatly extended.

Whether or not that could be accomplished depended on a number of circumstances. One factor on the credit side of the ledger was that he was now possessed of many thousands of acres of excellent farming and grazing lands. Another advantage was that in the Indian tribes of the valley he had a potential labor force large enough to enable him to care for herds of cattle far larger than he was then running and at the same time to put numerous new fields of wheat, corn, and other crops under cultivation.

On the other hand, the difficulties of the task he had undertaken were such that only one of Sutter's boundless self-confidence would have thought himself capable of overcoming them. Perhaps the chief of his handicaps was his isolation from the rest of the world, a situation that made it almost impossible to obtain dozens of articles necessary to his colony's proper functioning.

Sutter's correspondence demonstrates his perennial concern over that problem. It was a rare letter that did not at some point ask his correspondent's help in overcoming critical shortages of one sort or another. Often it was a request (accompanied by the promise of prompt and liberal payment) that one of his rancher acquaintances favor him with some badly needed draft animals, or a milk cow or two, or perhaps a few bushels of wheat or corn or beans to plant in one of his newly laid out fields.

But even more frequent and importunate were his letters to the pioneer merchants at Yerba Buena and Monterey. These, like those to the rancheros, usually followed a fixed formula. He began by apologizing for his failure to pay for goods already received, then went on to compile a new and generally lengthy list of merchandise he wished to have sent him at the earliest opportunity. Even in those of his letters that were concerned with other matters he could rarely resist slipping in a request for some items of which he was in short supply. Thus in January, 1842, in his capacity as agent of the Mexican government in the valley, he wrote United States Consul Larkin at Monterey asking Larkin to assist two Americans who had recently arrived at the fort and who wished to remain permanently in California. Having concluded with, "I remain Dear Sir! very respectfully Your Most Obdt Servt," he added this postscript:

"If you have some Soap on hand I would be very much obliged to you, to send me about $50 or 100 worth by the first Opportunity."

Writing such letters was not only a laborious and time-consuming chore (for most of them were in Spanish or English, and in neither language did he ever come to feel at home); it was also damaging to his self-esteem. Humility was an attitude he would never have adopted from choice, yet more often than not the tone of his letters was that of a humble asker of favors. His need was so great that time and again he was obliged to cultivate the friendship of men whom he secretly despised, but on whose good will the success of his enterprise depended. His letter to General Vallejo, quoted earlier, is evidence that he sometimes permitted himself the luxury of being imperious, even arrogant. On most occasions, however, he found it prudent to be both humble and apologetic.

Typical of such qualities was a letter written in the summer of 1843 and addressed to William A. Leidesdorff, a native of the Dutch West Indies who operated a trading post at Yerba Buena.

"I am," he began, "ashamed to ask you, but at present necessity
compels me to beg once more your favor . . ." He went on to
explain that he was in need of a further supply of the brown
cotton cloth he used to clothe his native servants and others of
his personal staff—"who are in Rags and naked, and when
strangers come it looks very bad." The letter closed with the re-
assurance that "after having received this favor of you I will
no more trouble you until I have made a good remittance,
I . . . [close] in the hope that you will be kind enough to do me
this favor and you will see that you have done it not to an
ingrateful."

With him it was ever a matter of personal pride, of keeping
up appearances. Visitors to the fort must be favorably impressed
at what they saw. Even so abjectly begging a letter as this was
not too high a price to pay for having his Indians neatly clothed.

2   "MY FAITHFUL SERVANTS"

But it was not altogether because of the impression it
might make on strangers that Sutter disliked to see his natives
running about naked or clad only in ragged shirts and breech-
cloths. He had an interest in his Indian charges and a feeling
of responsibility for their welfare that was almost unique among
the frontiersmen of his day. The claim he often made that he
understood primitive peoples better than most must have had
some basis in fact. All the evidence indicates that he got along
well with members of such races wherever he came in contact
with them, whether the Indians of the trans-Mississippi frontier,
the Kanakas of the Sandwich Islands, the Aleuts of the far
north, or the native tribes of the Sacramento Valley.

In his later years he liked to tell of how when he arrived in
the valley he set about winning the friendship of the natives. As
he and his party first made their way up the river, the Indians
left their camps along the banks of the stream at the approach
of the boats and fled into the interior. Then, after the party had
gone ashore for the night, the natives gathered some distance
from the camp and watched the strangers' movements curiously.

His first task, Sutter explained, was to overcome the timidity of the savages and convince them that he and his fellows wished to be friendly. One means he used to bring that about was to visit their deserted camps and leave beads, bits of cloth, lumps of sugar, or other small gifts for them to find on their return. Another was to approach them unarmed and to address them in friendly tones, avoiding any sign of fear on the one hand or of threatening behavior on the other. By such methods the suspicion of the natives was gradually overcome. Before many weeks had passed, the tribes of the vicinity had so far overcome their fears that considerable numbers of them were encamped about the new settlement. Sutter then began training his untutored guests in the simple tasks that would, he hoped, make them useful members of the colony.

One circumstance that proved helpful in such efforts was that each of the valley tribes usually had a member or two who had formerly been stationed at one of the California missions. That had come about because, following the secularization of the missions in the early 1830's, many had returned to their ancestral hunting grounds and resumed their old way of life. Most of these had been taught to cultivate land or tend cattle or perform other tasks set for them by the mission fathers, and all could speak and understand at least a few words of Spanish. These former mission Indians proved useful to Sutter by acting as interpreters during his meetings with the chiefs of the local tribes, meetings that resulted in the chiefs agreeing to supply him with gangs of laborers. By such agreements the workers were required to serve for specified periods, usually two weeks, at the end of which time they were replaced by others. On being dismissed they were paid "wages" that in the early period were likely to consist of colored handkerchiefs, cotton shirts, or such other articles of wearing apparel as Sutter had been able to procure. (Incidentally, instead of being worn, these items were often hung to the branches of trees to ward off evil spirits.)

Because labor for labor's sake had never held any attraction for the Californian Indian, it was necessary for Sutter to keep his work crews under constant surveillance to prevent their deserting should an opportunity present itself. Accordingly, during the period the gangs remained on duty it was the custom to confine them each night in a stockade and to allow them out only during working hours.

Although such treatment of the natives was then usual in many parts of the frontier, it was the one phase of life at the fort that visitors most often found objectionable. For to crowd so many into so confined a space, without beds or sanitary facilities of any sort, and except for the time when they were at work, to keep them there considerable periods, seemed to many a shocking state of affairs.

One of those who held that opinion was a Swiss emigrant named Heinrich Lienhard, who arrived in California in 1846 and for the next several years served as clerk and "keeper of the keys" at the fort. Lienhard's recollections, although they were put down many years later, present a revealing picture of the day-by-day life at New Helvetia during those years.

Among his duties was that of locking up the work gangs each night " in order to prevent them from returning to their homes in the mountains." Since the stockade where they were confined had, as stated earlier, been provided with neither beds nor straw nor sanitary arrangements, he observed that "the condition of the place after ten days or two weeks can be imagined."

Lienhard also described the method of feeding the native workers:

> They were given cooked wheat that was thrown in troughs; the natives sat in front of these feeding pens and ate the steaming wheat with their dirty hands, stuffing it into the mouths with loud noises that sounded exactly like a flock of cackling geese. In addition, they were allowed a small amount of beef, which they preferred to eat either in the evening or early in the morning after it was cooked over hot coals. It seemed to give them keen enjoyment; they bolted the meat greedily, in spite of the ashes that clung to it.

In addition to such transient groups, a considerable number of natives lived permanently at the fort. Among them were the young braves of Sutter's personal bodyguard, a group that, in his words, "numbered about twelve or fifteen . . . mounted Indians under the command of a very intelligent sargeant." The guardsmen were quartered near Sutter's bedroom, "so that I could be notified if anything happened." These youths were prime favorites of the Captain, and in consequence their treatment was far different than that of the fieldworkers, whose lot could not readily be distinguished from slavery. The reason for his pleasure in his small private army is understandable: all his life he had pictured himself as a dashing military leader, and now at last he had a detachment of troops obedient to his commands. He made the most of the situation. Life at the fort was conducted with the disciplined austerities of an army post. "I had an hour-glass installed," he once recalled, "and during the night the guards struck the bell every time the sand ran out, and cried, 'All is well'; summer and winter at daybreak, the bell was rung for all hands to get up and go to work."

Nothing pleased him more than to impress visitors with the smart appearance and military bearing of his "home guard." "The Indian boys," he wrote, "were obliged to appear every Sunday morning for drill, well washed and neatly clad. Their uniforms consisted of blue drill pantaloons, white cotton shirts, and red handkerchiefs tied around their heads. They were very proud of this uniform. After drill they could visit their friends at the Indian villages, and spend the day as they pleased."

Although in later life he frequently referred to his Indians as "faithful servants" and boasted of his success at winning their friendship, there is evidence that their relations were considerably less harmonious than he pictured them in retrospect. As indicated earlier, one of his major problems was that of keeping them on the job. Despite the vigilance of their overseers they were constantly stealing away from the fields and gardens and cattle ranges about the fort and fleeing to the foothills, where from time to time they had to be rounded up and forcibly returned. The expeditions against the fugitives were usually conducted by Sutter's elite home guard, the members of which looked on the runaways as uncivilized savages to be hunted down and driven back like wild animals.

Yet another of the native's shortcomings that caused Sutter a great deal of trouble was his larcenous instinct. For among the white man's rules of conduct, the one he found hardest to comprehend was that having to do with the ownership of property. When a California Indian coveted something, whether it be a pony, a gun, a hunting knife, or some object of trifling value, his impulse was to help himself to it; even the likelihood that he would be caught and severely punished rarely proved a deterrent.

Heinrich Lienhard cites two examples of that all-but-universal trait:

> When slaughtering took place, I noticed that the choicest pieces of meat disappeared rapidly toward the rear of the fort. Having discovered that this was being done without Sutter's permission, I knew he wanted it stopped, so next time some animals were killed I kept an eye on the Indians. They did not know I was watching them, for I pretended to be occupied with other matters. Soon the Indians began to sneak to the rear of the fort with large pieces of meat. I cornered them where they could not escape, and made them return their plunder to the meat room, slapping their thick, vermin-infected heads . . .
>
> Our bakery was always being looted, too. Often, after bread had been made, I saw Indians leaving the room carrying large bundles. I began to watch, and one day when the bread was about to be taken from the oven, I sat where I could see every door that led outside. I confiscated one large package being carried off by a huge, overgrown boy, and thrashed him soundly.

3 SHIFTING LOYALTIES

When, on August 29, 1840, Sutter became a citizen of Mexico, Governor Alvarado, as stated earlier, conferred on him a further distinction by making him the official representative of the government in the Sacramento Valley. On assuming that office he was expected, among other things, to enforce "all the laws of the country, to function as political authority and dispenser of justice in order to prevent the robberies committed by adventurers from the United States, to prevent the invasion of savage Indians and the hunting and trapping by companies from the Columbia."

To one who himself had only recently arrived in the valley this seemed a large order. Yet during the first several years he made a conscientious effort to carry out these and other official duties. While he seems to have doubted the wisdom of some of the laws he was expected to enforce, with one of them—that excluding foreign hunters and trappers from the province—he was in full accord. For in that case his own fortunes were deeply involved, the reason being that, as noted earlier, the Hudson's Bay Company each year was sending parties down from Oregon to gather furs along the northern California streams—an activity that brought them into direct competition with Sutter's own bands of trappers. Governor Alvarado's failure to heed his appeals that strong measures be taken to bar the northerners from the province was a keen disappointment to him. Thereafter he grew steadily more critical of what he considered the weak and vacillating behavior of the officials at Monterey.

As time passed, however, Sutter was forced to revise his views as to the wisdom of excluding all foreigners from the province. It grew clear to him that if his colony were to survive and prosper he must not, as his official position required him to do, try to bar them from the valley, but on the contrary he should welcome them and urge them to remain. Belatedly he came to realize that the emigrants who were beginning to drift in over the newly opened trails were not only a prime source of the skilled workers he needed to operate the mills and shops he planned to establish, but they would also provide a market for the goods his industries would produce.

Sutter's eventual decision to cast his lot with the newcomers and against the government was made easier by his growing estrangement from the California leaders. "Vallejo and the others were jealous of my settlement," he once stated, "and resented my giving passports to all people who came from the north and east. I was friendly with the immigrants and encouraged immigration whenever I could, while the Mexicans disliked the Americans and were afraid of increased immigration."

Sutter's Fort was the first outpost of civilization reached by all but a few of these early overland parties. And because they invariably arrived with both men and animals spent from weeks and months on the trail, Sutter gained the gratitude of the groups by his hospitable welcome, by providing them with food and shelter, and by assuring them that they were welcome to stay on as his guests as long as they wished.

As time passed he came to look on himself as the chief champion of the emigrants' cause, as one who stood between them and those who would drive them back across the mountains. In November, 1845, he wrote a highly emotional letter to United States Consul Larkin telling of his determination to see that the party of emigrants then at the fort received just treatment at the hands of the authorities.

"I wish you . . . could come up here, to assist your respectable Countrymen with their family's," he began. "It is a pity to see them in a such a situation, as they are now; if it would not be in your power, or in the power of a Man of War to protect them, *I will do it.* All are protected here and before I will suffer an injustice done, to them, I will die first. The snow is on the top of the mountains, and their Animals are worn out. Some of them have spent all their property to come here with their family's, some others have plenty of money and other property, but they could not leave the Country before next month of May or Juin."

4 BARTLESON, BIDWELL, AND COMPANY

At the time this letter was written, the overland migration to California was already well under way; when Sutter first reached the valley six years earlier it had not yet begun.

Until 1839 the only white men to enter the province from the north or east were the far-ranging hunters and trappers, and even

their visits were few and far between. It was not until the spring
of 1841 that the first company of California-bound emigrants
headed westward from the Missouri frontier, intent on making
their homes in the west coast Mexican possession. This was the
Bartleson party, so called for its captain, a Missouri farmer
named John Bartleson. The large group—it numbered sixty-nine
men, women, and children—set off from Sapling Grove, Missouri,
on May 12 and during the first part of their journey followed
the trail to the northwest that had been broken by the fur traders,
the same route Sutter had passed over three years earlier. Then,
on reaching a point near the present Wyoming-Idaho border, the
company divided, some continuing on to the Oregon country,
while the others turned toward the southwest and entered the
barren region that lay between the Rockies and the Sierra.

— This second group—which has the distinction of having
opened the emigrant trail to California—numbered thirty-one
men, one woman, and one child. It was a young party, the majority being still in their twenties and the patriarch of the group
only a year or two over forty. Nearly all were frontiersmen, natives of the upper Mississippi Valley; hence, they were familiar
with the use of firearms and adept at handling the oxen and
mules that drew their heavily loaded wagons. They were, however, without experience at breaking trail over the hundreds of
miles of uncharted countryside that lay ahead.

Considering the odds against them, the group came through
better than might have been expected. Through the summer of
1841 they pushed westward, passing to the north of Great Salt
Lake and crossing the waterless plains of present-day Utah and
Nevada to the base of the Sierra. The next, and final, part of
their journey proved to be by far the most difficult. The passage
over the mountains began in early August; it was not until the
end of October that the bedraggled and half-starved group made
their way down the west slope of the range into the San Joaquin
Valley. During the crossing they had been forced to abandon
their wagons, to kill their animals for food, and to discard all
their possessions save what could be carried on their backs.

Several members of the party later wrote accounts of their experiences en route. One was Sutter's future employee, John Bidwell, an ex-schoolteacher who had just turned twenty-one when he reached California and who was to become and remain a distinguished citizen of the state until his death nearly sixty years later. On emerging from the mountains, Bidwell and a few companions made their way across the valley to Los Meganos Rancho, near the base of Mount Diablo. Los Meganos was owned by a close-fisted misanthrope named John Marsh, who had reached California four or five years earlier and, posing as a physician (although he had had no medical training), had succeeded in stocking his rancho by demanding that his professional fees be paid in horses, cows, and sheep.

In his memoir, Bidwell states that after a brief stay at the Marsh rancho he and several others decided to move on.

"We had already heard that a man by the name of Sutter was starting a colony a hundred miles away to the north in the Sacramento Valley," he wrote. "No other civilized settlement had been attempted anywhere east of the Coast Range; before Sutter came the Indians had reigned supreme. As the best thing to be done I now determined to go to Sutter's . . ."

As Bidwell and his three companions started up the valley rain began to fall and continued without a break during their entire trip. Fording the swollen streams so slowed their progress that they ran out of food. Moreover, their situation was complicated by the fact that although game was plentiful, wet powder made their guns useless. It was a damp and hungry group that filed through the gate at the fort after eight days on the trail. "Sutter received us with open arms and in princely fashion," Bidwell recalled, and went on to comment on their host's "most polite address and most courteous manners."

Sutter in turn was so favorably impressed by his guest that he offered him a post as one of the chief assistants. During the next several years the young man served his employer well. As noted earlier, he acted for a time as overseer at Fort Ross while the movable property there was being transferred to New Helvetia. Later he took over the management of Hock Farm, Sutter's ranch on the Feather River. Later still, in 1849, Bidwell acquired a 22,000-acre ranch in the upper Sacramento Valley. Over the years he greatly increased his holdings and gradually developed them into one of the most valuable fruit-growing properties in the state.

5   THE ADVANCE GUARD

John Bidwell was but one of many recently arrived emigrants who found employment at the fort. Its ambitious owner had need of all who applied; it was his boast that he had never turned anyone away. "I have plenty to do for 60 or 80 men," he wrote John Marsh early in 1841, and the time was not far off when he would have several times that number on his payroll.

The first considerable addition to his original staff was made in the summer of 1840. This was a party of five men who had come down from Oregon on the schooner *Lausanne,* landed at Bodega Bay, and from there made their way overland to New Helvetia. Of these, the best remembered is Peter Lassen who, after several years plying his trade of blacksmith at the fort and elsewhere, left Sutter's employ and, like Bidwell, acquired large holdings in the upper valley. During the next decade Lassen became one of the largest landowners in the northern end of the state. Today his name is preserved in a mountain, a national park, a California county, a creek, and an early trail across the mountains.

Another member of the Bartleson-Bidwell party who held a responsible position at the fort was Charles Flügge, a literate German whom Sutter had known at St. Louis and who for a year or two after his arrival in California served the Captain as his "clerk and adviser." A third member of that same group was another German, Henry Huber. For a time Huber had charge of the first of the fort's industries to yield its owner a profit; namely, the distillery where the strong native *aguardiente* was made from wheat, corn, and the wild grapes that grew along the river banks.

The active year 1841 saw, too, the arrival at the fort of a numerous scientific party: six whaleboats and a launch bearing up wards of sixty men under the command of Lieutenant J. Ring-gold, U.S.N. The visitors were members of a government explor-ing expedition commanded by Lieutenant Charles Wilkes, the ships of which had dropped anchor in San Francisco Bay on August 14.

The appearance of Ringgold and his party, who were engaged in exploring and charting the river, gave Sutter an opportunity to play the role he most relished: that of greeting his visitors hospitably and entertaining them as elaborately as his limited facilities permitted. He recalled:

> I received information of their coming before they reached the landing place. Whenever strangers came into the valley, my Indians gave me notice of their approach, telling me whether they were white men, as they called the Americans, or Califor-nians . . . I immediately dispatched a clerk to establish the iden-tity of the visitors. The clerk was very glad when he saw the American flag. I at once sent down saddle horses for the officers and fired a salute when they arrived at the Fort. They were very much interested to find a flourishing establishment in this wilderness, and it made a very good impression upon the Indians to see so many white men visiting me . . . Ringgold was survey-ing the Sacramento River, and the following day he continued his journey, going as far as the Buttes [a group of rugged hills in the center of the valley about fifty miles north of the fort, now known as Sutter Buttes]. Two of his men deserted and Lieu-tenant Ringgold requested me to arrest them, but I could not find them. Afterwards they came out of their hiding place, and I employed one of them in my tannery.

Meanwhile Sutter had been making an effort to comply with the provision of his grant that required him to recruit twelve families who would purchase part of his land and settle there permanently. This proved to be no easy task. During the begin-ning 1840's the number of emigrants reaching California was still quite small, and few among them were willing or able to pay the cash, or goods, or services Sutter demanded in exchange for his land. A second requirement of the grant—namely, that the purchasers be Mexican citizens and the heads of families—presented less difficulty. For a year's residence in the province made the foreigner eligible for citizenship, and in order to qualify as a family man he had only to share his cabin with a squaw.

Perhaps the first to receive title to a portion of Sutter's New Hevlvetia grant was Theodore Cordua. Cordua was also a native of Germany; after varied experiences in South America and elsewhere, he had reached California in 1842. In exchange for some merchandise Cordua had brought with him, Sutter gave him a square league of grazing land on the Yuba River near its confluence with the Feather. This he stocked with horses, sheep, and cattle, and, on the site of present-day Marysville, built a one-story adobe ranch house that became a regular stopping place for those traveling between California and Oregon. During 1842 and 1843 several others acquired land in exchange for services rendered at the fort, but by the end of the latter year their number was still short of the required twelve. By then, however, Sutter considered his position so secure that he no longer felt obliged to abide by the terms of his grant.

Meanwhile the preliminary phases of the great westward migration had moved a step nearer. In the fall of 1843 the largest single group yet to make the overland trek reached the fort. These, some forty in all, were led by Joseph B. Chiles, a veteran of the Bartleson party two years earlier, and a far-ranging trapper named Joseph Reddeford Walker. The Chiles-Walker party had taken the by then well-traveled Oregon Trail as far as Fort Hall; then, because of a shortage of provisions and the lateness of the season, it had divided into two sections. Chiles, with about a dozen mounted men, unencumbered by wagons, had hurried on ahead, taking a northerly route to Fort Boise, then swinging southwest and entering California at its extreme northeastern corner.

In the interim the larger party, which was led by Walker and included four women and five children, had turned toward the south, proceeded down the east side of the Sierra, and crossed over the summit into the Owens Valley. During that crossing they, like the Bartleson party before them, had been forced to abandon their wagons and nearly all their other possessions. From the Owens Valley they packed over the Walker Pass into the southern end of the San Joaquin Valley. Then, having proceeded some distance up the San Joaquin and crossed over the Coast Range, they eventually reached the ranch of John Gilroy near the present town of that name.

The other group, having covered more than a thousand miles after leaving Fort Hall on September 16, reached New Helvetia on November 10, with both men and animals near exhaustion from the rigors of the trip. Besides the leader, Chiles, this part of the expedition included P. B. Reading, Samuel Hensley, Milton McGee, and four brothers named Williams, all of whom later became prominent in California affairs. Of their adventures en route Sutter stated in his *Reminiscences:* "They had had several hard fights with the Indians; McGee had fallen into a bear trap during one of these fights." He added: "When these men came to the Fort, I placed a number of them in my employment. Reading became my bookkeeper and Hensley I made super-cargo of the schooner [the *Sacramento,* which he had acquired from the Russians] and superintendent of my business at the [San Francisco] Bay."

Hensley and Reading remained with Sutter for several years. Hensley took a leading part in the Bear Flag revolt of 1846; then, during the early months of the gold rush, he and Reading operated a miners' supply store at the fort. Later still, in 1851, he helped organize the California Steam Navigation Company which for several decades enjoyed a virtual monopoly on the freight and passenger traffic on the Sacramento.

Reading's career was no less eventful. In 1844, partly through Sutter's influence, he was granted the Rancho Buena Ventura, a three-mile-wide strip of land at the northern end of the valley, and which extended nineteen miles along the west bank of the Sacramento River. During 1846–47 he took part in the conquest of California as a member of the California Battalion, attaining the rank of major. He then returned to the north where the adobe ranch house he built on his property became noted as a center of hospitality in that then remote region. After the gold discovery

Reading helped develop the rich Trinity River mines. In 1851 he became a candidate for governor of California, and although he failed of election he thereafter remained an influential figure in the affairs of the state until his death in 1868.

The two-pronged Chiles-Walker expedition was the last large company to reach California for a full year. "After that, immigration continued in small parties," Sutter stated in his dictation to Bancroft. "They were usually just strong enough to protect themselves against the hostile Indians. All immigrants were hospitably received by me. I took into my service as many as I could, and the others could stay under my roof as long as they liked."

That quiet interlude, however, was the calm before the storm. For by the mid-1840's the question of the annexation of California by the United States had become a major political issue in Washington and elsewhere throughout the nation. For some time letters and articles describing the attractions of the region had been appearing in Eastern and Middle Western newspapers, and in scores of towns and villages all over the land groups were laying plans to migrate to the new Utopia. The result of this heightened interest was that, by Sutter's account, less than two years later "all the buildings and houses of my settlement were filled . . . with wet, poor, hungry immigrants—men, women and children. Sometimes the houses were so full of people, that I could hardly find a place to sleep."

But before that day arrived, not alone Sutter's little community but all California had been jarred from its normal routine by a new series of events.

five

Warfare—California Style

---

1 CAPTAIN OF MILITIA

Not the least colorful chapter of Sutter's by no means drab career was that during which he, who all his life had been fascinated by the pomp and display of military life— and who knew nothing of the realities of warfare—found himself commanding a regiment of troops during one of Spanish-California's far from sanguinary civil wars.

This unexpected development came about because at the time of his arrival in 1839, and for some years prior to that date, the Californians had been growing progressively less satisfied with the men sent from Mexico City to rule over them. The consequence of their discontent was that in 1831, and again in 1836, they staged revolts against their governors, sent them back to Mexico, and replaced them with men of their own choosing. It was as a result of the 1836 uprising that Juan Bautista Alvarado, who served as governor during Sutter's first three years in California, came to occupy that office.

Then, in 1842, Mexico's president, Antonio López de Santa Anna, alarmed at the growing number of foreigners arriving in California and at the threat they posed to his country's hold on the province, dispatched a new governor northward. The latter's instructions were to see that the laws prohibiting any but Mexican nationals from owning land in California, or from settling there permanently, were strictly enforced. The man who received that assignment, and along with it the titles of Governor, Inspector, and *Commandante-General*, was Manuel Micheltorena, a general in the Mexican army. With him were sent some 250 soldiers to reenforce the small number of regular troops already in the province.

For a time this new arrangement seems to have worked out to the satisfaction of all concerned. Micheltorena proved to be a man of amiable disposition who exerted himself to win the friendship and support of both the native Californians and the naturalized citizens. In that attempt he was eminently successful insofar as Sutter was concerned. As we shall see, Sutter became one of his staunchest supporters in the conflicts that presently developed.

The source of the trouble between Micheltorena and a majority of the Californians was the contingent of unruly soldiers he brought with him. For the *cholos*, as they were known, were for the most part, decidedly a bad lot; nearly all were ex-convicts who had been released from the jails at Mexico City and elsewhere and sent to California not only to bolster the defenses there but also—and perhaps mainly—as a convenient means of getting them out of the country.

Although the new Governor tried hard to keep his dubious army under control, it was not long before the penniless conscripts (who had not been paid in many months) had shocked residents at Monterey and other towns by committing all manner of misdeeds, ranging from petty theft to assaults, burglaries, and like offenses, including attacks on the local señoritas.

In the eyes of the Californians the depredations of his hated *cholos* more than outweighed the Governor's constructive accomplishments in other fields. The latter included his conciliation of the local priests by restoring to them some of the church property of which they had been deprived when the missions were secularized nine years earlier. He also established the beginnings of an educational system in California, and instituted reforms designed to ease growing political rivalries between residents of the northern and southern halves of the province.

Such services, however, were not enough to placate those who had suffered at the hands of the lawless *cholos,* and a secret movement got under way aimed at forcing Micheltorena from office and sending him and his convict army back to Mexico. Among the leaders of that plot were Sutter's old benefactor, Juan Alvarado, whom Micheltorena had succeeded as governor, and José Castro. These are the two who, with Alvarado's uncle, General Mariano Vallejo, had led the coup of 1836 that had ousted Governor Nicholas Gutiérrez from office and installed Alvarado in his place. This time, however, Vallejo refused to join in the plot; instead he urged his friends and acquaintances, including Sutter, to refuse to take sides in the upcoming struggle.

But the Captain was in no mood to heed such advice. By the time Micheltorena became governor in 1842 Sutter was already on bad terms with both Alvarado and Vallejo—Alvarado because as governor he had, as stated earlier, refused to take strong measures to exclude the Hudson's Bay Company trappers from the valley, and Vallejo because of real or fancied slights that he believed were due to jealousy on the General's part at Sutter's success in buying out the Russians. Because of his strained relations with both men, Sutter was anxious to assure himself of the friendship and good will of the new governor.

One of his fears was that his enemies might be first to gain the ear of Micheltorena and give him a misleading account of the nature of his activities at the fort. He therefore dispatched his friend, Carl Flügge, who had recently become a member of his staff, to seek out the newly arrived official and intercede on his behalf.

"Flügge met Micheltorena at Los Angeles, where the Governor resided during the first months of his reign," Sutter later recalled.

> He explained to him that I had no evil intentions against the Mexican government and only resented encroachments from the Californians. The latter were constantly interfering with my business, and General Vallejo in particular had repeatedly thrown obstacles in the way of my communications with the Bay . . .
>
> The new Governor appeared satisfied with Flügge's represen-

tations . . . He wrote me a very kind letter, stating that he had
nothing against me.

The two men exchanged letters from time to time, but nearly
two years passed before they met. That came about because in
the summer of 1844 the Governor's superiors at Mexico City, having belatedly become concerned for the safety of the country's
northern possession, instructed him to organize a military force
that could reenforce the regular army in the event of attack by
a foreign aggressor. One of the first steps taken by Micheltorena
when he set about assembling his civilian army was to make
Sutter a captain of militia and put him in charge of recruiting and
training volunteers on the northern frontier.

To the martial-minded Sutter this was, of course, a highly gratifying assignment. For now at last, after years of deception and
pretense, he had an authentic military title of which he could
boast. The newly created captain set about his duties with enthusiasm. Before the summer was over his headquarters, which
already presented something of a military aspect, took on the appearance of an armed camp. Both his own workers and settlers
in the valley, as well as strangers who chanced to be passing
through, were assembled at the fort, provided with firearms and,
under the direction of two of his employees who were veterans
of the German army, daily put through several hours of strenuous
drill.

These preparations were still going on when, early in October,
1844, the Captain received a message from Micheltorena ordering
him to Monterey. It was while he was responding to that sum-
mons that he first heard rumors that the Governor's enemies were
plotting to force him from office. In his *Reminiscences* he stated:

> On the way to the capital I visited James [his full name was
> James Alexander] Forbes, the British vice-consul, at his resi-
> dence near San José. Forbes, having married a daughter of the
> country, was naturally in the secrets of the Californians and
> knew everything that was going on. He told me that the Cali-
> fornians were preparing to attack Micheltorena and send him

and his troops out of the country . . . As a matter of fact, the revolutionists were ready to blockade the General at Monterey, to send him back to Mexico, and select a Governor from their own people . . . I was well aware of what we could expect if the Californians were to succeed in their scheme . . .

Sutter hastened on to Monterey where, if one is to accept his own version, he was given a hero's welcome. "I was," he stated, "received with the highest civil and military honors"—the high point of which was an elaborate dinner tendered him by Michel-torena. "After the banquet, the Governor and I, as Captain of the Mexican Militia, reviewed the garrison lined up in parade, and in the evening a large balloon was sent up into the sky." All in all, it was a memorable day in the life of the former Burg-dorf drygoods merchant.

But his stay at Monterey was not all devoted to such matters, pleasant as they were. Sutter had several subjects of serious import that needed to be discussed with his friend the Governor. For one thing, there were the disquieting rumors he had picked up from Vice-Consul Forbes; clearly it was his duty to pass these on to his host, who was also his superior officer. But no less important from his standpoint was a plan he had had in mind for months, one by which he hoped greatly to increase his holdings in the valley. And what better occasion to bring that up than now, when the Governor's subjects were plotting a rebellion and when he might have desperate need of Sutter's help in putting down the rebels? Clearly this was the time to make known his wish to extend the limits of his colony.

To be sure, the amount of land Sutter already owned was far from niggardly. By the terms of the New Helvetia grant, which Alvarado had awarded him three years earlier, he had received eleven square leagues within an area that extended from below the junction of the Sacramento and American rivers on the south to well above that of the Feather and Yuba on the north. His aim now was to consolidate his possessions by a second grant that would give him title to all the land within the boundaries of the original grant. The inclusion of these marginal or, as they were called, *sobrante* lands would more than triple the size of his holdings, making him the owner of an empire of truly princely proportions.

Sutter was aware that Mexico's hold on California was growing less secure year by year, and that if he hoped to gain this further concession it would be well to act promptly. Moreover, the trend of recent events was favorable to his hopes. The threatened revolt had put him in a strong bargaining position, for there was every likelihood that Micheltorena would soon have need of the troops then in training at the fort. It might, indeed, have been the Governor's realization of that fact that accounted for the warmth of Sutter's welcome.

The precise nature of the discussions that took place between the two during their October meeting is not known. What *is* known is that on February 5 of the following year Sutter received the hoped-for *sobrante* grant and thereby became the owner of more than 225 square miles of rich farming and grazing lands in the heart of the Sacramento Valley.

2   THE SMELL OF POWDER

John Bidwell, who had accompanied his employer to Monterey, later wrote an account of what had transpired during the visit. One point he made was that Sutter feared that the insurgents, aware of his friendship with Micheltorena, might try to take him prisoner on his way back to the valley. He accordingly abandoned his plan of returning by land and instead slipped out of the harbor on a ship bound for Yerba Buena. Then, on reaching that village, he boarded his launch, the *Sacramento*, and proceeded up the river.

Bidwell's narrative describes further developments:

> In a few days the first blow was struck, the insurgents taking all the horses belonging to the Governor at Monterey, setting the Governor and all his troops on foot. He raised a few horses as best he could and pursued them . . . However, I understood

that a sort of parley took place at or near San José, but not battle, surrender or settlement.

Meanwhile, having started to return to Sutter's Fort, 200 miles distant, I met the Governor returning to Monterey. He stopped his forces and talked to me half an hour and confided to me his plans. He desired me to beg the Americans to be loyal to Mexico; to assure them that he was their friend, and in due time would give them all the lands to which they were entitled. He sent particularly friendly word to Sutter. I then went on to the mission of San José and there fell in with the insurgents, who made that place their headquarters. I stayed all night and the leaders, Castro and Alvarado, treated me like a prince. The two insurgents protested their friendship for the Americans and sent a request to Sutter to support them.

According to this observer, the question of what side they should support in the coming revolt was carefully considered by the foreigners assembled at the fort. Governor Micheltorena was the choice of all but a few. "He had been our friend," wrote Bidwell, "he had granted us land; he promised, and we were sure we could rely upon, his continued friendship; and we were sure, indeed, we knew, we could not repose the same confidence on the native Californians."

Sutter's account of the situation is in the same vein. "When I reached New Helvetia," he reported, "I immediately began preparations for the expected campaign. I organized and drilled companies, and my fort had all the appearances of a military camp. All the settlers in the valley were enthusiastic for the cause and joined me heartily."

As events were to prove, neither Bidwell's nor Sutter's statements as to where the sympathies of the settlers lay were wholly correct. Not all the Americans in the valley favored Micheltorena and his *cholos*. Some supported the Californians in their fight for home rule, while others argued that the matter was one for the natives to settle among themselves and that all others should remain aloof. But Micheltorena's implied promise to be liberal to those who aided his cause counted heavily with the land-hungry newcomers, and a clear majority elected to fight on his side. The upshot of these discussions was that early in December Sutter, disregarding messages from Vallejo, Marsh, and others urging caution, dispatched a courier to Monterey informing the Governor that the men under his command were ready to come to his aid whenever they were needed.

The bearer of Sutter's message was his longtime servant, Pablo Gutierrez, a Mexican youth whom he had first met at Santa Fe and who had accompanied him on most of his subsequent travels. Because in order to reach Monterey Gutierrez would have to pass through enemy territory, elaborate precautions were taken to prevent the letters he carried from falling into the hands of the Castro-Alvarado faction. On his first round trip to the capital he managed to get through safely; however, on the second—he was then bearing word that Sutter's army was on the march—he was not so fortunate. At a point in the Santa Clara Valley near present-day Gilroy he was intercepted by a squad of Castro's men; the message, which had been sewed into the lining of one of his boots, was found. He was given a brief trial, then was hanged as a spy from the limb of a nearby oak.

By then there was no turning back. Having assembled and trained and equipped his small force, the prospect of leading it into battle filled its commanding officer with visions of military glory. Attempts to dissuade him from what to many seemed a foolhardy exploit were impatiently brushed aside. Here was an opportunity to realize a long-standing ambition, and nothing must be permitted to deprive him of it. General Vallejo's temperate and rational letter of December 18, in which he outlined his own reasons for remaining neutral and advised Sutter to do likewise, was ignored. And when one of his former employees, Charles M. Weber, who then lived near the Castro-Alvarado headquarters at San José, appeared at the fort to present the case of the Californians, Sutter refused to listen. Instead, he had Weber and his two companions thrown into jail where they remained for the duration of the campaign.

Sympathy for the cause of the insurgents cost Sutter's Mount Diablo neighbor, John Marsh, an even greater indignity than that meted out to Weber. In a curt message dated January 3, 1845, and signed "J. A. Sutter, Commander in Chief of the forces of the Sacramento," the rancher was ordered to provide Sutter's men with horses, oxen, a two-wheeled *carreta*, and sundry other items, and himself to join the campaign against Micheltorena's enemies—all under threat of being put in irons and sent to join Weber in the guardhouse at the fort. Marsh accepted the lesser of these alternatives: that of serving as a private in Sutter's army. Thus, throughout the campaign that followed, the owner of the huge Los Meganos Rancho trudged along as a lowly foot soldier in the ranks while Sutter rode in state at the head of the column. Although he did not realize it at the time, his harsh treatment of his neighbor was a major mistake of judgment on Sutter's part, and one that in the end would cost him heavily.

But that was still some weeks in the future; meanwhile Captain Sutter was riding high. As head of what he proudly termed "the largest military force ever assembled in the north" he held un-challenged authority over the fortunes of everyone who lived in the region. It was a heady experience for the power-loving Sutter, one that, judging by his frequent references to it in later years, became and remained one of the high points of his career. While recalling the experience during his dictation to Bancroft more than thirty years later, he announced: "The whole country stood in awe of me!"

His account of the campaign—which in a number of respects differs from other versions—begins:

> At the end of December I received marching orders from the Governor. On the first day of 1845 we left the Fort with music and colors flying for Doctor Marsh's farm near Mount Diablo. My force consisted of several hundred men: a company of eighty-five riflemen under Captain John Gantt, a former officer of the United States army; a company of over one hundred In-dians, well drilled and commanded in German by Ernst Rufus, with Jacob Düe and Rufino, the Chief of the Mokelumnes, as lieutenants; a small squadron of cavalry, native Californians who had deserted Vallejo and joined me; and a detachment of artil-lery. At the Fort I left a garrison of about fifteen white men

and thirty Indian sharpshooters in command of Major Reading. The cavalry and artillery took the land route, while the infantry was embarked on my schooner. We all met at Los Meganos.

Having requisitioned "two bullocks . . . also one yoke of oxen" from Los Meganos's close-fisted owner, Dr. Marsh, and forced the Doctor himself to join up "as a common soldier," Sutter led his expeditionary force on to the south, his announced intention being to come to the rescue of Micheltorena's beleaguered force at Monterey. This proved to be unnecessary, for at word of the approach of Sutter's column the insurgents abandoned their blockade of the capital and started withdrawing down the coast. Their objective was the pueblo of Los Angeles, where anti-government sentiment was strong. At a public meeting held there early in January, a resolution aimed at ousting Micheltorena from the governorship and replacing him by Pio Pico (who had held that office briefly a dozen years earlier) had been adopted. Thus the opposition Sutter had expected failed to materialize, and he and his volunteers entered the Salinas Valley unopposed. There they were joined by Micheltorena's regulars, and toward the middle of January the combined force set off in pursuit of the insurgents.

So far all had gone well. Up to that point there had been only one complication—and that a minor one. During a stop at the Mission San José on the march to Monterey the resident padres had received them so hospitably that, in Sutter's words, "some of my men could not resist drinking too much of the wine which the major domo placed before them, and they became intoxicated." However, Sutter, who "knew I had some bad customers among my riflemen," was equal to the occasion. "Before we set out the next morning [for the nearby pueblo of San José]," he stated, "I sent orders to the alcalde to close all places where liquor was sold."

At their meeting place in the Salinas Valley the troops were divided into two columns—"the Governor commanding one and I the other"—and the pursuit began. It was a leisurely movement.

For in the California of the day, warfare, like every other form of activity, was never conducted with unseemly haste. Nearly a month was consumed on the march from the Salinas Valley to Santa Barbara, a distance of less than two hundred miles. Much of the time it rained heavily, and weeks of slogging over muddy trails, sleeping in wet blankets, and eating the scanty, ill-prepared food convinced many of Sutter's volunteers that the romance of war had been grossly exaggerated. The result was that a goodly number took French leave and headed back to the valley. What was even worse, a number of the discontented ones, believing they had more to gain by changing sides, slipped away and joined the ranks of the opposition.

But despite these defections and a growing feeling of dissatisfaction among his soldiers, Sutter's military ardor was undiminished. One reason for his unswerving loyalty to his chief might well be that it was during their stay at Santa Barbara that Micheltorena made good his promise of awarding him the hoped-for *sobrante* grant, thereby making him one of California's largest landowners.

The diminished army resumed its march, laboriously dragging themselves and their equipment—the latter included Sutter's cherished "Russian fieldpiece," a small brass cannon mounted on a cart and drawn by a yoke of oxen—over the steep mountain pass south of Santa Barbara and down to the valley beyond. There at last they came in sight of the enemy, and both sides made ready for a major test of strength.

In this, as in most other phases of the campaign, accounts of subsequent happenings differ widely, depending on which side the sympathies of the narrator lay. All versions agree that the engagement was brief and that it was the insurgent forces that gave ground. Castro's own explanation of the withdrawal was that he ordered it because the rain had dampened his soldiers' powder and rendered their weapons useless. According to Castro, and to several other sources cited by Bancroft, that first "battle" of the campaign consisted only of "two or three cannon shots . . . fired at long range."

Sutter's version of the engagement, though possibly less accurate than the others, is much more dramatic.

> During the night it rained very hard. The hills became slippery, men and horses fell and rolled down the ravines. When day broke I found myself in sight of the Mission Buena Ventura, but not more than half my command had come up. A council of war was held. Captain Gantt believed that not half the guns would go off, and Lieutenant Felix Valdes did not think we were strong enough to make the attack. Estrada likewise considered an attack by broad daylight as inadvisable, since we had not arrived in time for a night attack. Only the captain of the Indian company, Ernst Rufus, . . . was confident, and said that the muskets of his company were in good order, for his Indians had taken good care of them.

Sutter's account goes on to state that notwithstanding the qualms of his fainthearted advisers he was determined to launch his attack. One reason for his decision was that "the enemy would hardly expect us in such weather"; moreover, a fandango had been held at the mission the night before, and he reasoned that Castro's troops were "probably still half drunk and asleep." His narrative continues:

> Taking with me as many men as I could gather, I made a charge upon the town. The merry-makers of yesterday were panic-stricken and fled in every direction. Since we came out of the woods, they could not tell how strong we were; hence they did not stop running until they came to an open space about three-quarters of a mile away where they tried to form ranks. They began to swear at us, as was their fashion, calling us thieves and all kinds of bad names.
>
> I sent Bidwell to Micheltorena to ask permission to pursue the enemy. But the Governor believed it would be better to continue the march together.

The Captain's account of this, his first brush with the enemy, ends on a frustrated note:

"If we had followed up our advantage," he commented, "we could have easily routed them."

3 CAHUENGA

The first skirmish was over, but the decisive battle of the war was still to come.

The Castro-Alvarado forces continued to fall back until they reached Los Angeles. There the leaders spread reports of atrocities allegedly committtted by Micheltorena's convicts and of the reign of terror that would ensue should they capture the town. The consequence of that tactic was that virtually every able-bodied male hastened to join up and help repel the barbarians. Among the new recruits were a considerable number of foreigners, including about forty Americans who had recently arrived by way of the Santa Fe Trail.

On the morning of February 19 the reenforced Californians moved out from Los Angeles to challenge the approaching enemy. The two forces came in sight of each other at Cahuenga, a former mission property in the San Fernando Valley a few miles north of the pueblo. That night the armies camped on opposite sides of the valley, with Micheltorena's men occupying the crest of a hill exposed to a wind and sandstorm that blew down their tents and, in Sutter's words, "made rest impossible."

The engagement began at daybreak on the twentieth and, in the best military tradition, was preceded by an exchange of artillery fire on both sides. The bombardment could not have been very effectual, however, for Bancroft states that the Castro forces had but two small cannon and Micheltorena three—one of which was the fieldpiece Sutter had brought with him from New Helvetia. Nonetheless, the sound of gunfire was loud enough to be clearly heard in Los Angeles where, according to one contemporary account, the women and children gathered on a hilltop and prayed for the safety of their loved ones.

Sutter's description of this, the climactic engagement of the campaign, begins:

At daybreak we prepared for the attack. The fife, the bass drum, the three small drums, belonging to my company, gave the signal . . . At sunrise we began to march against the enemy, the cannon and infantry in front and the cavalry on the two flanks. Micheltorena was mounted and in the field. He had command of the artillery and the infantry, while I commanded the cavalry. The first shot from our cannon broke the wheel of one of their fieldpieces. The enemy became frightened and those in charge of the cannon took to their heels.

In Sutter's opinion, this was another lost opportunity. "Had we rushed upon them immediately," he commented, "we might have secured the victory." But instead of permitting him to launch a frontal attack on the retreating foe, Micheltorena ordered the Yankee riflemen under Captain Gantt to take up an advanced position along the river bank. Presumably the purpose of that maneuver was to prevent the enemy from attempting a flanking movement from that direction. But whatever its purpose, it proved to be a grievous tactical error. For from their new position the Americans had a closer view of the troops facing them, and thereby learned that among them were many of their fellow countrymen. The result was that the war was temporarily forgotten while the men of both sides visited back and forth, exchanging news and views and, in some cases, renewing old acquaintance.

Under the circumstances it was inevitable that the Americans should ask one another why they were fighting on opposite sides in a war in which they had no direct concern. It was then that John Marsh, who all the while had been smarting under the treatment he had received from Sutter, saw his opportunity. What, he asked, were they to gain by keeping Micheltorena and his rabble army in California? To the argument that the Governor had promised to be liberal in the matter of granting land to those who supported him, Marsh pointed out that if Micheltorena were deposed his promises would almost surely be repudiated by his successor.

To support the Doctor's arguments, the leader of the southern wing of the insurgent party, Pío Pico, was sent for. Bancroft states that when Don Pío appeared he explained to the foreigners that "Micheltorena's grant and promises were worthless, because lands could not be granted legally to any but Mexican citizens." Pío Pico, who hoped to succeed Micheltorena, assured the Americans that if he became Governor "they would be in no way oppressed, that their present occupation of lands would not be disturbed, and that as soon as they chose to become citizens he would give them legal titles."

The result of this period of fraternizing with the enemy was that when Micheltorena presently ordered the Americans to advance, his order was ignored.

Sutter's description of what happened next well illustrates the seriocomic mood in which the entire campaign had been conducted:

> I saw treachery lurking behind guns and said to Micheltorena, "I shall go and see why Gantt does not advance." To my great surprise, I found his men casting ballot to determine whether they would stay on our side or go over to the enemy. The Americans in our ranks said that they would not fight against the Americans on the other side. Moreover, Castro had received reenforcements from San Diego and our men began to get frightened. Dr. Marsh, who was there as a private, was a good talker and knew how to stir up mutiny.
>
> I said sharply to Gantt, "What do you mean by not obeying orders?"
>
> He replied insolently, "We are voting to see who wants to stay on this side and who wants to go over to the other side."
>
> "This is the time to fight and not to vote," I replied angrily.

Sutter tried hard to counteract Marsh's arguments and convince the wavering volunteers that it would be to their advantage to continue to support the Governor. But when it grew clear that the men were determined to have no further part in the fighting he gave up the attempt and started back to rejoin his chief.

Subsequent events were thus described by Bancroft:

"On his [Sutter's] way back to the general's position, he and Bidwell, his aide, were surrounded and captured by a party of

Californians . . . and after a brief detention at the rancho of Cahuenga, were sent under patrol . . . to Los Angeles, where they were lodged in the house of Abel Sterns."

Bancroft, who cannot be counted among Sutter's warmest admirers, added this comment: "There is room for suspicion, though there is no proof of the fact, that Sutter's capture was not altogether against his will, being merely a prearranged method of 'honorably' deserting Micheltorena's cause. It was evident from which corner the winds were soon to blow, and it was high time for the wily Swiss to trim his sails accordingly."

4 PEACE WITH HONOR

Whether Sutter's capture came about by accident or design, it was accomplished in a way that caused him a minimum of inconvenience. Then and later, his captors treated him much more leniently than might have been expected in view of the role he had played in the campaign. For in addition to allying himself with Micheltorena and his *cholos*, he had violated one of the cardinal rules of the frontier by arming his Indians with muskets and sending them against the whites. Yet, according to his own account, when his captors took him to the insurgent headquarters, Alvarado "embraced me like an old friend," then dispatched a messenger to summon Castro, from whom he received an equally warm welcome.

During his brief confinement at the Cahuenga adobe, the prisoner—to whom the formalities of military etiquette had always meant a great deal—protested indignantly that he was not being accorded the respect due one of his rank.

> While I was in my cell . . . an officer entered with a strong guard and demanded my sword. As I handed it to him, I thought to myself that things really looked dark to me. Fortunately, I saw an officer by the name of Eugenio Montenegro, a captain of cavalry, whom I knew very well. I beckoned to him and said, "You can do me a great favor. Tell your superiors that they know nothing of the usages of war, if they put an officer of my rank

under a common guard!" This had the desired effect. My sword was given back to me, I was invited into another room where the officers were drinking and was asked to join them.

The defection of the Americans under Captain Gantt reduced Micheltorena's already depleted army to a point where he realized that further opposition was useless. Accordingly, on the morning of February 21 the Governor raised the white flag of surrender. A treaty of capitulation was drawn up and signed the following day. By its terms Micheltorena agreed to lead the remnant of his army to San Pedro and embark on a ship that would take them first to Monterey, then to Mexico. On their part, the victors magnanimously bound themselves not to punish any of those who had taken up arms against them.

Thus the war ended on an amiable note, with the deposed governor accompanying his *cholos* out of the country, and with Pío Pico and José Castro, respectively, heading the civilian and military departments under the new regime. Estimates vary as to the losses sustained during the engagement at Cahuenga, but all agree that they were small. One eyewitness account fixed the casualties as one horse killed and one mule injured. In addition, the wheel of a gun carriage was struck by a cannonball and badly damaged. And so, another of California's revolutions passed into history.

But although Sutter, along with others who had backed the losing side, had only to pledge allegiance to the new regime in order to have his former rights and privileges restored, the experience nonetheless was a costly one to him. For one thing, it dealt a heavy blow to the image he had built of himself as an able and resourceful military tactician. Despite his efforts in later years to make it appear otherwise, it must have been clear even to him that his role in the campaign was considerably less than heroic. Although he continued to take pride in his title of captain (and later, by special act of the California legislature, that of general), from then on his references to past military triumphs were heard less frequently. There were even occasions when he went so far as to confess that his story of having served as captain in the Swiss Guard of Charles X of France had been an exaggeration.

Besides damaging his self-esteem, the ill-starred venture put him in trouble on a number of other counts. His material losses were heavy. "I had fitted out most of the men at my expense," he once recalled, "and failing in my purpose, I lost it all—money, horses, arms, and provisions." He estimated that the campaign had cost him 150 horses—animals that were badly needed to carry him and his men back to New Helvetia. All in all, there was truth in his comment that "I was really the greatest sufferer. Defeat meant much more to me than to the Governor."

It was a chastened group that set off from the Los Angeles pueblo in mid-March on the long trek home: the Captain himself, his faithful aide John Bidwell, several other whites, including a Dr. Townsend and Juan Vaca, plus a large number of Kanakas and Indians. All were mounted on horses Sutter had managed to buy—on credit—from a Los Angeles resident whom he had befriended earlier at the fort; the party was, however, without reserves of food and without funds to buy any along the way. Accordingly, it was decided to avoid the coastal settlements—the residents of which were unlikely to extend favors to supporters of the unpopular ex-governor—and instead took an inland route across the mountains and up the length of the uninhabited San Joaquin and Sacramento valleys.

The two weeks that followed were a time of trial and hardships, of riding many hours daily across a barren countryside, of a persistent shortage of food for men and animals, of brushes with unfriendly Indians, and of fording a succession of rainswollen streams.

The spent and bedraggled group that arrived at the fort on April 1 bore little resemblance to the high-spirited band of amateur soldiers who, with flags waving and bugles blowing, had set off to the wars three months earlier.

six

Wagons Westward

---

1 POLICING THE FRONTIER

While Sutter was absent on his maladroit attempt to keep Micheltorena in the governor's chair, things had been going badly at the fort.

In order to safeguard his colony against possible attack by the insurgents, he had left behind a force of fifteen white men and about thirty Indians under the command of one of his faithful assistants, Pierson B. Reading. But the fighting—such as it was—had all been at points far removed from New Helvetia, and the garrison there, after the manner of troops in barracks, had lapsed into almost complete idleness.

The consequence was that on his return the Captain learned that although ample spring rains had given promise of abundant yields of wheat, corn, and other crops, the planting season had come and gone without a field having been plowed or an acre sown to seed. This, as events were to prove, was a major setback. For he had already fallen far behind in his payments to the Russians and had counted on that year's harvest to restore his credit with them and with others to whom he was heavily in debt.

A second situation he faced on his arrival was of even more pressing concern. While he was absent, a band of Indians had raided two ranches in his part of the valley and made off with a number of horses and cattle. Then, soon after his return, the same band staged a third raid, during which a rancher was killed. Sutter's status as an official of the provincial government had not

93

been altered by the change of governors; he was still *Coman-dante militar de las fronteras del norte y encargado de la justicia,* and in duty bound to keep the peace within his district. Accordingly, after only a few days at home he again took the field.

This time his confidence in his ability to plan and execute a successful military campaign was justified. For in this, as in his other forays against the recalcitrant savages, he was uniformly more successful than experience had shown him to be in more former workers to return to the fort and resume their old duties that, far better than most Californians of the day, he understood the temperament of the natives, a circumstance that enabled him in some degree to gain their confidence and respect. His method of dealing with his untutored charges was a skillful combination of persuasion and force, of fair treatment to those who abided by the strict rules he laid down, and of prompt and severe punishment to those who disobeyed.

Sutter's success in that field required a high degree of patience and forbearance. For by all accounts, the California Indian bore little resemblance to the lordly savage pictured in novels of the Fenimore Cooper school. One close observer of the local tribes, Lieutenant Joseph Warren Revere, U.S.N., thus described them in his *A Tour of Duty in California,* written in 1846:

> They are docile, mild, easily managed, and although lazy and unthrifty, will work tolerably well for short periods at making adobes, getting in crops, and doing farm work generally, taking in payment, with great avidity, beads and toys of the cheapest kind, handkerchiefs, cottons, and other common dry goods.

Revere found them to be "offensively dirty" both in their persons and living quarters, and added that in order to keep them at their assigned tasks they had to be "closely watched and occasionally punished severely."

It was from such unpromising material that Sutter was obliged to recruit all but a few of the big crew of laborers needed to man his colony and keep it growing.

Throughout the first weeks after his return he had need of all his forcefulness and skill in dealing with the natives. For during his absence not only had the wild foothill tribes grown bolder in their raids on the outlying ranchos, but many of his own semi-domesticated Indians had seized the opportunity to slip away and join their marauding brothers. In his effort to persuade the former workers to return to the fort and resume their old duties Sutter could be patient as well as forbearing. However, when he set out to round up the band that had raided the rancho of his friend Thomas Lindsay, killed its owner, and driven off three hundred head of cattle, he was in no such conciliatory mood. For the slain man had served with him in the Micheltorena campaign, and Sutter was determined that the punishment of his murderers must be prompt and severe.

Having assembled a force of some twenty men—both whites and Indians, and all seasoned fighters—he picked up the trail of the fugitives and stolen animals, caught up with them and, in a brief but fiercely fought exchange, routed them with heavy losses, and recovered the animals. It was a costly victory. For, stated Sutter, at the height of the fighting, "my clerk and loyal companion during the recent campaign, Juan Vaca, was shot at my side." Vaca was the attacking party's only fatality, but several others were wounded. Sutter's account concludes: "I was, as usual, the first to charge, and a number of arrows pierced my clothing. Yet I escaped without injury."

There were other clashes with the Indians during that spring and summer of 1845. In June the numerous Mokelumne tribe, whose chief, Raphero, had provided Sutter with many of his best workers, suddenly went on the warpath and, in Sutter's words, "threatened to massacre the farmers, and to burn their houses and wheat fields." Sutter suspected that Raphero's revolt had been instigated by José Castro. It was his contention that Castro, the new commander-in-chief of the army, was jealous of his growing importance and had chosen that means of embarrassing him by demonstrating that he was unable to keep the Indians of his district under control. Sutter decided to adopt forceful methods to put down this latest rebellion. He accordingly assembled and armed all the available men at the fort and, with Pierson

B. Reading as second in command, set out in pursuit of the rebels.

The expedition got off to a bad start. On reaching the Mokelumne River, the improvised raft they had built to cross the stream was capsized, causing the loss of a number of firearms and most of their ammunition. Despite that setback the party pressed on and, having located the rebel stronghold, immediately launched an attack. Taken by surprise, the Indians offered but slight resistance. Chief Raphero was captured and brought back to the fort. There Sutter, serving in his judicial capacity, presided over the prisoner's trial and its end sentenced him to death. As a lesson to other chiefs who might be tempted to follow the dead man's example, Sutter had Raphero's head put on display near the main gate of the fort. Evidently the grisly object remained there for some time, for it was seen and commented on by visitors to the fort late that year.

The active year 1845 saw yet another outbreak of violence between the Indians and whites, one that for a time caused widespread uneasiness among residents of the valley. The natives involved in this dispute were, however, not the normally peaceful California Indians but members of the belligerent Walla Walla tribe from the Oregon country. A party of Walla Wallas consisting of thirty-six braves and a number of squaws and children came down from the north that year and camped in the vicinity of the fort. The chief of the party was a youth named Leicer, who had received his education at a missionary school in the Willamette Valley. While visiting at the fort one day Leicer became involved in an argument with one of Sutter's employees, a Kentuckian named Grove Cook, who was then in charge of the distillery. During the quarrel that followed—which assertedly was over the ownership of a mule—guns were drawn and fired, and the Indian was killed. The shooting took place in Sutter's room at the fort, although he himself was not present. On learning of the death of their chief the Walla Wallas hurriedly set off on their return to Oregon, taking with them a number of horses that had been stolen from ranchers in the valley. Next morning Sutter dispatched a posse to retrieve the animals, but they returned empty-handed, having been unable to overtake the fleeing party.

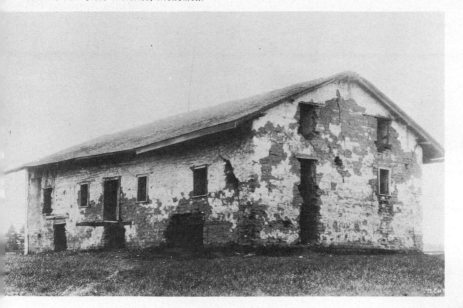

This central building was all that remained of the original fort when this photograph was taken in 1888.

Fort Ross in 1828. From a drawing that first appeared in Auguste Duhaut-Cilly's Voyage Autour du Monde, published in Paris in 1835.

Sutter in his uniform as a major general in the California Militia, to which office he was appointed by the State Legislature in 1853.

John Bidwell, who reached California in 1841 as a member of the Bartleson party. He entered Sutter's employ that same year and during the

Sutter's Fort in April, 1849. From a drawing by W. R. Hutton.

Sutter's Office. One of the restored rooms in the central building at the fort.

The Bear Flag. A replica of the device raised by a party of settlers from the Sacramento Valley who captured Sonoma in June, 1846 and set up the short-lived California Republic. The original flag was destroyed in the San Francisco fire of 1906.

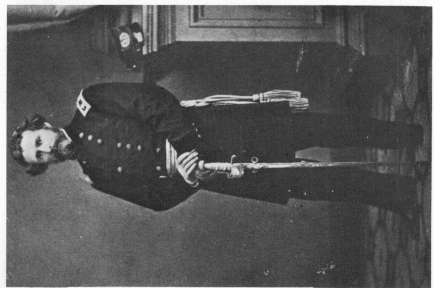

Major General John C. Fremont—U. S. Army.

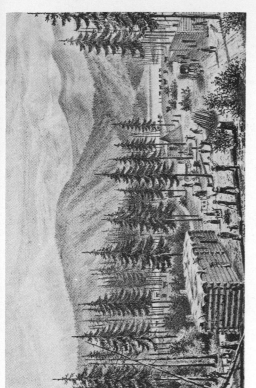

Camp at Donner Lake. This drawing, based on a description furnished by a survivor, pictures the cabins in which members of the ill-fated Donner party spent the winter of 1846–47.

Samuel Brannan, Mormon elder, chief of a large party of Mormon émigrants who reached California in 1846. Brannan played a leading part in spreading abroad news of the gold discovery; for several years he operated a profitable trading post at the new city of Sacramento.

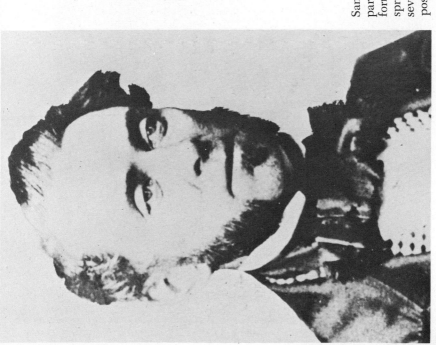

Monday 24th this day
some kind of mettle was
discovered was found in the tail race that
that looks like goald first discovered by James Martial, the Bos of the mill.
Sunday 30 clean & has been
all the last week our metal
has been tride and proves to
be goald it is thought to be
rich we have pict up more than
a hundred dollars wolth last
week

February. 1848
Sun 6th the wether has been clear

Page from Henry Bigler's diary recording the finding of "some kind of mettle" in the tailrace of the sawmill. This entry, made on Monday (January) 24th (1848), is important because it fixes the precise date of the discovery.

Sutter's Mill, from a painting by Charles Nahl. The tail race from which James W. Marshall picked up the first flakes of gold is shown in the foreground.

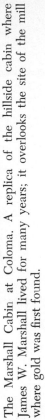

The Marshall Cabin at Coloma. A replica of the hillside cabin where James W. Marshall lived for many years; it overlooks the site of the mill where gold was first found.

James W. Marshall, carriage-maker and carpenter, who reached California in 1844. Three years later, in partnership with Captain Sutter, he undertook to build a sawmill in the Sierra foothills, and by so doing set off the gold rush of 1849.

A Pocket Gold-Weighing Outfit
Every well-equipped miner carried one of these gold scales on which
he weighed each day's take and calculated—at $12 per ounce—the
amount of his earnings.

Gold Rush Currency
These gold and silver slugs were privately minted in San Francisco
in the early 1850's to provide the residents with a medium of exchange more convenient than the gold dust that had been universally
used earlier.

A Coloma Store. One of two stone buildings, dating from the 1850s, still standing in this, the earliest of the mining towns. The iron shutters on the doors and windows were a characteristic feature of business architecture throughout the Mother Lode. In the foreground is a primitive stamp-mill dating from the early quartz mining era.

Mining on the American River. This view taken by the pioneer photographer, Robert H. Vance, shows the elaborate methods in use by the placer miners in the late 1850's by which the water was diverted from its normal channels and the beds of the streams mined.

Sacramento City, 1849. From a lithograph based on a drawing by C. V. Cooper. The city had then been in exist-

Hock Farm, Sutter's home on the Feather River, to which he moved in 1850, and where he spent his final years in California. From "Gleason's Pictorial Drawing-Room Companion," September 6, 1851.

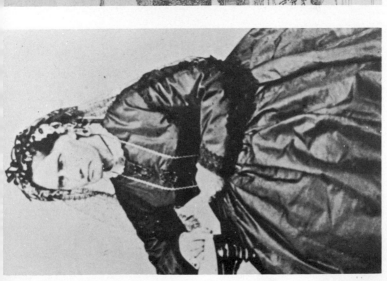

Mrs. John A. Sutter, the former Anna Dubeld, who rejoined her husband in California in 1850.

Emil Victor, Sutter's second son, in his uniform as
an officer of the California National Guard

John A. Sutter, Jr. From a painting by an unknown
artist

Alphonse Wilhelm, the youngest of the Sutters' four children, who became a member of William Walker's filibustering expedition to Nicaragua.

Anna Eliza Sutter, the Sutters' only daughter.

John A. Sutter during his last years. From a photograph made in the late 1870's.

Mades Hotel, Washington, D. C. It was in this modest hotel, which stood on the southwest corner of Pennsylvania Ave. and Third St., that Sutter died on June 18, 1880.

When the Walla Wallas reached their home grounds and reported the death of young Leicer, Dr. Elijah White, a missionary and Indian agent in the Willamette Valley, sent a strong protest to Governor Pico, American Consul Larkin, and Sutter, demanding that Cook be tried and, if found guilty, properly punished.

In a letter to Larkin, written from New Helvetia on July 21, Sutter warmly defended his employee's action. In it he stated that Cook had been threatened with a rifle by the Indian youth, adding that during his visits to the fort he had conducted himself in "a very saucy and haughty manner." The letter concluded: "Dr. White says that Leicer (the pupil of the Missionary) was by no means viciously inclined, but we believe here all that Leicer was a great Rascal."

An investigation of the affair was ordered, presumably by either Larkin or Governor Pico, but whether the order was ever carried out—and if so, what conclusion was reached—is unknown today. However, the episode was not forgotten for some time. Hostility occasioned by the shooting persisted among members of the Walla Walla tribe, and rumors that they were planning a retaliatory raid into the valley caused recurrent alarm among the settlers. In the fall of 1846 such rumors reached a point where hurried preparations were made to render the fort more secure against attack by the northerners. But the threatened invasion never materialized, and residents of the valley soon had more pressing matters to occupy their time.

2 TO BUY A FORT

The newly resurgent Indians were not the only problem besetting Sutter's New Helvetia, or indeed all California, as 1845 drew to a close.

During the year there had been numerous indications that drastic changes in the affairs of the province were imminent. First, the expulsion of Micheltorena and his army had weakened Mexico's hold on California almost to the breaking point. The Californians' long-standing desire for self-rule seemed about to be realized. But there was evidence, too, that they were likely to gain their independence only to lose it again. For by then they had come to realize that the chief threat to their security lay, not in their indolent, ineffectual home government at Mexico City, but in the land-hungry republic on the far side of the continent.

In California, as elsewhere, the fact that the administration at Washington was committed to a policy of extending the country's boundaries to the shores of the Pacific had long been an imperfectly kept secret. One clear indication of that plan had been the seizure of Monterey by Commodore Thomas Ap Catesby Jones, U.S.N., in the fall of 1842, under the mistaken belief that the United States and Mexico were at war. Another such hint had been the visit to California of John C. Frémont's party of soldier-explorers in the spring of 1844; and yet another was the annexation of Texas, which took place by Act of Congress in the early spring of 1845 shortly after Texas had gained her independence from Mexico.

The result of all this was that by the time the year 1846 opened, most Californians were convinced that the territory's transfer to the sovereignty of the United States was not only inevitable, but that it could not be much longer delayed. Moreover, the anticipated change-over was looked on, if not with enthusiasm, at least without profound regret by a majority of the inhabitants, including many of the old-time Spanish-California families. However, members of the Pico-Castro-Alvarado group—who had recently gained control of the government and, after the fashion of the time, were conducting its affairs largely for their own profit—were understandably unwilling to surrender California's independence (and along with it their own lucrative offices) without a struggle. And so the group's major effort since taking office had been to stir up resentment against those Americans who were already in the province and to attempt to prevent others from joining them.

The governing party's leaders realized that if they hoped to check the flow of emigrants into the country they must exercise much closer supervision over affairs at Sutter's Fort than had been the case during previous administrations. Because it stood in the center of the valley, the fort was the spot to which all but a few of the pioneer overland parties made their way on first reaching California. Hence it was obvious to the Pico-Castro group that if this rising tide of emigrants was to be checked and the northern and eastern frontiers closed, Sutter's policy of welcoming the newcomers and of inviting others to follow them would have to be reversed.

It became a question of how this strategically located stronghold could be removed from Sutter's control, transformed into an advance military post, and occupied by a force of Mexican soldiers strong enough to turn back future parties of American emigrants. One ingenious means of accomplishing that end was seriously considered: that of buying the mortgage Sutter had given the Russian-American Fur Company when he purchased the Fort Ross properties four years earlier, then of forcing him to turn over to them his Sacramento Valley holdings in settlement of that long-overdue debt. Negotiations between Pico and the Russian company's agent at Yerba Buena had in fact reached a point where a preliminary agreement was drawn up and signed. However, when it was learned that the document would have to be approved by the company chiefs at St. Petersburg the Californians lost interest. Rather than submit to so long a delay they decided on a new approach to their problem—that of buying the property direct from its owner.

The result of that decision was that on the morning of November 11, 1845, Sutter learned from the Indian boatman who operated a ferry across the Sacramento that a party of white men had arrived on the west bank and were waiting to be rowed across. He later recalled:

"I sent Bidwell to see who they were and what they wanted. The visitors turned out to be General José Castro, Colonel Prudon [a Frenchman then living at Sonoma], Jacob Leese, and Andres Castillero, *comisionado* from Mexico . . . They came with an escort of about fifteen mounted soldiers by way of Sonoma . . . Castillero had been sent by President José Herrera to regulate affairs in general, and to make peace with the new government. At the same time he was commissioned to effect the purchase of my Fort in order to garrison it and put a stop to the flow of immigration."

Accounts of the meeting that followed differ so widely that at this late date it is impossible to determine what really transpired. Sutter's own version of the interview, however, is specific enough. Bancroft quotes him as saying: "They entered at once upon the purpose of their coming: they told me that the government wished to buy my Fort and all its improvements and that they were authorized to pay one hundred thousand dollars for it."

The Captain goes on to state that the thought of selling his fort had never occurred to him, and that the Mexicans' offer was, therefore, a complete surprise.

> Thereupon I withdrew to my office in the same building and held a consultation with Bidwell, Reading and Locker [Loker]. I told them what I had been offered for the establishment, and they all thought that it was a very large sum. After they had discussed the matter for some time, their thoughts turned naturally to their own interests. "What shall we do?" they asked. "And what will all the settlers in the valley do if you abandon us to the Mexicans?" This brought about my decision. I felt that I was in duty bound to continue my protection of the immigrants.

The contention on Sutter's part that it was loyalty to his employees and to other American residents of the valley that caused him to reject Castillero's offer is hard to reconcile with the views he expressed at the time negotiations for the sale were in progress. For example, in a letter to General Castro, written in the spring of 1846, we find him urging that the sale be consummated as promptly as possible in order that Mexican soldiers could be stationed at the fort before the many Americans expected that year began to arrive.

> I advise Your Worship to put a respectable garrison at this point before emigrants from the United States enter the country. The time for their arrival is the middle of the month of next September. According to the reports there may be some thousands of souls, but not 10,000, as they say.

Since I believe the government will buy my establishment, I will put everything in the best order. To this large new house that Your Worship has seen I am now adding one more story, and I will fit it up as soon as possible for barracks fit to hold some 200 to 300 soldiers, and inside there will also be plenty of room for the troops. I wrote also to Señor Victor Prudon in regard to this matter . . .

The $100,000 supposed to have been offered by the Mexicans was looked on at the time as a high price to pay for the property. According to some accounts, however, other offers were even more liberal. Sutter himself on another occasion stated that he was given the option either of accepting $100,000 cash for the fort or of trading it for the lands in the Santa Clara Valley that had once been the property of the San José mission. Still another version was that of J. Ross Browne, a California journalist of the period, who, writing in the 1860's stated that "Castillero was empowered to pay as much as $100,000; and actually offered Sutter in addition several fine tracts of mission lands now worth millions."

On the other hand, Bancroft, after weighing the available evidence, concluded that in all likelihood the proposal that they purchase the fort was first made, not by the Mexican officials, but by Sutter himself. In support of that view he quoted Bidwell's statement that "Sutter was inclined to dispose of his lands and fort." Bancroft also quoted from a letter Sutter wrote Larkin a few days after the meeting at the fort, in which he stated: "I am now on most friendly terms with Don José Castro and Señor Castillero"—which elicited this comment from Bancroft: "A flat refusal to accede to their wishes would hardly have led to a state of things so satisfactory."

In any event, there is no lack of evidence that the purchase was seriously considered by the Mexican officials, or that some influential Californians were in favor of paying even the admittedly high price Sutter had demanded for the property. About ten days after the Sutter-Castillero meeting General Vallejo—whose brother-in-law, Jacob Leese, had been present— wrote his friend, Mexico's ex-President Bustamante, stating that

Sutter had offered to cede his fort to Mexico on payment of
$100,000. Vallejo added: "I grant that this is a high price to
pay for a few pieces of cannon, a not very scientifically constructed bastion, some fosses and moats, ten or twelve adobe
houses, and corrals of the same material; but the security of the
country is what is to be paid for, and that is priceless."

Bancroft summed up his conclusions by pointing out that Sutter's claims of having been offered $100,000 for his fort were un-
supported by evidence from any other source. He added that at
the time such claims were made—that is, in the mid-1870's—a
bill asking compensation for his losses was before the United
States Congress; hence, had he been able to convince the lawmakers that he had refused so large a sum for his property in
order to protect the interests of the Americans in the valley, that
would hardly fail to gain a sympathetic hearing for his bill.

Sutter's own account of the incident, dictated more than thirty
years later, ends on this embittered note:

"Often have I regretted not having sold New Helvetia at that
time, because for this great sacrifice I have been rewarded with
nothing but ingratitude."

3 NEW TRIALS

At the time of the Castillero-Castro party's visit in mid-
November the fort was crowded with Americans, most of them
newly arrived from beyond the mountains. For in 1845 the number of overland emigrants was substantially higher than in any
previous year. The parties had begun drifting in in early summer,
and had grown in number and size as the season advanced and
the time drew near when snows would block the mountain passes
until late the following spring.

The first considerable group to arrive that year came by way
of Oregon and reached the fort in mid-July. Among its forty
members was a thirty-three-year-old carpenter named James
Marshall, who was eventually to undertake to build a sawmill
in partnership with Sutter and by so doing play a leading part
in an event that was to capture the attention of the entire world.

Through the summer and early fall other parties straggled in, most of them smaller groups numbering twenty or less. All showed the effects of the ordeal they had been through. Some had lost so many animals that they had had to abandon their wagons and nearly all their possessions. Many were weakened and ill from the hardships of the trail, and all but a few were without means of support until they could establish themselves in the new land.

But whoever they were and whatever their condition, all received a cordial welcome to the fort. For nothing so pleased the genial host as to welcome the newcomers with courtly grace and offer them the hospitality of his establishment for as long as they wished to stay. "Sutter received us with open arms and in princely fashion, for he was a man of the most polite address and the most courteous manners, a man who could shine in any society." Thus John Bidwell had written of his first arrival in 1841, and his remarks were echoed by numerous others during the years that followed. In March, 1844, John C. Frémont, having reached California on the first of several expeditions to the coast, wrote that ". . . we were met a short distance from the fort by Capt. Sutter himself. He gave us a most frank and cordial reception—conducted us immediately to his residence—and under his hospitable roof we had a night of rest, enjoyment and refreshment which none but ourselves could appreciate."

There is little doubt that Sutter would have welcomed all who found their way to New Helvetia and offered them such hospitality as the place afforded solely out of a desire to be helpful, and without any expectation that he might profit thereby. But it so happened that by doing a kindly act to the travel-weary strangers he was also serving his own best interests. For he well knew that the success of his colony depended, as much as any other factor, on the number of emigrants who could be prevailed on to settle permanently in the valley.

His correspondence of the period makes frequent reference not only to his desperate need of farming implements, tools and machinery of various sorts, but also of men qualified to use them. And, born optimist that he was, he was always prophesying the imminent arrival of so many emigrants that his shortage of skilled workers would soon be at an end. Thus, in a letter to Larkin dated July 15, 1845, he announced jubilantly that "a very large Company" would reach the fort "in about 8 or 10 weeks from Now."

This party, the size of which he estimated at "more [than] 1000 souls," had been organized by a young Ohioan named Lansford W. Hastings; it had set off from Independence toward the middle of August, nearly a month after Sutter's letter to Larkin. This was not to be Hastings' first visit to the West Coast. He had made an overland trip to Oregon three years earlier, and from there had continued on to California. He was entertained by Sutter at the fort in July, 1843, and it was during that visit that he told his host of his plan of recruiting a large company of settlers and leading them out to California the following year.

On returning home Hastings embodied what he had learned during his western travels—plus a great deal of misinformation— in a book entitled *The Emigrant's Guide to California*, which was published at Cincinnati in 1845. During the next several years Hastings' *Guide* was used by a number of California-bound emigrant parties, most of whom had reason to regret having followed its advice. For the *Guide* recommended leaving the established trail near Fort Bridger, in present-day Wyoming, and taking what became known as the "Hastings Cutoff." The latter was an untried route that swung to the south of Great Salt Lake and meandered through hundreds of miles of broken, arid country before rejoining the main trail near the headwaters of the Humboldt River. Parties that went that way uniformly suffered severe hardships and heavy losses of animals, wagons, and other property.

Hastings' second expedition, which was originally scheduled to start in the spring of 1845, had to be postponed until late summer. Moreover, when it eventually got under way, it was drastically reduced in size; instead of the one thousand Sutter had been led to expect, the party that set out from Independence numbered only ten. Because they had got so late a start, it was necessary for them to travel fast in order that they might make the

Sierra crossing before the passes were blocked by snow. Accordingly, no wagons were taken along; each of the ten men was mounted on a horse and carried his belongings—which were limited to food, clothing, and a few other essentials—on the back of a pack mule.

All during that fall and early winter Sutter impatiently waited the arrival of this party which, according to his letter to Larkin, he believed to be composed of "familys from Kentucky and Ohio, and a good many young enterprising Gentlemen with some Capital to improve the Country . . ." He was sadly disappointed at the size and condition of the group of exhausted men who finally reached the fort on Christmas Day, 1845, having passed over the crest of the mountains only a few hours ahead of the first heavy snowstorm of the winter.

But notwithstanding the small size of the Hastings party, the number of emigrants who reached the fort during 1845 was substantially higher than in any previous year. The first considerable group to appear was the McMahon party which, as mentioned earlier, had come down from Oregon. It reached New Helvetia on July 10, and five days later Sutter, in his halting English, thus described its members in one of his letters to Larkin: "All of this people have a decent appearance and some very useful Men amongs them. Some of them will remain here, and the Majority will spread over the whole Country, like usual; a good many will come to Monterey and present themselves to you."

In a postscript the Captain listed each member of the party by name, occupation, and country of origin. The list throws light on the type of emigrants who were then entering California in growing numbers. Of the forty-three members, thirty-nine were natives of the United States; two Germans, one Frenchman, and one Canadian made up the remaining four. Well over half were listed as farmers; the others followed a variety of trades. Among them were two blacksmiths, four carpenters (one of whom was James W. Marshall), two hatters, a tailor, a soap-maker and chandler, a sawyer, a sailor, a saddler, and a shoemaker.

Having started from Oregon, the McMahon party arrived several months ahead of the main body of 1845 emigrants—the latter were, of course, obliged to travel much greater distances. Moreover, the Mississippi Valley groups were not able to set out until the grass on the prairies was high enough to provide forage for the animals. Hence, it was late spring before they left Independence, St. Joseph, or the other frontier assembling points, and, since the journey commonly took five or six months, it was likely to be mid-September or later before the weary travelers were cheered by their first sight of New Helvetia's adobe walls looming up ahead.

In a document known as *Sutter's Diary*, which the Captain wrote in the mid-1850's, the entries for the fall of 1845 include a number of such items as these:

"September 27th. A large party of emigrants arrived. On the 30th I dispatched a party of men to assist them.

"October 7th. Another large party arrived (about 60 wagons). Visitors and letters from the U. States."

The party mentioned in the October 7 entry numbered approximately one hundred men, women, and children, which made it the largest overland group yet to reach California. Led by John Grigsby and William B. Ide, its members had assembled at Independence in April, reached Fort Hall—approximately the halfway point—in early August, and spent the final days of September dragging their wagons over the Sierra passes. Although Sutter's note implies that the entire party reached the fort on October 7, such was not the case; the arrival of the wagons was spaced over several weeks. In an account written some years later, one of the party's leaders, William Ide, explained that once they were safely out of the mountains, "our emigrants . . . all made a rush for the long-sought California; ambitious to be the first—not waiting much for one another; the best teams leaving the rest; everyone looking out for himself only."

The piecemeal arrival of the Grigsby-Ide party is recorded, too, in the "New Helvetia Diary," another day-by-day account of happenings at the fort, which begins in September, 1845, and continues, with occasional breaks, until May of 1848. The entry for October 15 reads in part: "G. M. Smith came in from the Mountains with some two or three more from the Waggons and reported the Waggons mostly onto the plains." On the 17th the entry states: "5 Waggons from the Mountains, arrived last night about 12 Oclock." Two days later, this: "Last night one more wagon arrived from the Mountains belonging to Mr. Hess; today two more wagons arrived belonging to Mr. Todd and Mr. Rolette—four or five Waggons more are expected immediately." The 20th brought another five wagons (the entry for that day adds: "engaged a number of them to work at the Fort"); the 21st brought "a number more"; the 23rd, one wagon; the 24th, three; and the 25th, four, including that of the party's leader, William B. Ide.

4 CAPTAIN FRÉMONT

Not every overland party that reached the fort during the fall and winter of 1845 was made up of emigrants who had been drawn to California by reports that choice farming and range land was to be had for the asking, and who intended to choose a spot to their liking and grow up with the country.

One exception to that rule was the party headed by the celebrated soldier-explorer-intriguer John C. Frémont who, with his almost equally well-known guide, Kit Carson, unexpectedly put in an appearance on December 10. This was Frémont's second visit to the fort, his first having been, as recorded earlier, in the spring of the previous year. On that occasion he and his men had remained several weeks recuperating from their difficult winter crossing of the Sierra and assembling animals and supplies for their return to the States.

It was the publication of Frémont's account of his earlier (1844) expedition—which had had a wide reading in the eastern part of the country—that first drew general attention to California's attractions as a place to live and, incidentally, established its author's reputation as an intrepid trailbreaker. The expedition that brought about his reappearance at the fort in December, 1845, was the third he had undertaken in four years. As the head of what was ostensibly a scientific and exploring expedition numbering sixty-two men, he had headed west in the spring of 1845 and followed the, by then, well defined central trail as far as the Great Salt Lake. From there he had proceeded by way of the Humboldt Valley to the base of the Sierra and turned south to the body of water now known as Walker Lake. Then, because winter was near and supplies were low, the party divided. Frémont, with fifteen men, headed dirctly across the mountains, his destination Sutter's Fort, while the larger group, led by Joseph Reddeford Walker, took a southerly route and crossed the range over today's Walker's Pass. The plan was for the two groups to rejoin at a spot called the River of the Lake at the southern end of the San Joaquin Valley.

On the day Frémont made his second visit to the fort Sutter chanced to be absent at Yerba Buena. Young Bidwell, who had been left in charge, welcomed the visitors hospitably and put the facilities of the colony at their disposal. As was the case on his first visit, Frémont's needs were many and urgent. He informed Bidwell that he would need sixteen mules—one for each member of his party—to replace their exhausted animals, together with a number of pack-saddles and the use of the fort's blacksmith shop while the mules were shod. On being told by Bidwell that fewer than sixteen mules were available at the fort, and that a shortage of coal would delay shoeing such animals as could be supplied him, Frémont angrily left and rejoined his party, which had meanwhile made camp a few miles up the river.

Much disturbed at the other's behavior, Bidwell followed the captain to his camp and, by promising to make a special effort to round up the required number of animals, succeeded somewhat in placating him. That he was able in large part to make up his promise is evident from this laconic entry in the *New Helvetia Diary*:

"December 12th. Delivered 14 mules to Capt. J. C. Frémont." Early the following day, December 13, the party broke camp and headed down the valley, with the intention of joining Walker and his men as they emerged from the mountains.

A little more than a month later Frémont was back at the fort.

His return had come about because the Walker party had failed to appear at the rendezvous. After waiting several weeks Frémont and his men had made their way to the north again, where he planned to stay until contact with the main body of the expedition could be reestablished. This time he appears to have been in a more friendly mood and less critical of the treatment accorded him during his December stay. In any event, when on the morning after his arrival in the vicinity he and Sutter unexpectedly met, the meeting was cordial on both sides.

Sutter's description of that encounter has an added interest because it illustrates with what formality the rules of social and military etiquette were observed at his remote outpost:

> On January fourteenth, 1846, Captain Leidesdorff, vice-consul for the United States at Yerba Buena, and Captain Hinkley, captain of the port of Yerba Buena, arrived on a friendly visit. Since both men were in uniform, I put on my Mexican uniform too, and rode with them toward a certain spot on the American River which Leidesdorff wished to select for a grant. We had proceeded only a mile or two from the Fort when we noticed a camp. While I was wondering what camp that could be, I saw Kit Carson coming up to me. "Where is Captain Frémont?" I asked him. "Over there in his tent," was the reply, "he is tired and not up yet." I asked Kit Carson to call him out, introduced my companions to him, and told him that we were on a little expedition up the river. I invited him to join us on our return and to dine with me at the Fort. Frémont said that he had arrived at the spot late at night and that he would remove his camp to the bank of the river near the Fort. This he did while we continued on our journey up the American River. On my return I ordered the firing of a salute of seven guns and prepared a sumptuous dinner. Frémont returned to his camp the same night, and Leidesdorff and Hinkley left for Yerba Buena the next morning.

Frémont's movements during the remainder of his stay in California, and the part he played in events that were soon to get under way, are described in a later chapter.

5   A BENEVOLENT DESPOT

When the eventful year 1846 opened, the fort had been in existence a little more than half a decade. During that brief period the site had been transformed from an uninhabited wilderness into a cluster of canvas tents and brush-covered shelters, then to an assemblage of cabins, corrals, and modest adobe buildings, and finally into a large and flourishing agricultural, industrial, and trading center. Few of those who visited the spot during these years failed to express their surprise at finding a settlement of that size and variety so far removed from other outposts of civilization.

Several firsthand descriptions of the place as it was in the early and middle 1840's have been preserved, and although these differ in matters of detail, there is general agreement as to its principal features. The fort stood on a slight knoll that elevated it a few feet above the surrounding plain, and was bounded on the north by a shallow slough that emptied into the American River slightly more than a mile distant. The main buildings were grouped within an irregularly shaped area measuring approximately 425 by 170 feet, and were enclosed by a wall three feet thick at the base and some fifteen feet high. The wall, like the more important buildings, was made of sundried adobe bricks.

It was the wall that was mainly responsible for the fact that, in California and elsewhere in the West, Sutter's colony came to be universally referred to as a "fort." For once it was built, the design of the structure left no doubt that its purpose was to make the settlement secure from enemy attack, whether by hostile Indians or others. At its northwest and southwest corners stood solidly built two-story bastions, on the upper levels of which cannon were mounted and so placed that they could be brought to bear on an attacking force approaching from any direction. At a number of other points, too, the wall was pierced by portholes through which guns could be fired. Still another cannon was placed before the main gate, beside which an Indian sentry was stationed during daylight hours; usually, too, an armed patrol was maintained outside the walls throughout the night. All of which made the spot, in P. B. Reading's words, "the largest and best fortified fort in California."

The main building, the colony's headquarters and, for a time, Sutter's residence, stood near the center of the enclosure. It was a rectangular, two-and-a-half story structure, its outer walls of adobe bricks and its floors, partitions, and the supports of its roof of timbers hand-sawed from trunks of the great oaks that grew all about. A series of shed-like structures were built against the inside of the wall; these housed the workrooms of those artisans who produced whatever was needed to make the community self-supporting: the shops of the wood and metalworkers, of cooper, saddler, shoemaker, weavers, and other craftsmen. The uses to which such rooms were put varied from time to time; hence it is rarely possible to fix their locations except in general terms. At one period Sutter's private quarters were three connecting rooms just inside the main gate. Other buildings within the enclosure were storerooms, a kitchen, and sleeping quarters for the domestic staff and for guests, also a small gristmill operated by mule power and a distillery for the manufacture of *aguardiente*. Outside, and close to the old landing place on the American River, was a tannery where the hides of cattle, deer, and other animals were cured and prepared for the market. There were also corrals for the domestic animals, sheds for the storage of wheat and other agricultural products, and, a little distance away, the camp where lived the small army of Indians who planted and harvested Sutter's crops, watched over his cattle, and performed whatever other work was needed to carry out the ambitions owner's plans.

John Bidwell, in an article published in the *Century Magazine* for December, 1890, thus described one phase of that complex operation—the harvesting and thrashing of the wheat:

> Imagine three or four hundred wild Indians in a grain field, armed, some with sickles, some with butcher-knives, some with pieces of hoop iron roughly fashioned into shapes like sickles, but many having only their hands with which to gather by small handfuls the dry and brittle grain; and as their hands would

soon become sore, they resorted to dry willow sticks, which were
split to afford a sharper edge with which to sever the straw.
But the wildest part was the thrashing [sic]. The harvest of weeks,
sometimes of a month, was piled up in the straw in the form
of a huge mound in the middle of a high, strong, sound corral;
then three or four hundred wild horses were turned in to thrash
it, the Indians whooping to make them run faster. Suddenly they
would dash in before the band at full speed, when the motion
became reversed, with the effect of plowing up the trampled
straw to the very bottom. In an hour the grain would be thoroughly thrashed and the dry straw broken almost into chaff. In
this manner I have seen two thousand bushels of wheat thrashed
in a single hour. Next came the winnowing, which would often
take another month. It could only be done when the wind was
blowing, by throwing high into the air shovelfuls of grain, straw,
and chaff, the lighter materials being wafted to one side, while
the grain, comparatively clean, would descend and form a heap
by itself. In that manner all the grain in California was cleaned.
At that day no such thing as a fanning mill had ever been
brought to the coast.

Another phase of life at the fort during 1846 was described
by Edwin Bryant, a journalist who had led one of the many
overland parties that arrived that year. Like so many others, the
journalist was made welcome to New Helvetia and hospitably entertained at dinner by its host. In his book, *What I Saw in California*, which was published in New York in 1848, Bryant wrote:

> Captain Sutter's dining room and his table furniture do not
> present a very luxurious appearance. The room is unfurnished,
> with the exceptions of a common deal table standing in the cen-
> ter, and some benches which are substituted for chairs. The table
> when spread presented a correspondingly primitive aspect of
> viands. The first course consisted of a good soup served to each
> guest in a china bowl with silver spoons. The bowls, after they
> had been used for this purpose, were taken away and cleaned
> by the Indian servant, and were afterwards used as tumblers
> from which we drank our water. The next course consisted of
> two dishes of meat, one roasted and one fried, and both highly
> seasoned with onions.

I am thus particular, because I with to convey as accurately as I can the style and mode of living, in California, of intelligent gentlemen of foreign birth who have been accustomed to all the luxuries of the most refined civilization.

From this last sentence it is evident that, during the dinner for Bryant, Sutter had followed his usual custom of regaling guests with fanciful tales of the select social circles in which he had supposedly moved before coming to America.

Over the involved enterprise he himself had created, the Captain ruled with the authority of a benevolent but stern despot. Every phase of the operation received his close attention. Visitors reported that he began each morning with a series of interviews with assistants, both whites and Indians, during which the previous day's accomplishments were reviewed and orders for the coming day were issued. It was a difficult and trying task he had set for himself. For as his colony grew in size and complexity, the number of problems he was daily called on to face increased to the point where, according to his later testimony, he was sometimes tempted to give up the struggle, to sell out for whatever his property would bring, and start again under less demanding conditions elsewhere.

However, such moods soon passed. For so far as his personal fortunes were concerned, Sutter all his life was a confirmed optimist; however dark the present might seem, for him the future was full of bright promise. If, as happened in 1843 and again in 1844, the number of arriving emigrants fell far short of his expectations, he was unconcerned; next year they would be counted by the thousands. When a dry spring, or a lack of wheat to sow, or of men or implements to plant and harvest it, brought on a crop failure (and so deprived him of revenue desperately needed to maintain his credit), his letters to his creditors cheerfully ignored such catastrophes and instead of painted glowing pictures of the next season's prospects.

His habitually sanguine mood is evident in another of his letters to Thomas O. Larkin—one of the more patient of his long-suffering creditors—this one dated July 22, 1845. The fact that a lack of rainfall had resulted in a disappointingly small yield from his wheatfields is passed over with a few words, whereas the ambitious program of planting he had mapped out for the coming season is described in detail. He is, he states, planning to sow 600 *fanegas* of wheat in the fields about the fort, and an additional 200 *fanegas* at Hock Farm, the ranch he was then developing on the Feather River.

Of course he could see nothing but success for that venture. Once next year's crop was harvested, "all my debts will be paid, and I will have a very large Amount over." To succeed in his efforts and "make this business sure," he believed he had but to work out some means of irrigating his farmlands. This he proposed to do by building a dam across the American River, which would divert the water into a canal, and, as it flowed toward his wheatfields, would be made to turn the wheels of the flour and lumber mills he planned to build. "Great advantages will come of this business," he wrote, and went on to announce that the Russian colonies in Alaska offered a steady and profitable market for whatever foodstuffs he would be able to produce.

His letter made clear, too, that the fortune he was about to make would not be derived from agriculture alone. His other wealth-producing enterprises, he stated, were also in flourishing condition. The outlook for a profitable fur-gathering season had never been brighter. Come September, he planned "to fit out canoes for the Rivers, lakes and Bays," and to send another party over the route taken by Frémont on his recent trip across the Sierra where, Frémont had told him, "there are plenty of Beavers . . . never disturbed before by trappers."

Then followed these prophetic sentences:

> A great Advantage for this Establishment is that we have the best quality's of timber close by. It is only thirty miles from here where I have 9 white Men and 10 Indians employed, sawing the best Kind of pine, making shingles of pine and Cedar . . . In this Cedar and pine wood I intend to build a sawmill . . .

This was the sawmill about which a great deal more was to be heard during the next several years.

seven

The Yankees Take Over

· 1   THE "YEAR OF DECISION" OPENS

The beginning of 1846 found California facing an explosive situation on several fronts.

The native Spanish-Mexican population, having grown tired of the shabby treatment accorded them by their distant rulers, were in the process of severing all ties with Mexico City and establishing home rule. A second numerous class was made up of foreign-born residents who had taken out Mexican citizenship, received liberal grants of public lands, in many cases married local *señoritas*, and come to wield considerable influence in the affairs of the province. Like a great majority of the native-born Californians, these too were nearly all in favor of casting off the yoke of Mexico. However, members of that group, many of whom had become merchants or traders, were as a whole better informed of world conditions than the other Californians, and because they knew that local political developments were being closely watched by a number of foreign nations, they were convinced that California could not long keep its independence if it should become a separate state. By and large, the naturalized Californians favored the ultimate transfer of the province to the country from which they had come, whether that be England, France, Russia, or the United States.

A third class of residents—and by far the fastest growing of the three—were the Yankee emigrants who were flowing into California over the newly opened overland trails. These were a

115

heterogeneous lot, a representative cross section of the American
frontiersmen who, for well over a century, had spearheaded the
westward push. A restless, independent, self-reliant breed, impatient of restraints of any kind, they had little in common with
the other two varieties of Californians; indeed, their interests
clashed at so many points that they inevitably came to share a
mutual suspicion and distrust.

The Californians looked on the Americans as trespassers who
had entered the country illegally (as indeed they had), and who,
by their behavior while in the province and by their refusal to
obey orders to leave, had shown an arrogant disregard for the
country's laws. On the other hand, the frontiersmen, who all their
lives had been accustomed to roam at will wherever they chose
to go, hotly resented attempts by the Mexican officials to place
what they regarded as unwarranted restrictions on their freedom
of movement.

The conflicting aims of these opposing factions placed Sutter
in a highly uncomfortable position. For he had close personal
and business dealings with all three groups, and he well knew
that if his enterprise were to succeed, he must continue to enjoy
cordial relations with each. With the foreign-born merchants and
traders—to most of whom he was heavily in debt—it was essential that he maintain his credit by convincing them that he would
soon be in a position to settle his long-overdue accounts. In that
attempt he never quite succeeded, but thanks to much letter
writing, occasional token payments, and repeated promises of
larger payments to come he was able to put off the day of reckon-
ing from month to month and year to year.

Of more immediate concern to him was the problem of how
to retain the confidence and trust of the other two groups;
namely, the rulers of the province and the horde of newly arrived
Yankees. Here Sutter's dilemma was that he was caught between
two warring factions and obliged to win and hold the good will
of both. A further complicating factor was his own divided loyal-
ties. On the one hand, his natural hospitality—plus a realization
of where his own best interests lay—led him to welcome the
overland parties to the fort and to allow them to remain as long

as they wished. But balancing that, he was an official of the Mexican government, with, as he sometimes boasted, the power of life and death over everyone in his district, and as such it was his duty to enforce the laws of the province—including barring foreigners from taking up permanent residence there.

For a time the Captain succeeded in treading a precarious path between these increasingly hostile groups. Throughout that difficult period his correspondence shows him unabashedly playing both sides of the street. In his letter to General Castro, quoted from earlier, we find him urging the Mexican government to buy his fort and station troops there as a means of turning back the Americans expected to arrive that fall. This letter was dated early in 1846. Yet only a few months earlier, on November 5, 1845, he had written United States Consul Larkin vehemently denouncing the Mexicans for their attempts to bar the Yankees—a message that built up to a climax in which he announced that "before I will suffer an injustice done, to them, I die first."

It is hard to find a logical basis on which these two opposing viewpoints can be reconciled—but then, consistency in thought or action had never been one of Sutter's strong points. He was capable of supporting both sides of any controversial issue, at least until he could determine what effect the outcome would have on his own interests. Long before the year 1846 had ended, however, the question of which side he should support in the controversy then raging had been answered.

2 FRÉMONT VS. CASTRO

Soon after John C. Frémont's return to the fort following his unsuccessful attempt to rendezvous with the remainder of his party under Joseph Walker, he and his men again set off toward the south. This time his destination was Monterey, where he planned to ask the Mexican officials to allow him and his followers to remain in California until the spring of 1846, when the mountain passes would again be free of snow. With the help of Consul Larkin, the desired permission was granted him—but with the proviso that during the remainder of their stay his party must remain in the interior, avoiding the coastal settlements.

This condition is believed to have been imposed on him at the insistence of General Castro, who resented the presence in the province of so large a group of armed men (it numbered approximately sixty), and who, like most Californians, was skeptical of Frémont's contention that his party was on a friendly, non-military mission.

Castro's suspicion as to the nature and intentions of the Frémont expedition seemed to be confirmed by its leader's subsequent behavior. For instead of returning to the Sacramento Valley as he had been instructed to do, the Captain—who had meanwhile been joined by Walker and the balance of his command—proceeded only as far as the Salinas Valley, a day's march from Monterey. There, on a hill called Gavilan Peak, the united party made camp, surrounded the spot with a hastily thrown up fortification of logs, and on the highest point on the hill hoisted an American flag.

This action on Frémont's part brought a prompt and angry message from Castro charging him with having violated "the laws and authority of Mexico," and concluding with this ultimatum: "You will immediately on receipt of this . . . return with your people out of the limits of this territory. If not, this office will take the necessary measures to cause respect to this determination."

After three days had passed, during which Frémont's men continued to strengthen their position, giving no indication that they intended to leave, the Mexican general, on March 8, issued this proclamation:

> *Fellow Citizens:* A band of robbers, commanded by a Captain of the United States Army, J. C. Frémont, have without respect to the laws and authorities of this department daringly introduced themselves into the Country and disobeying the orders of Your Commander in Chief and the Prefect of the District by whom he was commanded to march forthwith out of the limits of our Country and without answering their letters he re-

mains encamped at the Natividad, from which he sallies forth, committing depredations and making scandalous skirmishes.

In the name of our native Country, I write you to place Yourselves under my immediate orders, at Headquarters where we will prepare to tame the ulcer, which should it not be done would destroy your independence and liberty which you all always sacrifice Yourselves, as will Your Friend and fellow Citizen.

(Signed) *José Castro.*

During the next few days a flurry of heated correspondence passed back and forth between Castro, Frémont, and Larkin, with the last-named, in his capacity as United States Consul, attempting to play the role of peacemaker. On March 8 Castro wrote Larkin repeating his threat to expel Frémont by force should the latter continue to defy his orders. Larkin in turn reported the quarrel to the Secretary of State at Washington, then dispatched a courier to Frémont's camp informing the Captain that Castro had recruited a force of two hundred men and was preparing to move against him. "Your encamping so near the town [that is, Monterey] has caused much excitement," he stated at one point. "The natives are firm in their belief that they will break you up, and that you can be entirely destroyed by their power; in all probability they will attack you . . ."

Whether Castro's threats or Larkin's reasoned arguments were responsible for Frémont's decision to withdraw is unknown; in any event, he presently broke camp and "slowly and growlingly" returned to the central valley, intending to continue on to Oregon.

March 21 found him once more at the forks of the Sacramento and American rivers, adjacent to the fort. His party remained there several days, then broke camp and resumed their leisurely march on up the valley. Something more than a week later Sutter received the disquieting news that Frémont, who had stopped briefly at the Peter Lassen ranch near the northern end of the valley, had taken with him a number of horses that he had bought from a group of Indian horse thieves in that area. The

stealing of horses and cattle by roving bands of natives was an
evil Sutter, along with the other landowners in the region, had
been making every effort to stamp out. Whenever livestock bearing the brand of any of the rancheros was found in the possession
of the Indians, the animals were returned to their rightful owners
and the thieves were severely dealt with.

In his dictation to Bancroft, Sutter stated that, having learned
that Frémont had bought a number of the stolen horses, "paying
five yards of calico and a few beads for each," he had sent the
American officer a message protesting his action and asking that
the animals be returned to their owners. "I was still a magistrate
and an officer of the Mexican Government at the time," he added,
"and I deemed it my duty to enter this protest. Frémont made
no reply to my letter and never forgave me for writing it."

The stage was now set for the next act of the unfolding
drama.

The *New Helvetia Diary* contains this laconic entry under date
of April 28, 1846: "Arrived Mr. A. Gillespie from Yerba Buena
also Mr. Stepp from Daylors, departed Sicard for Bear Creek."
Of the subsequent movements of Messrs. Stepp and Sicard and
the reasons therefor, nothing is known. Those of Gillespie, however, and information about that gentleman himself, is extensive.

The "Mr. A. Gillespie" of the diary was Archibald H.
Gillespie, a lieutenant of the United States Marine Corps, who
had recently reached California from Washington bearing messages for Frémont from a number of high government officials.
These included letters from Secretary of State Buchanan, from
Frémont's influential father-in-law, Senator Thomas H. Benton
of Missouri, and probably—though that point has never been
definitely established—verbal instructions from President Polk
himself. Traveling incognito and posing as a tourist in quest of
health, Gillespie had reached the province by a roundabout route
that included a land crossing of Mexico and a sea voyage from
Mazatlán to Monterey by way of Honolulu.

On reaching the mainland Gillespie had hurried to Sutter's
Fort, where he learned that Frémont and his men had left for

Oregon more than a month earlier. "He asked me for horses and a guide to overtake him," Sutter later recalled, then added disconsolately, "I allowed him to take my favorite mule, for which I had paid $300; he returned it wind-broken, and that was the only profit I got out of this affair."

By the time Gillespie overtook him, Frémont had already crossed into Oregon. The pair met on the shore of Klamath Lake on the evening of May 9. Precisely what was the nature of the information and instructions Gillespie imparted to the Captain at their meeting has long been a matter of debate. The common assumption is that Frémont was told that the authorities at Washington believed war with Mexico to be inevitable, and that—as Josiah Royce writes in his closely reasoned analysis of the situation—he was "instructed to use his force to attempt what was possible, in the way of stirring up the American settlers and any other available persons against the authority of the Department, so as to get us the territory in advance of the declaration of war."

At any event, following his meeting with Gillespie Frémont and his men at once turned about and hurried back to California.

When it became known at the fort that the Frémont party had returned to the valley, the news was far from welcome.

Ever since their arrival in California nearly six months earlier their presence had been a source of embarrassment to Sutter, who later complained that he had found the unpredictable behavior of the expedition's leader "extremely mysterious," and that his habit of "flitting about the country with an armed body of men" had needlessly stirred up ill feeling against the United States among natives and foreigners alike. It is not surprising that Sutter breathed a sigh of relief when Frémont eventually left for Oregon Territory, or that word of his return was received with a notable lack of enthusiasm.

Sutter's dislike of the headstrong captain—a dislike that was cordially reciprocated—was based only in part on such matters as his defiant action at Gavilan Peak, his dealings with the Indian horse thieves, and his belligerent attitude toward the Californians in general. The true source of grievance against the American officer was that by his actions he had further complicated the already difficult position Sutter occupied in his dealings with the settlers in the valley on the one hand and the Mexican officials on the other.

For the enmities engendered by Frémont's visit had once more put Sutter in a situation that called for the exercise of whatever tact and diplomacy he was able to muster. To have made known his dislike and suspicion of the American by refusing to provide him with the supplies his party needed would have destroyed the picture of himself he had been building up as the friend and benefactor of the valley emigrants and the chief champion of their rights. Conversely, his loyalty to the provincial government, of which he was the official representative in the valley, was already being questioned at Monterey, and it was therefore desirable that he lose no opportunity to provide Governor Pico and General Castro with evidence that he had their interests at heart.

In his effort to extricate himself from that dilemma Sutter followed his usual custom of trying to placate both parties. He provided Frémont with whatever he asked for in the way of provisions and animals and thereby helped speed him and his men on their way out of the province. Then, as a conscientious official, he duly reported the other's departure to his superiors at Monterey—taking care, however, to delay his report until Frémont was well beyond reach should Castro make good his threat to overtake and punish him.

Upon Gillespie's appearance at the fort several weeks later, Sutter had followed the same procedure. Gillespie was given a guide and transportation (including Sutter's favorite mule) to help him overtake Frémont and deliver his messages. Then, after another delay of nearly two weeks, he reassumed his role of loyal public servant and wrote Castro expressing his belief that Gillespie was not the innocent tourist he claimed to be but instead was probably a secret agent of the United States Government.

In his letter, which was dated May 12, 1846, Sutter wrote the Mexican general:

I think this gentleman is an officer of the United States Army . . . I told him this and he replied that he formerly was, but that he now has retired from the service. Who knows? It is my opinion that Senor Gillespie is a courier for Captain Fremont and who knows but that he may have important dispatches from his government . . .

By then, events in California were moving rapidly toward a climax.

On the morning of June 14—hardly a month after the above letter was written—a group of Americans from the Sacramento Valley staged a raid on the town of Sonoma, the northernmost of the Mexican settlements. The raiding party took the town's leading citizen, General Vallejo, and several others prisoner. They hoisted a flag above the plaza, bearing a crudely drawn grizzly bear, and proclaimed the formation of an independent California republic.

The events leading up to that exploit, which was to become known in California history as the Bear Flag Rebellion, can be briefly told.

On Frémont's return from Oregon he established his headquarters near a group of hills now known as Sutter Buttes in the center of the valley about fifty miles north of the fort. Soon after he and his party made camp there they were joined by a considerable group of American settlers. Most of the latter were recent arrivals who, having learned of Castro's threat to drive all Yankees out of the province, had fled to Frémont's camp for protection.

One of this group of leather-clad frontiersmen was a reckless, hard-drinking trapper named Ezekiel Merritt. Merritt and a number of his followers had no taste for waiting passively until Castro's army showed up; they advocated the strategy that they themselves take the offensive and strike the first blow. It was in keeping with that resolve that the first hostile move of the campaign was made. On June 10, learning that a herd of horses destined for use by the Mexican army was being driven from Sonoma to Monterey, Merritt and a force of twelve men overtook the cavalcade, captured the horses from the soldiers who had them in charge, and returned with the animals to Frémont's camp.

Although no shots were fired during that encounter, the incident came to be looked on by the group at Frémont's headquarters as the opening gun in a campaign to wrest California from Mexican control. Emboldened by the success of their initial coup, Merritt and his supporters, who by then numbered something more than fifty men, staged next a surprise raid on Sonoma, captured the town without opposition, and set up their short-lived California Republic.

3 THE BEAR FLAGGERS

The weeks that followed were a particularly difficult time for the "Lord" of New Helvetia.

Like Thomas Larkin, William Leidesdorff, Jacob Leese, and many other foreign-born residents, as well as the heads of some of the influential Spanish-Mexican families, Sutter had been looking forward to the day, which he believed to be imminent, when California would become a part of the United States. And, like the others, he had been both shocked and disappointed by the irresponsible action of the Bear Flag group, which had outraged the Spanish-Californians and ended all hope of bringing about the change by peaceful means.

Meanwhile, the Bear Flaggers' raid on Sonoma had been followed by a second encounter. The two forces involved were a company of about twenty American settlers under Henry L. Ford and a somewhat larger detachment of Castro's troops commanded by Captain Joaquin de la Torre. The two met unexpectedly on the morning of June 24 at the rancho of Camilo Ynitia in present-day Marin County about midway between the points where the towns of Petaluma and San Rafael now stand. A brief exchange of gunfire followed, most of it at long range. One Californian was killed and two wounded, whereas the Americans suffered no losses. The Mexican soldiers then withdrew and the "Battle of Olampali"—named for a nearby Indian

village—passed into history. It was the only action in the Bear
Flag Rebellion that incurred bloodshed.

Up to that point Frémont had refrained from taking an active
part in the affray. But from the beginning his camp in the upper
valley had been a rallying point for the insurgents, and there
is little doubt that he worked closely with their leaders. But once
the success of the movement was assured, he abandoned all pretense of neutrality and, after forwarding his resignation from the
Army to Washington, he openly assumed leadership of the
movement.

One of his first acts on taking charge was to transfer the rebel
headquarters from his remote and unfortified camp to Sutter's
stronghold. The reason he gave for the move was that the fort
was the only place in the valley where the settlers could successfully defend themselves against an attack in force by Castro's
troops.

"During the next few days Frémont made his appearance before the gates of my Fort with his entire force," Sutter later commented. "Merritt, Carson, and a great many settlers, in all about
a hundred men, were with him. I opened the gates of the Fort
and the soldiers came and went at their pleasure." He went on
to state that he had willingly cooperated with the Bear Flaggers,
that "Frémont regarded me as his ally" and that "by the single
act of throwing open my gates I had . . . thrown my lot with
the forces of the United States."

These remarks, however, were made three decades later, and
like many of his other statements during the final years of his
life, when he was petitioning Congress to reimburse him for the
loss of his property, they were intended to prove that he had
never wavered in his support of the American cause. But there
is evidence that such were not his sentiments at the time the
revolt took place. In point of fact, Frémont's action in taking over
the fort and stationing a detachment of troops there was a heavy
blow to Sutter's pride, and then and later he resented it bitterly.
This feeling on his part is understandable. For ever since he had
founded his colony more than seven years earlier he had been
its supreme ruler; now for the first time his authority had been

challenged and he found himself forced to play the role of underling.

Nor did Frémont do anything to spare the older man's feelings; on the contrary, he seems to have taken pleasure in adding to his humiliation. When Sutter, puzzled to account for Frémont's open hostility, asked his chief scout, Kit Carson, what had caused it, Carson replied succinctly, "Remember that letter"—the reference being to Sutter's message rebuking Frémont for dealing with the Indian horse thieves.

Frémont established his main camp near the American River, several miles distant from the fort, leaving the latter in charge of a detachment of ten men under one of his lieutenants, a topographical engineer named Edward Kern. "I believed at first that these men were to assist me," Sutter remarked, "but I discovered soon that they were left to act as spies over me."

A further source of discord between the two men were the Californians who had been made captive by the Bear Flaggers during the raid on Sonoma and who had since been confined at the fort as prisoners of war. The party was composed of four Sonoma residents: General Vallejo, Vallejo's brother Salvador, his former military aide, Victor Prudon, and his brother-in-law, Jacob Leese. All were men prominent in the affairs of the province, and all had been favorably inclined toward the American cause. Sutter, who was on friendly terms with the four (he and Vallejo having patched up their former differences) and had entertained them at the fort, now found himself acting as their jailer.

In his *Reminiscences,* he describes how he carried out that distasteful assignment:

> When the prisoners arrived at the Fort, I placed my best rooms at their disposal and treated them with every consideration . . . The gentlemen took their meals at my table and walked with me in the evening. Neither did I place a guard before the door of the room, nor did I order any soldiers to accompany us when we were walking. I thought that it was wholly unnecessary to be more severe with them. They were men of property and there was no danger of their attempting to escape.

He goes on to state that when word of his behavior toward the Californians reached Frémont, the latter "appeared again at the Fort and complained that I had treated his prisoners too kindly."

Frémont asked him bruskly: "Don't you know how to treat prisoners of war?"

"Indeed I do, Captain Frémont," Sutter retorted. "I have been a prisoner myself. Take charge of these men yourself; I don't want to have anything to do with them."

Vallejo and his companions were put in charge of John Bidwell, who, while he disapproved of the filibustering tactics of the Bear Flaggers, had joined Frémont's force and served with him throughout the campaign. Sutter later reported gleefully that "Bidwell . . . allowed them just as much liberty as they had enjoyed when they were in my care . . . I visited the prisoners frequently and often sat and talked with them until one day Dr. Townsend [one of Sutter's aides during the Micheltorena campaign] warned me not to be too friendly with them if I did not wish to become a prisoner in my own house."

The fact that Sutter was forced to play a subordinate role at the fort was not the most serious injury he suffered at the hands of his implacable enemy. For throughout Frémont's stay in the area he was busy signing up volunteers in order to strengthen his rag-tag army for the expected showdown with the Californians. So successful was his recruiting campaign among the employees at the fort that when he set off for the south he, in Sutter's words, took with him "all my workmen and all my best Indians."

This loss of almost his entire staff came at a particularly inopportune time. For Sutter was then well launched on a program of expansion that he believed would not only pay the debts that had been hampering his operation from the beginning, but would also for the first time make the colony completely self-supporting. In his letters written during the early months of 1846 he viewed the future with even more than his accustomed optimism. But that mood was short lived. For now of a sudden his mills and workrooms had all but ceased to function, his livestock was roving the ranges unattended, and virtually all his native hunters and trappers had marched off to war. So too had the crews on which he had depended to harvest and process the many acres of wheat and corn and other products then ripening in the surrounding fields.

The outlook was bad, but it could have been worse; only the fact that Frémont's season of authority was brief saved him from experiencing then the complete disaster that was to befall him three years later.

4   THE CONQUEST

In early June of 1846, while the ships of the United States Pacific Fleet were lying at the port of Mazatlán on the west coast of Mexico, their commander, Commodore John D. Sloat, learned that the United States and Mexico were at war.

For some time Sloat had had orders that in the event of hostilities between the two countries he was to hasten to California and seize and hold its seaport towns. Accordingly, he at once set sail for the north. His ships arrived off Monterey on the second of July and on the morning of the seventh 250 sailors and marines landed on the beach and marched to the old Spanish Custom House. There they stood at attention while an American flag was raised above the building and a proclamation stating that "henceforward California will be a portion of the United States" was read.

No opposition was offered to the occupying force at Monterey or at any place in the northern half of the province. On July 9 the United States sloop *Portsmouth* entered San Francisco Bay and the flag was raised above the plaza at Yerba Buena. On the same day a party from the *Portsmouth*, led by Lieutenant Joseph Warren Revere, reached Sonoma. The Bear Flag, which had flown over the town for a little more than three weeks, was lowered and was replaced by the new emblem. Following that ceremony an emigrant named William Scott—who had reached California a year earlier with the Grigsby-Ide party—was given an American flag by Lieutenant Revere and dispatched to Sutter's Fort with instructions to hoist it at sunrise on July 11.

Of these flag-raising ceremonies Sutter later wrote:

> A long time before daybreak I had the whole Fort alarmed and my guns ready. When the Star Spangled Banner slowly rose on the flag staff, the cannon began and continued until nearly all the windows were broken. Some of the people around the Fort made long faces, because they thought they would have had a better chance to rob and plunder if they had remained under the Bear Flag. The Sonoma prisoners, not knowing what was going on, were greatly surprised. I went to them and said: "Now, gentlemen, we are under the protection of this great flag, and we should henceforth not be afraid to talk to one another . . ." They all rejoiced that the anarchy was over.

Although the change of flags was heartily welcomed by Sutter, it by no means ended his troubles. Soon after the Americans landed at Monterey the Bear Flaggers were taken into the United States Army, made a part of a unit called the California Battalion and, with Frémont in command, set off to help complete the occupation of the southern part of the province. Sutter's position, however, was not much improved by their departure. For upon leaving, Frémont had placed the artist of his expedition, Lieutenant Edward Kern, in command at the fort; hence during the next several months Sutter was forced to continue playing a subordinate role in the direction of its affairs. One circumstance that made this particularly galling to him was the fact that he (who considered himself an authority on all things military) was obliged to serve under a man who, so far as soldiering was concerned, speedily proved himself a hopeless amateur. So great was Kern's ignorance of military procedures that it became necessary for Captain Montgomery, whose ship, the *Portsmouth*, was still at Yerba Buena, to send one of his officers to the fort to instruct the lieutenant in the ABC's of his profession.

The fact that in mid-August Sutter was himself taken into the Army and given the rank of lieutenant did not much improve his situation, for he was still outranked by the inept Kern. It is evident that this period long held unpleasant memories for him. In the reminiscent writings and interviews of his later years he invariably avoided making any reference to Kern's presence at the fort. By so doing he managed to give the impression that he had been in sole command of the "more than a hundred men, many of them my former soldiers" who were stationed there.

The weeks that followed were full of incident. Although such fighting as took place was nearly all confined to the southern part of California, the fort played a by no means unimportant part in the outcome. For one thing, it was the only fortified spot in the entire central valley, and thus was the place where the settlers congregated for protection both against hostile Indians and the troops General Castro had threatened to send against them. In addition, it was at the fort that volunteer military companies were recruited and trained and outfitted preparatory to taking the field against the Californians.

During the remaining months of the year events continued to move rapidly. On July 15—eight days after the flag was raised at Monterey—Commodore Robert F. Stockton succeeded Sloat as commander of the American forces in California. Stockton was a more aggressive leader than Sloat had been and less concerned with gaining and holding the good will of the Californians. It was he who had conferred the rank of major on Frémont and put him in charge of the California Battalion. Frémont then had led his force down the coast toward the southern settlements, encountering virtually no opposition along the way.

Up to that point all had gone well with the invaders. Seemingly the conquest of California had already been accomplished, and with a minimum of violence. But it was not to be quite that easy. In mid-August Stockton's naval force occupied Los Angeles, then withdrew to the north, leaving behind some fifty men under Lieutenant Gillespie. A month later the residents of that pueblo, resentful of restrictions placed on their activities by the occupying force, took up arms and, having surrounded Gillespie and his men, held them prisoners on a nearby hilltop. At length, however, a messenger managed to slip through the lines and carry word of the besieged party's plight to Stockton, who had meanwhile returned to Monterey. The Commodore at once dispatched a force of some 350 men to their rescue. But before the ship bearing the relief party reached San Pedro, Gillespie had signed an agreement with the Californians by which he promised to retire with his men to San Pedro and leave on the first available vessel.

But before the Gillespie party could embark, the shipload of reenforcements arrived from the north and the united force set out to retake Los Angeles. This time they were met by a determined band of Californians who, by their expert horsemanship plus their skillful use of their "artillery" (which consisted of a single small brass cannon), succeeded in halting the invaders and driving them back to San Pedro.

Emboldened by their initial successes, the residents of the Los Angeles area made ready to step up their resistance to the Americans, who by then were approaching from two directions. Frémont's battalion, more than 300 strong, was hurrying down the coast from the north, while to the east a contingent of Regular Army dragoons under General Stephen W. Kearny, having completed the occupation of New Mexico, was marching overland to join in the California operations.

It was Kearny's force that met the Californians in what proved to be the major engagement of the campaign. This was the Battle of San Pascual, the most sanguinary ever fought on California soil, which took place on December 6 at a point some thirty miles northeast of San Diego. During the hours-long engagement the Californians, under Andrés Pico—brother of Pío Pico, the last Mexican governor of the province—followed the strategy of falling back before the charge of Kearny's dragoons, then turning suddenly on the front ranks of their pursuers and inflicting heavy damages before reenforcements could be brought up. The result of a series of such brief hand-to-hand encounters was that the Americans lost seventeen men killed and nineteen wounded while the Californians' casualties were limited to twelve wounded.

Kearny's column reached San Diego on December 12 with men and animals near exhaustion from their encounter with Andrés Pico's elusive horsemen and from their long march across the desert from Santa Fe. Preparations then got under way for what proved to be the final phase of the campaign: the recapture of Los Angeles. On December 29 Kearny and Stockton, their combined forces numbering about 600 men, set out from San Diego and, on January 10, 1847, the American flag was again raised over the Los Angeles plaza, the occupying troops having this time encountered only token resistance. Three days later, on January 13, Frémont—who had finally reached the northern outskirts of the town on his march down the coast—met with Andrés Pico. Together they drew up and signed the Cahuenga Capitulation, which completed the take-over of California by the United States.

While the fighting was going on in the south Sutter had remained at the fort, busily occupied with matters growing out of the war. Although Lieutenant Kern was still the ranking officer there, the ex-artist had neither taste nor talent for the responsibilities of that office and so was content to shunt off his duties on his subordinate. Sutter, of course, was ready and willing to accept the assignment, and during the next several months much of his time was given over to such official duties. Not only was he active enlisting and outfitting recruits, both Indians and whites, and dispatching them south for service with the California Battalion; he also had the responsibility of maintaining order throughout the central valley. For with all but a few of the settlers serving with Frémont's force, there was an ever-present threat that hostile Indians would resume their raids on the semi-deserted ranchos and drive off the livestock.

Toward the end of 1846 that danger was enhanced by the arrival in the valley of a party of Indians belonging to the warlike Walla Walla tribe.

"They came down from Oregon to hunt and trade in the valley," wrote Sutter, "and to seek justice for the murder of a young chief, the son of Yellow Serpent, who had been killed some time before during a quarrel with one of my men. Their appearance at the northern frontier caused some of the settlers to flee post haste to my Fort, and the exaggerated reports caused such a panic throughout California that a massacre of the Walla Wallas was just barely averted."

Sutter met that situation by inducing the tribesmen to join in the campaign against the Californians, promising that the United States Government would pay them for their services. "Being a warlike people, many of them were glad to go," he added. Thus a contingent of Walla Wallas served in Frémont's army during the final weeks before the signing at Cahuenga. After the end of hostilities, however, they presented Sutter with a new problem. In his *Reminiscences* he stated:

"When they returned to New Helvetia, they had not yet received their pay and, believing that I had deceived them, threatened to declare war on us. I pacified them by giving them a lot of old, broken-down government horses, stamped U.S., that were roaming about the Fort. On their return to Oregon, they behaved very badly and did a lot of damage. They caught and maltreated a number of Indians from California tribes and stole horses from me and the other settlers."

5 "ORDEAL BY HUNGER"

Fully occupied though he was with matters pertaining to the war, Sutter yet was obliged from time to time to turn aside from such concerns to play host to parties of newly arrived emigrants. In general, such groups came through in good shape, needing only a brief period of rest in order to recover from their months-long marches.

But this was not always the case; some groups arrived in California in such weakened condition that rescue parties had to be sent out to accompany them on the last leg of their journey to the fort.

The first hint that one such party was facing what might be serious trouble reached the fort in early fall of 1846. Toward the end of September two travel-worn emigrants appeared, bringing word that a company numbering close to one hundred men, women, and children was making its way across what is now central Nevada with many of its animals lost and with supplies of food dangerously low.

On learning of that emergency Sutter acted promptly and with his accustomed liberality. By his orders five packmules were loaded with dried beef, flour, and other necessities and dispatched across the mountains. Heading that rescue mission was Charles Stanton, one of the two men who had brought news of the party's plight; the other, William McCutchen, had become ill and so remained at the fort. As guides Sutter sent two native youths whom he described as among his "best Indians."

Nothing further was heard of the slowly approaching party for more than a month. Then there appeared at the fort one James Reed, who had been expelled from the company following a quarrel during which he had fatally stabbed a fellow member. Reed brought more disquieting news. It was already October when he had left the party. Yet despite the lateness of the season and the need for haste if the mountains were to be crossed before winter snow blocked the passes, the expedition, headed by elderly, cautious George Donner, had then been proceeding deliberately down the Humboldt Valley, still a number of days' travel from the base of the Sierra.

The next several weeks set the stage for the coming disaster. On October 19 Stanton with his two Indians and five packmules met the party, which by then had reached Truckee Meadows, near present-day Reno. A day or two later the long and difficult climb toward the distant summit began. The end of October found the company strewn out along the trail, most of them at an altitude of 7,000 feet or higher. They had reached the vicinity of Truckee (now Donner) Lake when they experienced their first heavy snowstorm. Between October 31 and November 3 the by then thoroughly alarmed party made several attempts to draw the wagons up to and over the summit pass. When their efforts were defeated by the continuing storm, they returned to their former campsites, put up improvised shelters, and waited for a break in the weather that would permit them to make a new attempt.

But the winter of 1846–47 was exceptionally severe. The succession of storms that began in late October continued with only brief interruptions until the following April. All but buried beneath massive snowdrifts and with their supply of food nearly exhausted, the now desperate party had no choice but to attempt to break out of their prison. Twice during November some of the stronger members set out for the Sacramento Valley, their purpose not only to summon help but also to conserve food for those who remained behind. Both parties reached the summit, then were forced by continuous heavy storms to abandon the attempt and return to the cabins.

On December 16, during a temporary break in the weather, still another attempt was made. This party, made up of ten men and five women, all wearing improvised snowshoes, succeeded in crossing the divide, and after more than a month of fighting their way down the snow-blocked canyons, eventually reached the foothills and stumbled into the camp of a tribe of friendly Indians. Of the fifteen who had started, however, only seven survived the ordeal. Among those who lost their lives was Charles Stanton, who more than two months earlier had led the first rescue party across the mountains from the fort. On the return trip Stanton had grown too weak to keep up with his companions and, rather than slow their progress, had courageously urged them to continue on without him.

After a brief stay at the rancho of William Johnson near the eastern edge of the valley, to which they had been guided by the Indians, the survivors were escorted to the fort. There their emaciated appearance and the tales of suffering they had to tell warned their listeners that a tragedy of major proportions was in the making. Although most able-bodied men were absent fighting in the south, plans at once got under way to go to the relief of those still trapped in the mountains. By the end of January a party of seven men, each with a heavy pack of food strapped to his back, had started up the mountains. Traveling day and night with only brief periods of rest they reached the first group of snow-covered cabins on the evening of February 18 and were greeted as saviors by the starving occupants. The rescuers learned that the marooned party, once their meagre food was exhausted, had been reduced to cooking and attempting to eat oxhides, shoes, or whatever else have promise of sustaining life—and finally, after all else had failed, of consuming the flesh of those who had already starved to death.

Because the amount of food the rescuers had been able to carry would sustain the entire party for only a brief period, it was imperative that all those able to travel start down the mountain at once. Accordingly, a company of twenty-two refugees, fifteen of whom were children, was assembled and on February 22 the journey began. The passage of this group, like that of the earlier snowshoe party, was marked by intense suffering from cold, fatigue, and the perennial lack of food. Two of its members died en route, and only the fortunate meeting with a new relief party struggling up the mountain trail prevented a further heavy loss of life.

This newest relief expedition—the third sent out from the fort since word of the emergency had first been received—was headed by James F. Reed, the same Reed who months earlier had been banished from the Donner Party because of having been involved in a stabbing affray. Reed and his fellows reached the camp on Donner Lake on March 1; two days later they started back with another contingent of refugees, this one made up of one man, two women, and fourteen children.

For them, as for the earlier parties, the passage down to the lowlands entailed great hardships. Because of their weakened condition, the survivors' progress was painfully slow. Three days were consumed reaching the summit, and soon after they started down the western slope a protracted storm closed down and immobilized them for more than a week. To prevent themselves from freezing during that ordeal the group spent the days and nights huddled about a fire that had been built atop the snow on a platform of logs. As time passed, the fire's heat caused the platform to sink until it was eventually resting at the bottom of a deep pit. When the storm at length abated, Reed and the other members of the rescue team started down the mountain in search of help. Before they left they gathered a supply of wood for the marooned party, but they had no food to leave with them.

At the end of several days of breaking trail down the mountainside Reed and his companions were at the point of complete exhaustion when they providentially encountered yet another relief party struggling up from the valley. Having ministered to

Reed's little group, the new party hurried on to the spot where the emigrants were still gathered about the fire at the bottom of the pit. By the time the rescuers arrived three of the group were dead; here, too, there was evidence that the hunger-crazed survivors had resorted to cannibalism.

While some members of this fourth rescue party transported the weakened refugees to safety below—only two of whom were able to walk—the others pressed on over the summit. When they finally reached the snowed-in camps they found the once crowded cabins almost empty. Starvation had claimed all but a few of those who had remained there throughout the winter. This time but four of the survivors were in a condition to be escorted down to the lowlands; among them were three young daughters of the ill-fated party's leader, George Donner. Donner himself, his courageous wife, Tamsen, and a thirty-two-year-old German emigrant, Lewis Keseberg, were left behind. When, more than a month later, a final party reached the scene, only Keseberg was alive. All about was grisly evidence of the means by which he had managed to survive.

Of the eighty-seven members of the Donner Party who had left Fort Laramie the previous summer, only forty-five lived to reach California. It was by far the most tragic episode in the annals of the westward migration. The loss of life, however, and the suffering of those who survived, would have been even greater had not Captain Sutter and others at the fort responsed generously and courageously to each call for help. It was at the fort that the successive rescue expeditions were organized and outfitted, with the Captain himself always a liberal contributor of supplies and other necessities. And it was to the fort that the half-starved survivors were brought and where the owner provided them with food, shelter, and whatever else they needed to restore them to health.

eight

Prelude to Frenzy

---

1   TO BUILD A SAWMILL

During California's first year under American rule its population nearly doubled.

Members of the United States armed forces accounted for a goodly share of the increase. Among the military and naval units were Companies C and K of General Kearny's First Dragoons, which had arrived by way of Santa Fe, the sailors and marines aboard Commodore Sloat's Pacific Fleet, plus a number of lesser groups. The largest single contingent was the first Regiment of New York Volunteers, commanded by Colonel Jonathan D. Stevenson, which had sailed from New York on the transports *Thomas H. Perkins, Loo Choo,* and *Susan Drew* and reached San Francisco in March and April of 1847. By the time the New Yorkers arrived the fighting had ended; hence, the regiment was broken up and single companies, or parts of companies, assigned to various places up and down California, one of which was Sutter's Fort.

"On May 24, 1847, a detachment of . . . the New York Volunteers arrived at the Fort to relieve my Indian soldiers," Sutter states in his *Reminiscences.* "The commander of the detachment was Lieutenant [Charles C.] Anderson, to whom I turned over the command of the Fort [note that Sutter ignores Lieutenant Kern, who was really in charge there]. The detachment consisted of one-half of Company C, which was quartered at New Helvetia, while the other half of the company was stationed at Sonoma. The officers of the detachment ate at my table, and the enlisted men cooked their own rations. The New York Volunteers remained at the Fort for several months . . ."

A second substantial increase in California's population—this one a party of civilians—had taken place some nine months earlier. In late July, 1846, the 450-ton ship *Brooklyn*, five months out of New York by way of Honolulu, unexpectedly entered the bay and dropped anchor off Yerba Buena Cove. The *Brooklyn* carried seventy men, sixty-eight women, and more than one hundred children. Nearly all were members of the Mormon Church who had come west with the intention of founding a colony somewhere on the Pacific Coast.

The company was headed by Samuel Brannan, a picturesque and energetic Elder of the church, who was soon to play an influential part in local affairs. The emigrants brought with them a large assortment of tools, equipment, and other material needed to sustain themselves on the frontier. Their party was the first contingent of what was expected to be a large-scale migration of church members from the former headquarters of the sect at Nauvoo, Illinois, where some of the tenets of their religion, notably those having to do with plural marriages, had subjected them to persecution.

A second large party of Mormons, this one more than three hundred strong, arrived in January, 1847. This was a military company, the so-called Mormon Battalion, which had been recruited from among Mormon communities in Iowa and elsewhere in the Middle West. The battalion had been mustered in at Council Bluffs on June 16, 1846, and after being outfitted at Fort Leavenworth in mid-August had set off for the west coast. Their uncommonly long and arduous march took them first to Santa Fe, then across hundreds of miles of semi-desert to San Diego. It was not until the following January that the travel-worn column eventually arrived. Thus they, like Stevenson's water-borne New York Volunteers, did not reach the scene of the fighting until the war was over.

When their enlistments expired, members of both the Mormon

Battalion and Stevenson's Regiment were given the option either of re-enlisting and returning east with their units or of being mustered out in California. Most of Stevenson's men and virtually all the Mormons elected to remain in the new land, where they believed their opportunities would be greater than at home. However, it was not the intention of the Mormons to remain in California permanently; instead, they planned to march inland and join their brethren at a new headquarters their leader, Brigham Young, had recently founded on the shore of the Great Salt Lake.

The Mormon Battalion was disbanded at Los Angeles in late July, 1847, and the next day its members set out on the long trek to Utah. Their route took them into the lower San Joaquin, then up the valley to Sutter's Fort, which was reached slightly less than a month later.

One of the party, a young Virginian named Henry W. Bigler, kept a diary during that journey and later. His entry for August 26 reads:

> Laid by while some visited the Fort, where there was a blacksmith shop, and got the animals shod, for some of them were tender footed. The price for shoeing was one dollar for each shoe made and nailed on. We learned there was plenty of grain and unbolted flour and peas to be had. Unbolted flour . . . was worth eight dollars per sack, peas one dollar and half per bushel. Captain Sutter seemed to have plenty of everything in the shape of cattle, horses, mules, grain, etc. Several of our boys concluded to stop here and go to work for Sutter, as he was wanting to hire and was offering pretty fair wages, as the boys thought, and fit themselves up and come on [to Salt Lake] next spring.

Bigler and most of the party left the fort on the morning of the 27th and headed eastward. They had not gone far when they heard news that caused most of them to turn about and return to the valley.

On September 6, while they were camped at Donner Lake— where evidences of the tragic events of the previous winter

were still to be seen—they were met by their fellow church-
man, Elder Brannan. Brannan was returning from Salt Lake
where he had tried—unsuccessfully, as it proved—to persuade
Brigham Young to establish the church headquarters in California rather than Utah. He brought a message from Young stating
that the amount of food on hand at Salt Lake was barely enough
to sustain those there. He, therefore, advised those former members of the Mormon Battalion who did not have families waiting
for them at the Utah headquarters, or who could not bring
enough provisions to last them through the coming winter, "to
return to California and go to work and fit themselves out with
plenty of clothing, stock, provisions, etc.," then to join the new
community after the first crops were harvested the following
year.

On receiving this message thirty members turned about and
retraced their steps to Sutter's Fort, which was reached on the
afternoon of September 14. One of their number was Bigler,
whose diary entry for that day reads:

> After eating a bite of dinner we sent three men to see Cap-
> tain Sutter. Late in the evening they returned reporting
> [that] . . . he was willing to give the whole of us employment.
> He would either hire us by the month or by the job. He was
> intending to build a mill and wanted mill timbers got out and
> a race cut about three miles long. He would pay $25 per month
> for working on the race or he would give twelve and one-half
> cents a yard. We talked the thing over among ourselves that
> night and the next morning we closed a bargain with him to
> work on the race for twelve and a half cents per yard to be
> paid in cash. He was to board us, but we were to do our own
> cooking.

2 MARSHALL'S "GOLD MINE"

The millrace the Mormons contracted to dig was part of
an ambitious plan Sutter had had in mind for some time; that
is, the building of a large gristmill on the American River some
distance northeast of the fort, which was to be operated by water

brought from that stream through a three-mile-long canal. The Natoma mill—it was so called from an Indian village near its site—was scheduled to be completed by the end of 1847. It was to have a capacity of forty bushels per hour—which, as its projector pridefully wrote his friend Larkin, "will grind what the whole Sacramento Valley will be able to produce in wheat."

The building of the gristmill was but one manifestation of a new spirit of enterprise that had become evident in Sutter's behavior during the first months following the American conquest. Never before—and never afterwards—did his prospects look so bright. Sutter himself was fully aware of that. "After the war, things prospered for me," he once wrote. "I found a good market for my products among the newcomers and the people of the Bay district. My manufactures increased and there was no lack of skilled mechanics. I had a number of looms, and the natives were taught to weave blankets and to make hats. People came to buy leather, shoes, saddles, hats, spurs, bridles, and other articles which were turned out by my shops."

But this was only one phase of the operation; the farming and cattle-raising activities were on an even larger scale.

"I had several hundred workmen in the harvest fields," he wrote "To feed them I had to kill four and sometimes five oxen daily." During the planting season thirty or more ox-drawn plows and harrows were daily in the fields preparing the ground for planting. Despite the crude implements and primitive methods then in use—his Indian workers were, in his words, "forced to reap the crop with sickles, thrash it with hoes, and winnow it in the wind"—it was possible in good years to harvest as much as 40,000 bushels. The herds of cattle that roamed the ranges of the New Helvetia grant contributed still further to the colony's booming economy. In later life Sutter once estimated that at the end of 1847 his holdings in livestock included 12,000 head of cattle, 2,000 horses and mules, between 10,000 and 15,000 sheep, and 1,000 hogs. He added plaintively: "My best days were just before the discovery of gold."

It was during that period, too, that Sutter launched yet another enterprise. This was one that, although no one could have fore-

seen it at the time, was to have a profound effect on his personal
fortunes as well as on those of countless others.

In his recollections of the period, written many years later,
John Bidwell thus explained the reasons behind that move by
his one-time chief:

> Sutter's many enterprises continued to create a growing de-
> mand for lumber. Every year, and sometimes more than once,
> he sent parties into the mountains to explore for an available
> site to build a saw-mill on the Sacramento River or some of
> its tributaries, by which lumber could be rafted down to the
> fort. There was no want of timber or of water power in the
> mountains, but the cañon features of the streams rendered raft-
> ing impossible . . . Yet, never discouraged, nothing daunted, an-
> other hunt must be made for a mill-site.

It was the pressing need for lumber to complete his new flour
mill at Natoma, plus a growing demand for the product from
the fast-growing settlement on San Francisco Bay (the name of
the village had recently been changed from Yerba Buena to San
Francisco), that caused Sutter to renew his quest.

Bidwell's narrative continues:

> The last search for a saw-mill site was by Jas. W. Marshall.
> Sutter had sent him with an outfit for a thorough exploration
> of the Sierra Nevada. After about a month he returned with a
> favorable report. This was in the fall of 1847. I wrote the agree-
> ment between Sutter and Marshall. The site chosen was the
> place now known as Coloma. Marshall, not a millwright but in-
> genious at almost anything, was to build the saw-mill and have
> a share of the lumber—Sutter was to furnish all the men, means
> and material.

Because this Coloma sawmill presently became a very well
known place indeed, virtually everyone who had a hand in its
planning or building—and a great many who had neither—later
recorded their versions of what took place. Hence, there is no

lack of documentary evidence bearing on events of the next few months.

The site Marshall chose for the mill was on the south fork of the American River, in a foothill valley about fifty miles northeast of the fort. Work began in early September, 1847, and continued through the fall and winter. During most of the construction period the number of workers averaged about twenty-five, seventeen of whom were Mormons. There was one woman in the group, a Mrs. Wimmer, wife of Peter Wimmer; she served as camp cook. The Wimmers, along with most of the others, lived in a cabin built of pine logs that stood on the nearby hillside, overlooking the millsite.

By mid-January, 1848, the mill was almost completed. One of the few tasks remaining was that of deepening the tailrace that was to carry the water back to the river after it had turned the wheel. As an easy means of accomplishing that it was Marshall's habit to leave the sluice gate open each night so that the water flowing through would wash away the sand and gravel. Each morning after shutting off the water he walked down the length of the ditch to see the result of the night's erosive action.

On one such morning—the date was January 24—Marshall chanced to notice some small flakes of shining yellow metal at the bottom of the race. His curiosity aroused, he asked an Indian helper to go to the cabin and fetch him a tin pan. Into it he scooped a few handfuls of sand and gravel from the edge of the stream; then, by moving the vessel in a circular motion, he washed away the lighter material. At the end of this primitive placer mining operation there remained in the bottom of the pan a small amount of the yellow metal, "about as much as a ten-cent piece would hold." Although Marshall was excited at what he had found, he was not yet wholly convinced that the metal was gold. The workmen at the mill were openly skeptical. Later when he announced to them that he "believed he had discovered a gold mine" he was greeted with derisive laughter.

But the doubts of the others failed to discourage the amateur prospector. Later that same day, according to Bigler's circumstantial account of the episode, he asked Bigler and another worker "to shut down the head gate early in the evening . . . and make all tight and I'll see what there is in the morning." This was done, and while the crew was at breakfast he went down alone to the race. Their meal over, the men had just started to work when Marshall came hurrying up, "carrying his old white hat and looking wonderfully pleased."

The reason for his pleasure soon became evident. He put his hat down on a workbench and as the others gathered about, showed them a heap of bright yellow fragments in the depression of its crown—fragments that ranged in size "from the smallest particle up to the size of a kernel of wheat or larger."

By this time their earlier doubts had vanished and the excited group, none of whom had ever seen gold in its native state, set about trying to hit on some means of identifying the particles. A number of tests were applied. One of the Mormons produced a five-dollar gold piece, part of his pay on being mustered out of the Army, and compared it with the specimens; the two appeared to be alike as to weight, though the coin was a bit lighter in color. Several grains were put on an anvil and pounded with a hammer; instead of crumbling under the blows they were flattened out to the thinness of paper. Other particles were subjected to heat and emerged from the fire unchanged. Finally, pieces were placed in a pot of lye that Mrs. Wimmer, who was making soap that morning, had on the stove; the strong chemical had no effect on the metal.

When no one could think of any further tests to apply, Marshall led the way back to the tailrace. "We all followed him," wrote Bigler, "and in looking close, we could see particles here and there on the base rock and in seams and crevices. Conjectures were it must be rich, and from that time the fever set in and gold was on the brain . . ."

3   AN ILL-KEPT SECRET

The scene now shifts to Fort Sutter. The time is three days later, on the evening of January 28. Here is Sutter's account of what happened:

Marshall [who had ridden down from the mill in a driving rain], dripping with water, hurried excitedly into my office next to the guard house. He asked to see me alone in the 'big house' where my private office and the clerk's office were located. I was utterly surprised, because the day before I had sent up everything he required, mill iron and provisions. I could not imagine what he wanted, yet I conducted him to my private rooms, which were furnished with old, clumsy laurel wood furniture made by the Russians at Fort Ross. We entered and I shut the door behind me. Marshall asked me if the door was locked. "No," I replied, "but I shall gladly lock it." I knew that he was a very strange man, and I took the whole thing as a whim of his . . . I supposed he acted so queerly because he wanted to tell me some secret which he considered important.

On being assured that they were safe from interruptions, Marshall asked for a pair of scales, which Sutter got for him from the fort's apothecary shop. Thereupon he "pulled out of his trousers pocket a white cotton rag which contained something rolled up in it." The "something" proved to be a small quantity of bright metal particles—Sutter estimated their weight at about an ounce and a half—the largest piece "not quite as large as a pea" and the smallest "hardly the size of a pin-head."

Marshall handed the specimens to Sutter, saying that he believed them to be gold. After examining them carefully the other agreed that they might indeed be gold; first, however, they must be submitted to tests. Thereupon he put a silver coin on one pan of the apothecary scale and the same weight of the unknown metal on the other, then immersed the whole in water. The result was that the side bearing the silver rose to the surface and the other sank toward the bottom. "Then I went to the apothecary shop, got *aqua fortis* and applied it," the Captain's account continues, and adds that the specimens were unaffected by the acid. "Finally," he stated, "I brought out a volume of the 'Encyclopedia Americana,' a copy of which happened to be on my book shelf, to see what other tests could be applied." A reading of the encyclopedia article on gold convinced him; there was no longer any doubt that gold has been found at his new sawmill.

Marshall, more excited than ever now that his yellow fragments had been positively identified, insisted that the two set off at once for the mill. When Sutter advised waiting until morning, pointing out the lateness of the hour and the fact that it was still raining heavily, his companion refused to listen. Instead, he mounted his horse and rode away into the darkness. Sutter, taking with him two native retainers, followed the next morning. He had been only a few hours on the trail when he "saw in the distance a human being crawling out from the brushwood." The stranger proved to be Marshall who, since he had left the fort the previous evening, had ridden fifty miles to the mill, changed horses, and come nearly half way back so as to accompany Sutter on the remainder of his journey.

Meanwhile, the workers at the mill, having learned that "Old Cap Sutter," as they called him, was on his way up from the valley, planned a surprise for him, one that they hoped would put him in a mood to share the bottle of *aguardiente* he usually carried on such trips. Accordingly, each contributed some of the dust he had collected and, early that morning after the water had been shut off, sprinkled it along the edges of the ditch. Having thus liberally "salted" the mine, they awaited "Old Cap's" arrival.

Bigler's diary explains the reasons why that carefully laid plot misfired:

Just as we were completing our breakfast, we saw Marshall, Wimmer, and Sutter coming, walking side by side, while the old gentleman was in the middle, very well dressed, walking with a cane. At this we stepped out into the mill yard and met them, and after passing the common salutations, we were invited to go along and have a general good time together in looking for gold. Right at this juncture one of Mrs. Wimmer's little boys came running past us down into the race and picked up nearly every particle and came running back almost out of breath, meeting us, holding out his hand and saying, "Father, see what I have found." Sutter, as soon as he saw it, jabbing his cane into the ground saying, "By Jo, it is rich." Here the joke was against us. We dared not say a word, but let the boy claim and keep the gold, lest we lose our expected drink.

But notwithstanding that contretemps, it seems safe to assume that Sutter's bottle was brought forth and shared with the others. For by Bigler's account, the entire party continued on to the millrace where "the Captain had the pleasure . . . of picking up here and there a few particles that had been left or overlooked by the boy." To the small amount he had himself gathered, the workers added from their own findings until he had "about an ounce and a half." The gratified Captain told the donors that he intended to have their gift fashioned into a ring "as soon as I can get hold of a goldsmith." Some time later the ring was duly made; according to its owner, it bore "my coat of arms" inside the band, together with the legend, "The first gold discovered in January 1848."

The generous welcome his employees had given him might of itself have been sufficient to cause Sutter to offer them the hoped-for libations; there was, however, another and stronger reason why he wished to retain their good will. For he had already begun to suspect that for him the gold discovery would not prove an unmixed blessing. Although from the beginning he appears to have realized its future importance, he was aware too that so far as his personal fortunes were concerned, it had come at a particular inopportune time—a time when his affairs were flourishing as never before and the scope and variety of his activities were expanding on all fronts.

It was not hard for him to forsee what was likely to happen to his various enterprises once it became known that gold in considerable quantities had been found at the new sawmill. In his mind he pictured his army of workers leaving their fields and cattle ranges and workbenches and hastening en masse into the foothills. Thoroughly alarmed at that prospect, he set about persuading the Mormons to remain on the job until the mill was completed, and urging them meanwhile to keep news of the discovery secret. This the workmen agreed to do, though not without some misgivings on their part. Of that phase of the situation Bigler wrote:

> Some and even most of the hands had a strong desire
> . . . [to] let the mill go and turn their attention to gold
> mining, but still they were afraid lest they could lose in the long
> run more than they might make. They knew they were getting
> pretty fair wages for their labor on the mill and it was sure
> pay, while on the other hand there was a risk to run. That was
> the way we reasoned among ourselves, but when Sunday came,
> down into the tail race we would go . . . [where] we could pick
> and crevice with our jack and butcher knives, and we hardly
> ever failed to get three to eight dollars and sometimes more . . .
> Still we were fearful to venture, and besides the mill was so
> near completed, we finally concluded to stick to the mill until
> she started.

The spot where the mill was being built was well beyond the boundaries of the New Helvetia grant. Sutter's next step, therefore, was to try to secure legal title to the site for himself and Marshall. This he sought to accomplish by negotiating a treaty with the Indians of the district by which, in return for supplying them with clothing, farming equipment, and other goods having a value of about $150 per year, he and his partner would receive a twenty-year lease to a large area of land surrounding the mill. Acting in his official capacity as Indian Sub-agent for the Sacramento district, Sutter drew up such a document and, after it had been duly signed by both parties, he dispatched it by messenger to Monterey. With it he sent a letter to Colonel R. B. Mason, the military governor, asking his approval of the agreement on the ground that "it will be of great benefit to the Indians by . . . furnishing them with food, clothing, etc. and [will] teach them habits of industry."

Neither the lease nor the letter made any mention of the fact that gold had been found on the property.

Although it seemed a shrewd move at the time, Sutter's treaty with the Indians proved to be a serious mistake of judgment.

Colonel Mason received Sutter's message on March 4; the next day he wrote this reply:

Headquarters Tenth Military Department,
Monterey, California, March 5, 1848.

Sir:

I last evening received your letter of the 22nd February, together with the lease to certain lands on the waters of the 'American fork,' a tributary of the Sacramento, made by certain Indians of the Yalesummy tribe to yourself and Mr. James W. Marshall.

The United States does not recognize the right of Indians to sell or lease the lands on which they reside, or to which the tribe may have a claim, to private individuals. It would therefore be improper for me to sanction any lease of lands made by Indians to individuals, because, after the war, should the United States extinguish the Indian titles to these lands, they would find them encumbered with private claims, which certainly would not be recognized; for, as soon as the Indians' titles to any lands are extinguished, they are at once a part of the public domain.

I am, respectfully, your obedient servant,

R. B. Mason,
Colonel 1st Dragoons, Governor of California.

Captain J. A. Sutter,
Sub-Indian Agent, New Helvetia

4 THE FEVER RISES

Not only did Sutter fail in his attempt to have the lease approved; that ill-advised action was also responsible for spreading abroad news of the gold discovery sooner than otherwise would have been the case. For Charles Bennett, the millworker whom Sutter had chosen to take the document to Monterey, and who himself had signed it as a witness, could not resist the temptation to share his knowledge with those he met along the way. "With him in a buckskin bag," wrote Bancroft, "he carried some six ounces of the secret, which, by the time he reached Benicia, became too heavy for him."

Bancroft went on to state that on arriving in Benicia Bennett stopped at the store of one Ed Pfister. There a group of townspeople was discussing the fact that evidences of coal had been found at the base of nearby Mount Diablo and speculating on what effect that discovery was likely to have on California's future. After listening for some time Bennett could no longer remain silent. "Coal!" he exclaimed disdainfully, "I have got something here which will beat coal, and make this the greatest country in the world!" Thereupon he produced his buckskin bag and poured its contents out on the counter.

Bennett's next stop was San Francisco. There too the bag was brought forth, this time in order that a local resident, Isaac Humphrey, who had had previous gold mining experience in Georgia, could pass on its contents. (Humphrey unhesitatingly pronounced the metal gold.) Again, during his stay at Monterey, Bennett, in Bancroft's words, "consoled himself for the failure of his mission by offering further glimpses of his treasure." Clearly, Sutter could hardly have chosen a less reticent messenger.

The Captain himself, however, was not much better at keeping the secret. Although he had pledged those at the mill to silence, he could not long resist the urge to share the exciting discovery with others. Thus we find him hinting to those about the fort that sensational news was in the making in the foothills. "One day," wrote his assistant, Heinrich Lienhard, "Sutter made some mysterious remarks about his sawmill, which was under construction, and said that . . . momentous changes might be expected. He accompanied his remarks with a broad smile." According to this same source, one day at the dinner table the Captain—"who for two or three weeks had been acting queerly"—produced some particles of metal which he had "tied in a dirty old rag," and showed them to his guests. "The small grains were yellow," stated Lienhard, "and we began to think they might be gold."

With others Sutter was even less prudent. In a letter to Vallejo, written on February 10, he announced jubilantly: "I have made a discovery of a gold mine, which, according to experiments we have made, is extraordinarily rich." Though in the past this pair had been on bad terms, the Spanish-Californian did not begrudge the other's seeming good fortune. To John Bidwell, who on a latter visit to Sonoma gave him details of the discovery, Vallejo commented: "As the water flows through Sutter's millrace, may the gold flow into Sutter's purse."

About that time yet another break occurred in the by no means impenetrable wall of silence with which Sutter had tried to surround happenings at the mill. This came about because in dispatching a wagonload of provisions to the spot, he put it in charge of a man who was even less adept at keeping secrets than Bennett had been. When the wagon arrived, the teamster, whose name was Jacob Wittmer, was greeted by one of the Wimmer children with the announcement that "a gold mine" had been found there. Wittmer, who knew nothing of the discovery, ridiculed the child's remark, whereupon his mother, indignant that anyone should question her offspring's word, not only showed her small hoard of "dust" to the teamster, but also gave him some.

This might not have been a serious breach of secrecy except for the fact that Wittmer had a weakness for the strong native *aguardiente*. On his return to the fort, bent on refreshing himself after his long trip, he visited the store Sam Brannan and George Smith had recently opened in one of the outlying buildings. When his proffer of gold dust in payment for a bottle of brandy was rejected by one of the proprietors, Wittmer suggested that he consult Sutter and learn whether or not the metal was genuine. This the skeptical merchant did, whereupon the Captain, recognizing the futility of further attempts at secrecy, acknowledged that the particles were really gold.

In recalling that episode nearly thirty years later, Sutter stated that instead of putting the hard-drinking Wittmer in charge of the wagonload of goods sent to the mill, "I should have sent my Indians"—which remark elicited this comment from Bancroft: "It seems that the gentle Swiss always found his beloved aboriginals far less treacherous than the white-skinned parasites."

But although news of the discovery was soon known not only

at the fort but at Sonoma, San Francisco, Monterey, and way points, at no place did it arouse any particular excitement. The reason the news was received so calmly can be readily explained. For one thing, the Californians were already aware that gold existed within the confines of the territory. There had been a number of earlier discoveries, the most important of which—in the Placerita Canyon of present-day Los Angeles County—had taken place as recently as 1842. In none of them was the metal present in quantities sufficient to make mining profitable, and accordingly such claims as were worked were soon abandoned. Another reason for the comparative indifference with which the news from the sawmill was received was that during the first several weeks no prospecting was done except in the immediate vicinity of the mill. Hence, no one as yet had any conception of the extent and richness of the gold fields.

It was mainly due to the Mormon workers at the mill, and in particular to diary-writer Henry Bigler, that the true significance of the discovery eventually came to be recognized. "I was the only one in the crowd who had gold badly on the brain," Bigler wrote. He went on to state that it was his habit to slip away from the camp each Saturday and Sunday, and on the pretext of hunting for game, "to examine every likely spot where I thought there might be gold."

On one of the first of his prospecting trips he chanced on what appeared to be a likely formation on the opposite side of the river about a half mile below the mill. He waded across the stream, and with a jackknife as his only tool, dug from the seams of the rock half an ounce of free gold. The following Sunday he revisited the spot and that time gathered "a little more than an ounce." But his weekly trips down the river soon aroused the curiosity of his fellows, and when on February 22 he returned from another visit to his secret claim, they demanded to know what he had been doing. Bigler replied by showing them his day's gleanings, "a little short of one ounce and a half of clean gold dust."

On his next visit to his "mine" Bigler was joined by four fellow Mormons. Despite the fact that high water in the river had covered most of the outcropping, by their joint efforts the group managed to gather more than five ounces of gold. Figuring its value at $16 per ounce, they estimated their winnings for the day at slightly more than $16 each, far more than the wages Sutter was paying them. Thereafter, although work on the mill continued—it was completed on March 11—the men devoted all their free time to the more lucrative business of gold mining.

The industrious Bigler meanwhile had written some of the Mormons at the Natoma gristmill telling them of the discovery and urging them to keep the news to themselves "unless it would be some one who could keep a secret." Toward the end of February three workers there, having announced that they were going deer-hunting, arrived at the sawmill and spent several days prospecting the streams and sandbars of the vicinity. Although they made no large strikes, they returned to Natoma bearing visible evidence of their success as gold miners.

It was in that manner that the gold fever, after an uncommonly slow start, began a gradual rise. First to become infected had been the workers at the site of the discovery, then the Natoma mill hands, and finally the labor force, both Indians and whites, at the fort itself.

Once the movement began, it spread rapidly. On March 7, some six weeks after Marshall first noticed the particles in the millrace, Sutter reported disconsolately that his entire staff, laborers and overseers alike, had joined the rush to the foothills, "and left me only the sick and lame behind."

5   EXODUS

Meanwhile, at the village of San Francisco, rumors of the discovery continued to be heard from time to time, only to be ignored by a majority of the townspeople. It was not until mid-April that interest reached a point where a delegation was formed to visit the spot and learn at first hand what all the talking was about. The group was composed of P. B. Reading, George McKinstry—both of whom were former employees of Sutter—and Edward T. Kemble, editor of the *California Star*, San

Francisco's first newspaper; they made the trip up the Sacramento aboard William A. Leidesdorff's schooner, the *Rainbow*.

After an overnight stay at the fort they left the next morning for the sawmill. Their host of the night before accompanied them, ostensibly as companion and guide, but probably also to do what he could to prevent their learning the true importance of the discovery. The youthful editor—Kemble was but twenty at the time—later wrote an account of the trip which was published in the *Sacramento Union* on April 5, 1873. In it he stated that besides Sutter, Reading, McKinstry and himself, the little cavalcade included two of Sutter's Indian boys, Antonio and José, who went along "to look after the animals and make camp."

All were mounted on horses except Sutter, who by preference rode a favorite mule, which he called "Katy." Kemble's narrative gives us this pleasant glimpse of Katy and her solicitious owner:

"Frequently that morning in crossing marshy places or ascending slippery paths the Captain would fall to the rear and be heard in low tones expostulating with his mule: 'Now, den, Katy—de oder foot! God bless me, Katy—de oder foot, child!' "

Arrived at the mill, the party was met by suspicious looks from Marshall and the Mormons, who well realized the purpose of their visit. They accordingly volunteered no information, and returned evasive answers to the visitors' questions. Their uncooperative attitude had the desired result. After a night and day at the scene, during which some perfunctory attempts at gold washing were made—Reading later remarked that their efforts had yielded "not enough to buy a drink"—the party returned to the lowlands.

In the May 6, 1848 issue of his paper Kemble wrote admiringly of the climate of the valley, of its "large" crops, "full-flowing" streams, "mighty" timber and "fragrant" flowers—but made no mention at all of the gold discovery. "Whether he walked as one blind and void of intelligence," commented Bancroft, "or saw more than his interests permitted him to tell, does not appear." In any event, the editor continued to deprecate the discovery long after his fellow townsmen had come to hold a contrary view. As late as May 20—by which time the rush to the mines was in full swing—he wrote: "Fleets of launches left this place on Sunday and Monday, closely stowed with human beings . . . Was there ever anything so superlatively silly?" In the same issue he pronounced the mines "all sham," a "takeoff" that had been "got up to guzzle the gullible."

Ironically, it was the *Star's* owner, Mormon Elder Sam Brannan, who more than anyone else was responsible for having set in motion the rush his editor so much deplored. Presumably, Brannan had first heard of the discovery from his partner, C. C. Smith, to whom Sutter's teamster, Jacob Wittmer, had offered gold dust in payment of a bottle of brandy at the Smith and Brannan store at the fort. On learning of that incident Brannan—who was never one to overlook an opportunity for a quick and easy profit—had hurried up from San Francisco. According to the *New Helvetia Diary,* he reached the fort on May 4 and next morning left for the mill, taking with him his partner, George Smith.

Brannan's examination of the gold fields must have been a hurried one, for the diary reveals that he left the fort on his return to the bay on May 8. But it soon grew clear that his stay at the diggings, brief as it was, had convinced him that the discovery was no mere flash in the pan. For on reaching San Francisco the exuberant promoter is credited with having strode down Montgomery Street "holding aloft a bottle of dust in one hand, swinging his hat in the other," and shouting at the top of his ample lungs: "Gold! Gold! Gold on the American River!"

It was his words that belatedly stirred his townsmen to action and sent them scurrying up the river, each avid to claim his share of the new bonanza.

nine

Crumbling Empire

---

1 THIS PUZZLING NEW ERA

One of the major ironies of John Sutter's story—and his life was a succession of ironies—is the fact that although the gold rush projected both him and his fort into world-wide prominence, its ultimate effect was to leave him a financial and spiritual bankrupt, and to reduce the establishment that was his chief monument from the position it had once held as the only outpost of civilization in California's great interior valley to the status of a mere way station on the route to and from the gold fields.

The disastrous effect of the discovery on Sutter's personal fortunes is the more striking because by all the rules of logic it should have presented him with a matchless opportunity. Sutter himself was well aware of that. In his later years he was frequently heard to lament that the gold rush should have made him "the richest man in the world." And when one takes into consideration the position he occupied when the rush began, it becomes clear that this was hardly an exaggeration. For one thing, he owned an immense area of fertile valley and foothill land, much of it adjacent to the richest of the gold camps. Thus he was in a position to provide the populous communities that soon sprang up there with virtually everything needed in the way of supplies, whether products of his fields and gardens and cattle ranges or goods turned out in his mills and workshops. In addition, the location of the fort, situated as it was at the junction

159

of two navigable rivers, made it inevitable that as the population of the area grew, a city would spring up on or near its site— a city that in due course would become the commercial, financial, and transportation center of much of California's rich central valley.

Why, it might be asked, did Sutter fail to gain the spectacular successes that appeared to be within his grasp? There have been a number of answers to that question. Sutter himself always maintained that he was the victim of cirumstances beyond his control. It was his contention that the sudden appearance of tens of thousands of gold hunters in what only a few months earlier had been a remote and sparsely populated land had brought about a complete breakdown of facilities for preserving law and order, and that in consequence he had been powerless to prevent the newcomers from helping themselves to his land, his crops, his livestock, and whatever else they coveted.

No one disputes the fact that in that respect Sutter's charges were well founded. There are any number of authenticated instances of depredations on the part of the horde that overran the valley, of horses and mules stolen, of cattle driven off or slaughtered, and of crops and other property wantonly destroyed. All of which was made easy by the fact that almost without exception his army of retainers, both natives and whites, had deserted him and joined in the pell-mell rush to the diggings, leaving his fields and mills and workrooms deserted and his herds of livestock to wander about the ranges with no one to look after them.

But it was not these circumstances alone that brought about the collapse of Sutter's empire. To one in his position such losses, substantial as they were, need have caused him no more than a temporary inconvenience. For his real estate holdings alone, had they been managed with ordinary prudence, would have had a value sufficient to repay him many times over for all his other losses. Moreover, his fort, as the oldest established and most favorably located settlement in the valley, was the logical trading center for the entire northern mining district, a region that extended from Mokelumne Hill and San Andreas on the southeast to Shasta City and Weaverville on the north and northwest.

The trouble was that life on the California frontier had been so completely changed by the gold rush that Sutter, who during the earlier period had conducted his affairs with reasonable shrewdness and good sense, found himself totally at a loss as to how to cope with this puzzling new era.

The brief entries on the pages of the *New Helvetia Diary* during May, 1848 (this valuable record of day-by-day happenings was permanently abandoned on the 25th of that month), reflect the quickened tempo of life at the fort once the rush got under way. May 1 was "a very bussi day" during which several men "went up to the Gold Mines," while a second party which had been at the sawmill returned to the fort; also, a Dr. Isabel "with 3 other men" arrived from down below (that is, San Francisco Bay) and left again the same day; presumably they, too, were heading for the mines. On May 2 "Messrs McKinstry & Bidwell left for Cosumney River" and, on the same day, "many loafers" likewise left. Entries for the 4th and 8th record the arrival of Sam Brannan and several companions, their two-day visit to the site of the discovery, and Brannan's return to San Francisco, taking with him his famous bottle of gold dust.

Thereafter the entries became little more than listings of arrivals and departures. On the 16th "a small launch arrived with many passengers and some Goods." On the 18th "Some families arrived from San francisco bound for the Mountains"; the entry for the 19th states "Arrived Messrs Norris, Ward and a great many others, all bound for the Mountains," and that for the 20th, "Continually new arrivals from Sonoma, San Francisco & Pueblo de San Jose. . ."

At the time these words were written, Sutter's view of the gold discovery was still untouched by disillusion. He looked on it as a providential stroke of good fortune, one that would fulfill all his hopes and compensate for his earlier trials and disappointments. In a letter written from New Helvetia on May 4 and addressed to a former employee named Heinrich Thomen, he tells

of finding gold "near my sawmill" and adds that "many considerable discoveries" had since been made. "Gold is found now
twenty miles from here and travels up to the sawmill in a width
of twenty to thirty miles and about forty miles in length; that
is, as far as we have traced it . . ."

Not only did he believe that the metal was widely distributed,
he was also convinced that it was present in unprecedented quantities. His letter to Thomen continues:

> It seems almost unbelievable how rich these placeros and
> mines have proved to be. Nothing equalling them has ever been
> found in Mexico, in Peru, or in Chile. The workers make at least
> an average of $4 to $5 per day, where the Mormons are operating
> [this spot later became known as Mormon Bar] one has found
> in one single washing $60. Business in the stores is quite active,
> Mr. Smith [C. C. Smith, partner in the firm of Brannan & Smith]
> has received in three days thirty ounces of gold . . .
> Messrs Abeck and Schmidts [and] Zimmerman [all three were
> former employees of Sutter] have formed a partnership, and they
> start tomorrow for the mountains for washing gold. Abeck has
> been there before and has made out very well. We shall see
> that Sutterville will immediately become a town, and another
> small town will spring up near the sawmill, which will give me
> a splendid market for my boards. My flour mill would have been
> finished by this time had not every one of the workers gone
> after gold, but it will be ready within three weeks time. I do
> not need to look now for another market for my flour, as within
> six months at least 3,000 souls will be hereabouts.

The "Sutterville" mentioned above was yet another enterprise
then engaging Sutter's attention. The town, which had been laid
out in 1844, occupied a wooded spot on the river bank about two
miles downstream from the confluence of the American and the
Sacramento. The site had been chosen by Sutter because its
slightly elevated position would, he believed, protect it from
winter floods that periodically inundated much of the surrounding
countryside, including the spot that then served as the fort's
embarcadero. During its first four years Sutterville had made

almost no progress; however, its frequent mention in Sutter's correspondence and in the *New Helvetia Diary* makes clear that its founder intended that it would ultimately replace the fort as the chief settlement of the valley.

2   THE EMPEROR ABDICATES

At one point during his 1876 interview with Hubert H. Bancroft, Sutter stated:

> The Fourth of July, 1848, I celebrated with a great banquet to which all the prominent men of the neighborhood were invited. Governor Richard Mason, Captain William Sherman, and Captain Joseph Folsom stopped on the eve of the celebration at my Fort, while on a tour of inspection through northern California and the gold districts . . .
> The day began with the hoisting of flags and the firing of the cannon. It being the first national holiday to be celebrated under the American flag, everybody was in high spirits . . . The table was set up in my old armory hall and Kyburz [Samuel Kyburz, a Swiss who then served as Sutter's major-domo], with the help of a number of women who were at the Fort at the time, had prepared an excellent dinner. We had beef, game, and fowl, and all the luxuries which a frontier life could offer. A French captain had just brought up in his launch a supply of good sauterne, brandy, and other drinks . . . All ate and drank freely, and soon general hilarity prevailed.

Sutter went on to state that in General Sherman's *Memoirs*—which had been published a year earlier, in 1875, and were then having a wide reading—the Civil War hero had accused him of partaking so freely of the toasts drunk at the dinner that he had ended up intoxicated. To that charge Sutter replied indignantly that he "was no more intoxicated" than the general himself had been, then added this philosophical comment, "A man cannot drink liquor without feeling the effects of it." By 1848 it was obvious to those who saw him often that Sutter had been "feeling the effects of it" with increased frequency of late. To be sure, there was nothing new in the fact that the Captain had a liking for the product of his own distillery. We have the word of Heinrich Lienhard—who became a Sutter employee in the fall of 1846—that he sometimes helped his befuddled boss to bed in order that he might sleep off one of his drinking bouts. But at that time such lapses appear to have been neither prolonged nor frequent, and in the free-and-easy frontier community no one save Lienhard (who had a broad puritanical streak in his makeup) seems to have given the matter any particular thought.

However, news of the gold discovery had, of course, greatly increased the number of visitors to the fort, and throughout the summer of 1848 Sutter continued to welcome the strangers with the hospitality that had become traditional at New Helvetia. The result was that in playing the role of host Sutter had the *aguard-iente* bottle brought forth so often that, according to Lienhard, most of his walking hours were spent in an alcoholic haze. Moreover, among those who benefited by his hospitality were always those who did not hesitate to take advantage of his condition, and by playing on his vanity flattered him into granting them concessions that subsequently proved to be extremely valuable. The result was that during the first months following the gold discovery he entered into a series of partnerships: to gather the metal in the foothills, to operate trading posts at the fort or in one or another of the new mining camps, and to speed the development of the town of Sutterville, to name but a few.

All such ventures promised to make quick and easy fortunes for their backers, and some did in fact yield handsome profits. But in most instances it was his shrewder partners who reaped the greater share of the rewards, and on the rare occasions when Sutter received his just share he could usually be persuaded to reinvest it in some highly speculative enterprise.

The truth of the matter is that even had the easygoing Captain been in full possession of his faculties he would have been no match for the conniving crew the gold discovery had attracted to the fort. All were bent on enriching themselves at the expense

of the man whose hospitality they were enjoying, who in his befuddled condition was an easy victim to their blandishments.

Such was the situation when Sutter's eldest son, John Augustus,
Jr., who had not seen his father for nearly a decade and a half,
reached California from Switzerland in the summer of 1848. Recalling that period later, he wrote:

"Already in San Francisco I heard some very strange and con-
tradictory rumors about my father and the state of his affairs.

"Some said he was the richest man on earth and did not know
himself his wealth; others on the contrary told me in confidence
that my father on account of his dreadfully loose and careless
way of doing every business transaction was on the brink of
ruin and that . . . he was surrounded by a parcel of rogues and
immoral men, which, instead of helping him, would only accel-
erate and in a short period accomplish his utter moral, physical,
and financial ruin."

Alarmed and shocked at what he had heard, the young
man—he was not yet twenty-two—boarded his father's schooner,
the *Sacramento*, which chanced to be in the harbor, and hurried
up the river to the fort. There he learned that most of the stories
he had heard were true. "Everything belonging to my father
was at everybody's disposal," he stated. He went on to relate that
the merchants who had recently opened trading posts in and
about the fort were furnishing goods to everyone who applied,
including the local Indians, and encouraging them to run up
"enormous bills," which were charged to Sutter's account.

At the time John, Jr., arrived, his parent was absent in the
gold country on one of his unproductive mining ventures. Not
until his return a week later did the reunion between the two
take place. It was a highly emotional meeting during which both
men wept. For the next few days all other concerns were put
aside while the two discussed family matters and jointly made
plans for the future. In the face of the Captain's unshakable optimism and his boundless confidence in his own business sagacity,
the young man's fears gradually subsided.

But he was not permitted to enjoy that feeling long. For he
soon learned that his father's involved affairs had reached a point

where something drastic would have to be done—and done at once—if a complete debacle were to be avoided.

The circumstance that had brought matters to a climax was a threat by officials of the Russian-American Fur Company—from which Sutter had bought the Fort Ross properties seventeen years earlier—that unless the long-overdue balance owed the company were paid promptly and in full, an attachment would be levied on all the Sutter property, wherever located. (Incidentally, the fur company cannot be charged with having acted with undue haste, in this matter, for despite numerous attempts to collect the annual installments as they fell due, Sutter had invariably been late with his payments and had made none at all for the past three years.)

Up until the time gold was discovered, the Captain had managed to put off his creditors, including the Russians, with pleas that a crop failure, or a bad trapping season, or some other mischance had left him temporarily short of funds, and with assurances that if they would be patient until the next harvest season payment in full would be forthcoming. In the past, such excuses had sufficed; now, with trading activities at the fort enormously increased and with signs of prosperity visible on every hand, Sutter's plea to the Russians for yet another extension of credit fell on deaf ears. Through its San Francisco agent, William A. Leidesdorff, the company began legal proceedings designed to prevent Sutter from disposing of any of his belongings until his debt—which amounted to approximately $19,000—had been settled.

Thus the summer of 1848 found the Captain in imminent danger of losing control of all he possessed. It was the timely arrival of his son that presented him with a possible means of averting that disaster. The plan he and his advisers—the chief of whom seems to have been his former employee, George McKinstry—worked out and put into effect was to transfer title to all the Sutter properties from father to son. One of the deeds covering that transaction, which was drawn up and signed in mid-October, states that "For and in consideration of fifty thousand dollars . . . to me in hand paid by John A. Sutter, Jr.," the older man conveyed to the younger all his lands in the Sacramento Valley, the Fort Ross property, the sawmill at Coloma and a square mile of land surrounding it, and a town lot in San Francisco. A second deed, executed that same day, transferred to John, Jr. personal property valued at $15,000 and including, among other items, 1,500 horses, 50 mules, 600 head of cattle, 20 saddles and bridles, and the schooner *Sacramento*.

While the legality of these transactions—the purpose of which had obviously been to prevent the fur company from tying up the property—is open to question, both Sutters then and later maintained that their purpose had not been to evade payment to the Russian firm but rather to safeguard the interests of all creditors alike. Seven years later, in 1856, John, Jr., wrote: "I knew very well that, if the country had been in a settled state . . . , this transfer would have been of no avail whatever, an attachment on the property having been levied before [the deeds were executed]."

Whatever the ethics of the transaction, the result was that young Sutter, who had been in the country less than two months and who was entirely without experience in business operations of any magnitude, unexpectedly found himself in control of a property of truly epic proportions. It is hardly to be wondered at that the young man felt a sense of inadequacy as he entered into his new duties.

3   JOHN JUNIOR'S DILEMMA

Once the transfer of his properties had been completed, a chastened John Sutter, no longer the swashbuckling lord of the New Helvetia empire, returned to the foothills, intent on restoring his diminished fortunes by a lucky coup at the mines.

This was Sutter's second such venture. The first had taken place some six weeks earlier and had been designed, he later explained, because only by that means could he hope to keep his native labor force intact.

"Other Indians engaged by white men to work for them," he stated, "had quantities of gold for which they bought all kinds of articles at the stores at enormous prices. When my Indians saw this, they too wished to go to the mountains to dig for the all powerful metal. At last I consented. I got a number of wagons ready, loaded them with provisions and goods of all kinds, appointed a caretaker [to look after affairs at the fort] and left with about one hundred Indians and a large number of Sandwich Islanders."

His party first made camp on the south fork of the American at a point about ten miles above Mormon Island. There it remained until the spot became so crowded with other miners that Sutter decided to move his unwieldy company elsewhere. The next stop was about twenty-five miles farther south, near the spot where the town of Sutter's Creek later stood. His account continues:

> The work was going well for a while until three or four traveling grog-shops were established within one and a half or two miles from the camp. Then, of course, the gold was taken to these places and spent in drinking and gambling, and the following day the men were sick and unable to work. My laborers, especially the Kanakas, became more and more indebted to me, and I found that it was high time to quit this sort of business in which I only lost time and money. I therefore broke up this camp too, and returned to the Fort where I disbanded nearly all the people who had worked for me in the mountains digging gold. The whole expedition proved to be a heavy loss to me.

(Other accounts imply that one reason for the failure of this venture was that the leader was himself a faithful patron of the traveling grog-shops.)

Sutter's second effort to profit by the gold discovery proved no more successful than the first. This time he made his way to Coloma, the community that had sprung up about his sawmill. There, in partnership with Lansford W. Hastings, he organized the firm of Sutter, Hastings & Co., developers of mining properties and dealers in miners' supplies. Born optimist that he was, Sutter could see only a shining success for this venture, as for all others. Writing to a friend in Europe, he estimated that during

the first six months he and his partner would reap a profit of
$100,000. When that operation also ended in failure he put the
blame on his partner. "Hastings was unworthy of my trust. The
business made good profits, but I lost money."

Meanwhile, back at the fort all was in confusion. John, Jr., a
mild and diffident youth, had little taste for the responsibilities
that had been thrust upon him. Yet he tried manfully to play
the role assigned him, his only purpose being, as he later wrote,
"to save something from the general wreck for my family." It
did not take him long to realize the complexity of his task. No
sooner did the news get about that he now controlled his father's
properties that he was besieged by men willing and eager to
profit by his inexperience. In the forefront of that clique were
those who, truthfully or not, claimed that the elder Sutter owed
them large sums of money, and who demanded immediate payment. So many such claims were made that young Sutter was
led to remark that he was "sure there was not a man in the
fort or in San Francisco . . . [or] in the country, with whom
my father had not unsettled accounts."

Not the least of John junior's problems was that of settling the
bills contracted by his father during his mining and merchandis-
ing operations in the gold camps.

Writing of that period he stated that "wagonloads of provisions of every kind, dry goods, etc., bought at enormous prices,
were taken off by him and his agents to his camps and
there . . . Indians, Kanakas, and white men robbed and stole
what they could; very little gold I ever saw from their labor.
On the contrary all the bills I had to pay afterwards with lots,
money, cattle, sheep, horses or anything I could lay my hands
on."

In his 1856 "Statement" the son reported that miners at the
diggings sometimes entrusted their gold dust to his father for
safekeeping, and that when they sought to reclaim it he "used
to give them orders on me, to repay them as well and as fast
as I could." Of the various partnerships the older man formed
during that period, John, Jr., stated that he—that is, the
father—"furnished provisions, Indians to do the work, etc., and

always the partners got the whole and sole benefit of it." A bit farther on in his reminiscence he added: "All this time hardly a day passed in which he, himself, and his clerks, partners, Indians, etc. were not on a general frolic intoxicated as I then already had had an opportunity of seeing . . . , I am sorry to say, more than once."

In order to pay off the clamoring crowd of creditors who daily besieged him, young Sutter was obliged to resort to all manner of money-raising devices. His first such venture, which he embarked on only a day after the property was put in his hands, was to join three others, Samuel J. Hensley, P. B. Reading, and Jacob R. Snyder, in setting up a trading post at the fort, a firm that became known as Hensley, Reading & Co. By the terms of their agreement, each partner undertook to furnish capital in the amount of $3,000 in gold dust, or its equivalent in property. In lieu of gold John, Jr. obligated himself "to procure suitable buildings at Capt Sutter's Fort for the operations of the aforesaid Company," to give it the use of the launch *Sacramento*—the largest ship on the river—and to grant it "the exclusive privilege to erect buildings" on the river front in what is now the city of Sacramento.

Some two weeks later, on December 1, the clause in the agreement giving Hensley, Reading & Co. the sole right to build on the river land was cancelled, the reason being that the partners had come to realize the impossibility of preventing others from settling there. For by then a large number of men and a growing volume of freight, all destined for the mines, were daily being landed at Sutter's embarcadero. The number of ships moored to the banks, and the great heaps of merchandise piled up on shore—some of it open to the sky, the rest protected by hastily thrown up wood and canvas shelters—all made it evident that this, and not the fort, was destined to become the area's leading settlement. Once that fact was clear, young Sutter and his partners prepared to lay out a town there.

The man who made the survey was Captain William H. Warner of the United States Topographical Engineers, who had reached California two years earlier with General Kearny's column. John, Jr. reported that as soon as word got about that the town was being established "everybody commenced to buy lots at the river at $500 a piece and in the vicinity of the fort at $250." Because he was, as he admitted, "entirely ignorant" of how to manage such transactions, he appointed Peter H. Burnett as his legal adviser and financial agent. Burnett—who less than a year later was to become California's first governor—had recently come down from Oregon where he had served as a judge of the territorial supreme court.

"I was to attend to all his law business of every kind," Burnett later wrote, "to sell the lots in Sacramento City, and collect the purchase money." For these services he received "one fourth of the gross proceeds arising from the sale of city lots"—an arrangement that in a period of a few months netted him a substantial fortune.

The launching of the new town was formally announced in the December 16 and December 23 issues of the weekly *California Star and Californian*, of San Francisco, then the territory's only newspaper:

PUBLIC AUCTION

Of Town Lots in the new Town of Sacramento,

Will take place at Sutter's Fort, in said town, on Monday the eighth day of January, 1849. The advantages which this sale now offers to merchants or mechanics wishing a residence near the mines, are too evident for comment. This sale also includes the lots lying at Sutter's Embarcadero, which is included in the town.

Maps of the new town can be seen at Maj. P. B. Reading's office in San Francisco, or at the proprietor's in Sutter's Fort. Dec. 2, 1848.

4   SACRAMENTO CITY VS. SUTTERVILLE

Although it was with funds derived from the sale of Sacramento town lots that John Sutter, Jr., was able to pay off the most pressing of his father's debts, the young man received no thanks for having performed that service. On the contrary, his action in founding a town at that point was bitterly resented by his parent and opened up a breach between the two that was never completely healed.

The quarrel came about because while the elder Sutter had long intended to build a town at a spot in the vicinity of the fort, he had definite ideas as to where it should be located, and the site he favored was not that chosen by his son.

"I had always been opposed to the plan of establishing the metropolis of the valley at New Helvetia," he once remarked. "The location was favorable enough, to be sure, but the land was so low that a rise of the river above normal would cause a flood in the town . . . For this very reason, I had started the town of Sutterville several years before the gold discovery. Sutterville was located about three miles below the Fort on rising ground, high above the level of the river. From Sutterville a high and dry wagon road to the mountains could easily have been built. The town prospered from the very start . . ."

Although Sutterville did in fact prosper for a time once the rush to the diggings got fully under way, its younger rival, Sacramento City, forged ahead. By the summer of 1849 the latter had become, according to the *New York Herald's* correspondent, Bayard Taylor, "quite a flourishing place" containing "some 300 Canvass Houses," and with lots in the business section bringing from $600 to as much as $20,000. On the other hand, Taylor, who visited Sutterville in October of that year, found the rival city to consist of "only some thirty houses, scattered along the bank for half a mile," and compared the few ships he saw moored there with the "forest of masts" that lined Sacramento City's embarcadero.

But Sacramento's triumph over the downstream settlement had not been accomplished without a struggle—one that further widened the breach between the two Sutters. The Captain was in the foothills during the winter of 1848-49, engaged in his disastrous trading venture with Lansford Hastings when he first learned that his son was laying out a town that would inevitably compete with his cherished Sutterville. The news so infuriated him that more than a quarter century later its memory still stirred him to anger. "Had I not been snowed in at Coloma," he told Bancroft in 1876, "Sacramento never, never would have been built!"

Two of the older man's former associates, George McDougal and George McKinstry, added fuel to this family feud. Incensed at John junior's refusal to grant them exclusive use of the new town's waterfront, they had hurried to Coloma and succeeded in further inflaming the Captain against his supposedly ungrateful offspring. By skillfully playing on his real or fancied grievances—and by keeping the brandy bottle close at hand—the pair, along with Sutter's current partner, Hastings, had little trouble turning his resentment of the son's behavior to their own advantage. The upshot was that by way of compensating them for having failed to gain control of the waterfront at Sacramento City, the Captain signed an agreement awarding the three eight hundred yards of land facing on the river at Sutterville.

This set off a brief but hard-fought struggle between sponsors of the two settlements, the prize being a lion's share of the heavy traffic of men and goods passing between San Francisco and the populous camps then springing up throughout the northern mines. The McDougal firm was first to move from Sacramento City to Sutterville. Then, in an effort to induce other Sacramento merchants to follow their example, McDougal and his partners made them tempting offers of free land at the rival town. Faced by this threat, young Sutter and his advisers countered by what Bancroft termed "a massive distribution of lots," designed to attract other business and professional men to Sacramento City and to persuade those already there to remain.

Although the adherents of Sutterville waged a vigorous battle, it soon grew clear that theirs was a losing cause, this despite the fact that the town's elevated site was clearly superior to that of its low-lying rival. One reason why few mercantile houses could be attracted to Sutterville is said to have been that Hastings who, with McDougal and McKinstry, controlled much of the town's business district, placed too high a price on desirable building sites. However that may be, most accounts agree that by the summer of 1849 Sutterville was already on the decline.

Meanwhile Sacramento City continued to move forward. Vessels of every type and size capable of navigating the winding river channel were arriving daily, each loaded to its fullest capacity. Immediately on landing, most of the passengers hurried off to the diggings, to be followed after a day or two by the bulk of the ships' cargoes, which had in the interim been unloaded and transferred to the backs of pack animals. By mid-May of 1849 Sacramento's first newspaper, the *Placer Times*, which had begun publication on April 28, reported proudly that the town's permanent and transient residents were being served by from twenty-five to thirty business houses. Among those the paper listed were a hotel, a printing shop, a bakery, blacksmith shop, tin shop, billiard room, bowling alley, plus the quota of bars, cardrooms and brothels usual in frontier communities of the day. Some of the businesses were housed in permanent quarters; the rest occupied hastily constructed shelters having wooden frames, with roofs and walls of canvas.

News of the gold discovery had spread rapidly and was arousing keen interest at places far removed from California.

In a letter dated September 1, 1849, J. A. Moerenhout, then French Consul at Monterey, wrote the Minister of Foreign Affairs at Paris:

> The growth and importance this new settlement [Sacramento City] has exhibited are among the marvelous things that are happening in this country. Last year I was at this place at the same season and there was not a house or even a tent there. Only a few little schooners lay in the port and the only business of any importance was a trade or barter carried on at the fort of New Helvetia. Now there is a town of 3,000 to 4,000 inhabitants there, with a quay lined with fine buildings, streets laid out and with a large volume of business that increases as communication with the placers and the interior becomes more regular and easy, and where . . . thirty-five ships were at anchor, the smallest of which was fifty to sixty tons.

Further along in his letter Consul Moerenhout wrote:

> Sutter's Fort or New Helvetia has lost all importance since
> the founding of the settlements [Sacramento City and Sutter-
> ville] on the Sacramento River. In the fort itself there is still
> a hotel and a few stores, but its business is languishing and there
> is no longer any such stir and activity as prevailed there at the
> time of my visit in 1848.

Before the rise of the two nearby towns, however, the fort too
had experienced a period of hectic activity.

On Moerenhout's first visit, in July, 1848, he had found the
scene there one of "frightful confusion." Men on horseback and
afoot were milling about outside the walls, while loaded wagons
were moving in and out of the gates, "some bringing goods from
the Sacramento landing, others taking them to the different mining regions." The open spaces within the enclosure were piled
with heaps of merchandise being offered for sale, and the noise
made by the crowds of buyers was such that "one would have
thought himself either in a Turkish bazaar or in one of the most
frequented market places of Europe." The Frenchman added
that "M. Sutter was not in his quarters and I had a great deal
of trouble finding him in the midst of all the crowd and tumult,
but when he was informed of my arrival he soon came and received me with his usual affability."

Space at the fort was then at a premium, and merchants, gamblers, and many others were eager to occupy quarters of any sort
and to pay the owner well for the privilege. "All around the
courtyard inside," wrote Moerenhout, "it is divided into cham-
bers and rooms, eighteen by thirty feet in width . . . Now all
is occupied and rented for gold." The big central building, which
the visitor termed the armory, was said to command $500 per
month and the rooms on the inner side of the walls from $150
to $200 each. Moerenhout added that "the total of the rent, ac-
cording to what M. Sutter told me, came to eighteen hundred
dollars a month, not including some houses outside, one of which
was used as a hospital. The whole enterprise soon would bring
him, he hoped, from two to three thousand dollars per month."

5 "THERE WAS NO LAW . . ."

When the above lines were written in the summer of 1848, Sutter's future looked bright indeed. To be sure, the industries he had been laboriously building up over the years were at a complete standstill. The fields of wheat and other crops that had been planted the previous spring remained unharvested. The new mills on which he had spent so much time and money and effort, and on which he had counted so heavily, both stood idle and would remain so permanently. The tannery, the wood and metal-working shops, and nearly every other activity in and about the fort had ceased to function, while his herds of livestock, deserted by their *vaqueros*, wandered aimlessly about, presenting every passerby with an open invitation to thievery.

But such losses, when they were measured against the apparently limitless quantities of gold being gathered in the foothills, seemed of little consequence. The rush to the diggings had sent the prices of goods and services of every sort to unprecedented heights. As we have seen, the deserted building and vacant rooms at the fort had all been rented for sums that a few months earlier would have been considered fantastic. Such horses, mules, and other animals still in his possession found a ready market at prices five or six times their normal value. The fort's ferry service by which a few of his loyal Indians continued to transport passengers and goods across the river at the embarcadero, and the schooner *Sacramento*, busily plying between the fort and San Francisco, were earning large profits. Finally, his immense holdings of fertile valley and foothill land had a potential value that, in Sutter's own words, promised to make him "the richest, wealthiest man on the Pacific Shore."

That he believed his new-found wealth to be inexhaustible is evident from the manner in which he proceeded to divest himself of it. He had never been prudent in financial matters even during the years when he was chronically short of cash; hence, it is not surprising that once he had ample funds on hand he launched into what his son described as "an orgy of extravagance." Dazzled by his sudden prosperity, and with his never keen business sense further dulled by nightly drinking bouts, he fell easy victim to the group of sycophants who had gathered about him—and who were the first to leave when he was no longer useful to them.

Speaking of such false friends during his interview with Bancroft in 1876, the disillusioned and defeated old pioneer said:

> I was the victim of every swindler who came along. I understood little about business and was foolish enough to have faith in men who cheated me on every side. Before the discovery of gold I had honest men around me like Bidwell, Hensley, Reading, etc. These had inspired me with confidence in human nature and caused me to trust many a sharper who was swept into California on the wave of the gold excitement.

By the time 1848 drew to a close, Sutter's inability to cope with conditions brought about by the gold discovery had become distressingly evident. With an ever-increasing tide of strangers overrunning and transforming all that had once been familiar to him, he came to feel himself an alien in his own land. Adding to his sense of insecurity was the fact that such attempts as he made to adjust himself to this puzzling new world had uniformly failed. It is hardly surprising that when, early in 1849, he received a bid of $40,000 for his semi-deserted fort, he accepted the offer with relief and retired to his farm on the Feather River.

It was not long after he went to live at Hock Farm that Sutter was called on to face still another situation that could hardly have been an unalloyed pleasure to him; that is, a reunion with the dour wife whom he had not seen in nearly fifteen years. It is significant of his feelings in that respect that the prime mover in the plan to bring the divided family together again had been not the father but the son. Sometime that spring John Augustus, Jr., had engaged Heinrich Lienhard to go to Switzerland and escort his mother, his sister, and two brothers out to California. By Lienhard's account, young Sutter paid him $4,000 for his services, plus an additional $8,000 to cover the expenses of the group while en route. Besides the four Sutters and Lienhard himself, the party included Mrs. Sutter's sister, Mrs. Schlaffi, and the latter's son, making seven in all.

Lienhard left San Francisco on the Pacific Mail steamer *Panama* on June 20, 1849, and returned with his charges aboard the same vessel on the twenty-first of the following January. After a reunion at San Francisco, the elder Sutter escorted the reunited family back to Hock Farm. There he installed them in his newly completed residence, a spacious, two-story frame house that had been built under the direction of his loyal and able assistant, John Bidwell.

For a period after he went to live at Hock Farm it appeared that Sutter's fortunes, which for many months had been at a low ebb, were likely soon to take a turn for the better. The thought of again having his children with him was a pleasant prospect to the gregarious Captain, of whom it was said that he was never wholly content except when surrounded by a crowd of admirers, and on whom the role of country squire at the remote Feather River estate had begun to pall. Moreover, what promised to be an opportunity to reassume his old place near the center of the stage—a position he had held ever since he had reached California more than a decade earlier—had come about in August, 1849. For it was in that month that John, Jr., having succeeded in paying off all the estate's most pressing debts, thankfully resigned his managerial post and transferred title to such property as remained back to his father.

But it was soon evident that the problems that had plagued the son during his stewardship had not all been eliminated; in fact, no sooner had the father reassumed control than they appeared in aggravated form. One of his first acts had been to dismiss John junior's agent, Peter H. Burnett, who had, in the Captain's words, "made a fortune too quickly to suit me." But he was presently to learn that the ousted Burnett was no worse than the men he chose to succeed him. Of the latter, he wrote:

> I commissioned other agents to place on the market the unsold lots of Sacramento, agreeing to let them have a rather high percentage of the profit. However, my choice did not prove to be a fortunate one. One of them made a fortune out of me in a very short time. As my agent he earned some $80,000 . . . The

next agent sold a great many lots and never accounted for them. Besides this he borrowed $5,000 on my account at 10 percent per month interest. He did not tell me a word about it and in 1856 the debt amounted to $35,000.

Meanwhile, what remained of his livestock was melting away even more rapidly than his real estate. The slaughter of his herds, which he had been patiently building up for more than ten years, reached a high point during the winter of 1849-50. During one period of heavy rain the Feather River overflowed, flooding the surrounding grazing lands and causing the animals to gather on the few knolls that remained above water. Thereupon, stated he, "people from the surrounding towns approached by boat and killed hundreds of animals."

He told, too, of one group of five men who during that same winter formed a partnership for the express purpose of slaughtering the Sutter cattle and who, having gained a monopoly of the meat market at Sacramento City, in the spring divided a profit of $60,000.

His losses of horses, mules, and sheep were equally heavy. On one occasion a herd of valuable horses was stolen from Hock Farm and driven to Oregon where they were sold for high prices. In the hope of salvaging something from his fast-disappearing herds he made a deal with a man named Owens by which, in return for half the profit, Owens was to kill and sell all animals that strayed beyond the boundaries of the farm. But that venture ended in failure. Later Sutter reported sadly: "Mr. Owens started his work by slaughtering a fine Durham cow that had cost me $300, and I had to chase him away."

After having had all but a few of his hard-won possessions wrested from him by men shrewder and less scrupulous than himself, it need surprise no one that in later life the disillusioned old pioneer came to look on the period of the gold rush as a time of infamy and dishonor.

"The country swarmed with lawless men," he wrote. "Talking with them did not do any good. I was alone and there was no law."

ten

Disintegration

---

1 BOOM AND BUST

One of the earliest views of Sacramento City, a lithograph drawn in December, 1848, by G. V. Cooper, shows several scores of substantial-looking buildings, some of them two or three stories high, covering an oak-studded plain that a year earlier had been almost completely deserted.

The scene depicted in the drawing is full of variety and movement. The section of the waterfront in the foreground—it was once the embarcadero of the fort where the *Sacramento*, Sutter's twenty-two-ton launch, was normally the only ship to be seen—is occupied by four ocean-going vessels and a number of smaller craft. Two three-masted schooners had been converted into storehouses and moored permanently to the river bank; a third is the pioneer side-wheeler *Senator*, the first steamer to enter the lucrative San Francisco-Sacramento run.

In the space between the river and the line of buildings facing Front Street great heaps of boxes and bales and barrels have been dumped. Tents and wooden sheds provide shelter of a sort for other newly landed merchandise; men afoot and on horseback are scurrying about; wagons and pack-mules are being loaded and dispatched to the mines. One Argonaut is transporting his possessions in the bed of a push-cart, and nearby two crowds have assembled, one to bid on goods being sold at auction, the other watching an open-air monte game.

Sacramento City's abrupt rise to prominence was accompanied by the equally rapid decline of its nearest neighbor, Sutter's Fort. Of the numerous books about the gold discovery that were hurried into print during 1849 and 1850 all but a few describe the fort as already falling into ruin. Typical of such works is S. M. Letts' *California Illustrated.* Letts visited the spot in July, 1849, to see a patient at a hospital that had been established there. "The fort, at the time of its construction," wrote he, "was an extensive work, but now it is all in ruins except the inner inclosure, in which are situated the dwelling, hospital and outhouses." By then nearly all the former tenants had moved to more convenient quarters nearer the river, and space no longer commanded the high rentals of a few months earlier.

Another visitor during that period was J. Goldsborough Bruff, member of one of the many mining and trading companies that had arrived in California to exploit the gold discovery. Bruff, a former draftsman for the United States Topographical Engineers, examined the fort with a professional eye. He described its plan as similar to that of two other well-known western outposts, Forts Laramie and Hall; its buildings were, however, "in a very dilapidated state." The hospital described by Letts continued to occupy the big main building for some months longer. In its issue for April 16, 1850, one of the town's several newspapers, the *Sacramento Transcript,* carried an advertisement announcing that the Sutter's Fort Hospital had recently been thoroughly restored and that it was now offering "comfortable accommodations" to patients. The proprietors concluded by stating that "being in a large adobe building, the institution is exempt from that extreme heat which is incidental to this climate during summer."

Sutter's Fort Hospital soon had need of everything it had to offer in the way of accommodations and services. For only a few months later, beginning in late October, an outbreak of cholera crowded the building far beyond its normal capacity. At the height of the epidemic the number of deaths in Sacramento rose to more than sixty a day; four-fifths of the residents fled from the town, and before the pestilence subsided it had claimed six hundred lives.

The appearance of the fort as it was in late 1849 and 1850—a place of leaking roofs, broken windows, sagging walls, and a general air of improvidence and neglect—is in marked contrast to that which it had presented to the world only a year earlier. The recollections of William R. Grimshaw, a twenty-three-year-old New Yorker who reached Sacramento in October, 1848, and went to work in Sam Brannan's store, indicate that during the winter of 1848-49 the spot was a very lively place indeed.

"In the middle of the fort," he wrote, "was a two story adobe building . . . , the lower portion of which was used as a bar room and with a monte table or two in it. The bar was crowded with customers night and day and never closed from one month's end to the other. The upper story was rented by Rufus Hitchcock & wife as a boarding house. Board was $40 per week; meals $2 each. The fare was plain and simple. We had plenty of fresh beef, beans, bread, tea & coffee, no milk . . . The few potatoes & onions that came into the market were sent to the mines as a cure & preventive of scurvy and brought such enormous prices ($1 each) as placed them entirely out of reach."

The scarcity of lumber and its fantastically high cost—$1 per board foot was the going price—were responsible for the fact that by 1853 all buildings in and about the fort, with the single exception of the big central structure, had been, in the words of an upstate editor, "completely razen." The reason was that the Sacramento residents, lacking sufficient lumber to keep pace with their town's extremely rapid growth, had turned to the fort as a readily available source of building material.

Under that concerted assault it was not long before everything standing—houses, workshops, corrals, even the massive outer walls—were leveled to the ground. Sharing their fate were other Sutter properties in the area, including his big unfinished flour mill at Natoma, on which he claimed to have expended more than $30,000. That structure was torn down board by board and the hand-sawed lumber used to build what for a number of years was Sacramento's leading hostelry, the City Hotel.

All the while his holdings in the Sacramento area were being demolished, Sutter had remained, not too patiently, in semi-retirement at Hock Farm. That attractive spot, which he had begun developing in the early 1840's with the thought of some day

making it his permanent home, lay on the banks of the Feather
River a few miles below its junction with the Yuba. A description
of the place as it appeared in the fall of 1849 is contained in
an official report of Lieutenant George H. Derby of the United
States Topographical Engineers. Derby's party, which was on a
map-making expedition in the region, camped across the river
from the Sutter farm on the night of October 15.

"This is the most beautiful situation I have seen in California,"
he wrote. "The river, which at this place is about six hundred
yards in width, is lined on either bank with majestic sycamores,
in a fine grove of which, upon the west bank, is situated Captain
Sutter's [first] farm-house, a remarkably neat adobe building
whitewashed and surrounded by high and well built walls enclos-
ing out-houses, corrals, &c. There are about 100 acres of excellent
land enclosed and cultivated upon the west bank, which yields
the most astonishing crops of wheat with very little labor. The
river is filled with salmon; and we observed two seines drawn
across the river, about a mile apart, from which I was informed
the occupants of the farm-house obtain a plentiful supply."

Of the natives of the area Derby wrote:

> About 200 yards above the farm-house is situated a rancheria
> of Indians, some 300 in number. This village consists of about
> 20 mud ovens, partly above and partly below the ground, with
> a small hole for egress in the side. They had just commenced
> the collection for their winter stock of acorns, and had many
> high baskets, containing probably forty or fifty bushels of this
> kind of provender, standing about. They were mostly naked, and
> kept up a dismal howling all night as a tribute of respect
> to one of their number who had departed this life the day previ-
> ous. They were suffering much from the prevalent fever [prob-
> ably malaria], as were the occupants of farm-house, several of
> whom were sick at this time.

2 PATERFAMILIAS

As we have seen, it was at Hock Farm that Sutter after
a lapse of fifteen years reassumed the role of family man. One

of his earliest acts as paterfamilias was to write his personable former assistant, John Bidwell (who had supervised the building of his handsome new Hock Farm residence), suggesting that Bidwell marry his twenty-two-year-old daughter, Eliza. From his standpoint that was a highly sagacious move on the Captain's part. For throughout their long and close association young Bidwell had invariably displayed industry, initiative, and sound judgment, as well as loyalty to his employer's best interests—all of which were qualities highly desirable in a son-in-law.

But Sutter's matchmaking efforts got him nowhere. Young Bidwell's reply, dated April 2, 1851, and written from his Arroyo Chico ranch on the site of the present town of Chico, was a diplomatically worded document that conveyed his respect and affection for the older man—and politely but firmly turned down his suggestion. He concluded with: "I desire to see you frequently, and to live, so long as we both may live, in terms of intimacy and friendship . . . But I cannot persuade myself to marry . . ."

Bidwell's decision, however, did not consign Eliza to permanent spinsterhood. She was a high-spirited girl with, according to her contemporaries, much more of her father's exuberance and liking for attention than the other Sutter children. Perhaps it was these qualities that made her the old man's favorite. One evidence of his affection for his only daughter is that when the beginnings of what promised to be a new river town appeared on his property a few miles below the farmhouse he gave it the name of Eliza City. For a time Eliza City's future looked bright, but its site was less convenient to travelers than that of its closest rival, Marysville—named for Mary Murphy Covillaud, a survivor of the Donner Party—which stood at the confluence of the Feather and Yuba rivers. The result was that during the next few years Marysville grew and prospered while Eliza City faded from memory.

Such was not the case with the young woman after whom the town had been named. A short time after Bidwell's prudent refusal to assume the role of bridegroom, Eliza was reported engaged to David Engler, a young Swiss emigrant who had been hired to give her brother Alphonse piano lessons. When Sutter learned of the romance he—who had once boasted that his children "could marry into the finest families of New York and Philadelphia"—ordered the penniless suitor off the premises. But Eliza was as strong-willed as her father, and she eventually won him over. The wedding, which took place on March 1, 1852, was a gala event attended by two hundred guests who were brought from Sacramento aboard a steamer that the bride's father had chartered for the occasion. Despite that auspicious beginning, the marriage failed to last. The pair were subsequently divorced and a few years later Eliza remarried, this time to a Sacramento physician, Dr. Franz Link.

During the years prior to their arrival, Sutter had often expressed pride in his absent family and his eagerness to be reunited with them. In the spring of 1846 he wrote John Marsh—his nemesis during the Micheltorena campaign two years earlier—at the latter's rancho near Mount Diablo:

"Yesterday I received at last some letters of my family and with the greatest of pleasure to see my eldest son, twenty years and 6 months old is on his way to California and will be here in about 6 or 7 months, his education is finished, likewise his aprentisage in one of the first counting houses in Switzerland, he speaks and writes several languages, and no doubt will be an able Clark. My Family remains in Switzerland for a year or two longer till the two younger Sons have received their education complete, the second [Emil Victor] is in a celebrated Agricultural Institut, the 3rd [William Alphonse] is in a Military school or Academie as Cadet. The education of my Daughter about 19 years old is completed like-wise, and it was a great pleasure to read all their letters out of which I can judge how the[y] received their education and was to my greatest Satisfaction."

This letter has its full share of the exaggerations and bombast usual with the Captain when he was discussing his own background or that of his family. The company where John, Jr., was serving his apprenticeship, which he called "one of the first counting houses in Switzerland," was in reality a small business firm in the village of Burgdorf. Nor did the "celebrated Agricultural Institut" or the "Military school or Academie" that the two younger sons were attending measure up to the high-sounding title he gave them.

As we have seen, Sutter's relations with his eldest son, when that youth finally reached California, were considerably less than cordial; there were, indeed, times when, according to Lienhard, he became so enraged at what he believed to be the other's mismanagement of his properties that he vowed to have him arrested and "sent back to Switzerland in chains." Moreover, there was some basis for the exasperation and annoyance with which the father normally viewed the son. John, Jr., was a conscientious and hard-working young man who carried out his difficult assignment with honesty and, on the whole, with reasonably sound judgment. But balancing that was a narrow-minded and prudish strain in his nature that both puzzled and irritated his liberal-minded parent. The free-and-easy customs of the frontier which the elder Sutter had always found precisely to his liking shocked and repelled his straitlaced son. From the beginning John, Jr., made no secret of his disapproval of his father's drinking bouts, his habit of keeping Hawaiian or Indian mistresses, and his other moral lapses.

As for other members of the family, Heinrich Lienhard found much to criticize in the way they had conducted themselves on the trip to California, particularly their demanding preferential treatment at hotels, restaurants, and on shipboard because they had been led to believe that their father was "the wealthiest man in California." Other commentators pictured the family in a less unfavorable light. John, Jr. was described as a serious-minded and well-intentioned youth whose only shortcomings were a too great reliance on his own judgment, plus an inability to equate his rigid moral code with the relaxed standards of the time and place. Eliza, the next child, had much of her father's generous and outgoing nature, yet on occasion could be "rude, boorish, and filled with boundless conceit." Less was known of the two younger children, Emil Victor and William Alphonse, who were twenty and seventeen, respectively, the year they reached California. Of their mother, the former Anna

Dübeld, daughter of the Burgdorf shopkeeper, Samuel Dübeld, most accounts agree that the stern and disapproving expression on her face as shown in existing photographs accurately reflects the lady's joyless view of life.

But if, as seems likely, domestic life at Hock Farm failed to come up to his expectations, Sutter was at pains to conceal the fact. By the summer of 1849 he had begun to receive gratifying evidence that his services to California during pre-gold rush days had not been completely forgotten. On June 3 the military governor, General Bennett Riley, called an election to choose delegates to a constitutional convention to be held at Monterey the following September. Sutter was one of four candidates chosen from the Sacramento area, the others being Sam Brannan, John McDougal, and Peter H. Burnett. The forty-eight delegates first met at Monterey's Colton Hall on September 3, and by holding day and night sessions were able to complete their task in a little less than six weeks.

During the long and frequently acrimonious debates that accompanied the framing of the document—the slavery question was responsible for most of the dissension—Sutter's voice was rarely heard, his chief role being that of "a sort of ornamental appendage" to the gathering. Nonetheless, he had his moments of glory. When, on October 3, the convention assembled for the last time, its presiding officer, Robert Semple, was ill and Sutter was chosen to take his place. While the delegates were signing the final version of the constitution, Governor Riley ordered a salute of thirty-one guns—one for each state of the Union, including California—fired from a battery in the nearby presidio. "Sutter has a great love for the noise of artillery," wrote Bancroft, "and was much excited by the discharge of the cannon, exclaiming over and over, 'This is the proudest moment I ever saw!'"

Next day the Captain was accorded still another honor, that of leading the delegation to the Governor's house and presenting him with the completed document. It was an occasion he long remembered. Years later he wrote:

"Preceded by the sargeant-at-arms, I led a procession with Senator William Gwin on one arm and Delegate M. M. McCarver on the other, followed by all the other members of the convention, as well as all the secretaries and clerks. I delivered an address to the Governor, thanking him for his assistance. In his reply Governor Riley remarked that this was the happiest day of his life. Then he had wine served of which he had a rich supply and many toasts were drunk."

Before the year was out Sutter again found himself briefly in the public eye. Once the constitution had been drafted, the next step was to have it ratified by the voters, who at the same time would choose state and local officers to put it into effect. Sutter later reported that while he was at San Jose on his way home from the convention friends there persuaded him to become a candidate for governor. Although he conducted a vigorous campaign, appearing not only at San Francisco, Sacramento, and way points, but also at a number of the mining camps, his was a losing cause. Election day, November 13, was cold and stormy over most of California and few bothered to go to the polls. Out of an estimated population of 170,000, less than ten percent voted. When the returns were in, it was found that Sutter had come in third in a field of five. Peter H. Burnett was the winner with 6,716 votes, W. S. Sherwood received 3,188, and Sutter but 2,201.

3   LAND TITLES

The fact that his gubernatorial campaign had failed by so wide a margin indicates that despite the honors accorded him at Monterey Sutter was no longer a figure of consequence in the eyes of the public. Along with many others who had once been prominent in California affairs, his name and accomplishments meant little to the thousands who had arrived in the wake of the gold discovery. Besides, like most of the other old-timers, Sutter had grown accustomed to the relaxed and unhurried tempo of life in the days before the gold rush, and to him the environment created by these brisk newcomers was both alien and hostile.

To be sure, there were some among the pioneers—Sam Brannan was a prime example—who had no trouble adjusting themselves to changed conditions and so were able to take advantage of the opportunities offered by this puzzling new age. To all but a few of that group, however, the finding of gold, instead of bringing wealth and security, had an opposite effect. That was almost universally true of the old Spanish-California families, the Vallejos, Alvarados, Peraltas and others, many of whom were obliged to devote the balance of their lives to long-drawn-out (and frequently futile) attempts to establish ownership of lands that had been seized and settled on by the newcomers.

Squatters, as they were called, played a leading part in speeding Sutter down the road to ruin. For the average '49er, particularly if he were a native of the United States, was no respecter of land titles granted by the former rulers of the province. In his view, California was conquered territory, and as a member of the conquering nation he considered himself privileged to settle wherever he chose, provided the spot was not already occupied by someone capable of forcibly ejecting him. And in a country where law enforcement agencies were rare and courts rarer, the landowner whose rights had been violated had no recourse save to attempt to drive off the trespassers, or else await the establishment of tribunals before which he could plead his case.

The first step toward remedying that chaotic condition was taken early in 1851 when Congress passed a bill creating a three-member United States Land Commission to pass on the legality of grants issued by the Spanish and Mexican governors. The Commission began hearings at San Francisco the following January, and all holders of grants were directed to appear and present proof of the validity of their claims. During the six years before its mission was completed, the Commission reviewed a total of 813 claims, of which 521 were confirmed and 273 rejected, 19 being "discontinued."

But that by no means ended the matter. The Commission's findings were subject to review by the federal district courts, and their decisions in turn could be appealed to the United States Supreme Court. This was an expensive and time-consuming process, one that often lasted the better part of a decade. The consequence was that even when the ultimate decision was favorable to the original grantees, their heirs or assigns, it was likely to be an empty victory. For in order to raise funds to finance the litigation many were obliged to sell most of their lands and to mortgage what remained. More often than not, the chief beneficiaries of the long-drawn-out legal battles were the attorneys, a number of whom grew wealthy from their fees from "land title cases."

Sutter's attempts to establish ownership of his lands followed the familiar pattern. His two grants—that of New Helvetia, awarded him in 1841, and the Sobrante grant, which he received from Governor Micheltorena during the 1845 revolution—were submitted to the Land Commission, which approved them on May 15, 1855. Thereupon the squatters who had preempted much of the land included in the grants appealed the Commission's decision to the District Court of Northern California, only to have that body confirm Sutter's title to the property. However, that decision was again appealed by the squatters and the case went to the United States Supreme Court. Another long delay ensued. When the court's decision was eventually handed down it reaffirmed the legality of the New Helvetia grant but rejected that of the Sobrante lands. One of the reasons given for setting aside the *sobrante* grant was that in awarding it Micheltorena had acted not in his capacity as governor of California, but as commander-in-chief of the military forces of the province.

Regardless of the grounds on which the court's decision was based, so far as Sutter's fortunes were concerned, its effect was catastrophic. At one stroke the amount of land to which he had held title was reduced from 230 to 75 square miles. But these figures fail to tell the full story. For the Supreme Court decision meant that at no time had he had a right to sell the *sobrante* land; hence, he was legally liable to reimburse the buyers of such land for any losses they might have sustained. How much it cost him to settle the rash of claims that resulted is not known. Years later in one of his petitions to Congress asking compensation for his losses he stated that in his attempts to establish ownership of his land he had spent a total of nearly a third of a million dollars.

The period from 1858, when the Supreme Court's adverse de-

cision was rendered, to 1865—the year he abandoned California
and moved permanently to the East Coast—saw a continuing decline in the fortunes of the aging and disillusioned pioneer. By
an extraordinary combination of poor judgment, misplaced confidence, and plain bad luck he had seen properties that in the
ordinary course of events would have made him many times a
millionaire melt away, leaving him not only almost penniless but
heavily in debt. By 1862 the few hundred acres that remained
of Hock Farm were said to be his only possessions of any value,
and there were rumors that this too was so heavily mortgaged
that he was in danger of losing it.

When word of the straits to which the once prodigal Lord of
New Helvetia had been reduced became known, a group of old
friends launched a movement designed to provide him and his
wife with a modest income to sustain them during their declining
years. The result was that early in 1864 the state legislature
passed a bill granting him $15,000, to be paid in monthly install-
ments of $250 over a period of five years. To Sutter that windfall
was certainly welcome, but he was at pains to make clear that
he did not consider it an act of charity. "It was not a gift of
the State to me, nor would I have accepted it as such," he once
explained. "This amount was only a return of the taxes which
I had paid on the sobrante land grant, later taken away from
me."

There are other evidences that as time passed, his fellow Californians had come to feel a sense of guilt at the treatment the
doughty old empire builder had received at their hands, and
they tried to make up for years of neglect by singling him out
for occasional honors. Thus in 1853, by special act of the legislature, he was a major general of the California militia. This was
an office that entailed no duties and carried no compensation;
nonetheless, it was one of which he ever after was inordinately
proud. Two years later a full-length portrait showing him in full
regalia, his general's uniform decked out with a profusion of gold
braid, was offered the state by the pioneer California artist, William S. Jewett. After considerable opposition on the part of the
economy-minded governor, John Bigler, the portrait was

purchased by the legislature for $2,500; today it hangs inside the north entrance of the capitol at Sacramento.

By the mid-1850's many Californians had come to look on the period prior to the gold rush as a romantic age, and on those who had lived there then as picturesque and adventurous figures. The result was that Sutter, who in the eyes of many personified that early era, was sometimes called on to take part in community celebrations. Clad in his glittering uniform and mounted—albeit insecurely, for he was never entirely at ease on horseback—on a spirited charger, he made a colorful figure as he led parades on Admission Day, July Fourth, and other patriotic occasions.

But despite such pleasant interludes when for an hour or two he received the homage of sidewalk crowds at Sacramento, Marysville, and other valley or foothill towns, as time passed Sutter's life became one of increasing solitude and neglect. By the beginning of 1860 he and his wife were much alone. Of the large crew of *vaqueros,* farmhands, gardeners, and household servants he had brought from the fort, only a few elderly Indians remained. Their three sons and daughter who for a time had enlivened the big house had all drifted away.

John, Jr., had been the first to leave; the breach between him and his parent was never entirely bridged, and after an unsuccessful business venture at Sacramento, the young man left California, where he had known only strife and contention, and settled permanently at Acapulco, Mexico. There the next child, Eliza, presently joined him, bringing with her her second husband, Dr. Franz Link. Emil Victor, the middle son, spent several years helping his father at Hock Farm, then left to try his luck at the mines. Disappointed at what he found there, he made his way to San Francisco where he became an official of a financial house.

The youngest Sutter child, William Alphonse, who was but seventeen when the family reached California, seems to have had more of his father's adventurous spirit than any of the others. In May, 1855, while still in his early twenties, he sailed from San Francisco as a member of William Walker's filibustering expedition to Nicaragua. Following the failure of that exploit Alphonse, as he was known in the family, returned to California, settled in the Mother Lode town of Nevada City, and died there in 1863, supposedly of a fever contracted during his stay in the tropics.

As the 1860's advanced it became evident that Sutter's stay at Hock Farm was near its end. It seemed that everything conspired to force him off this last remnant of his once immense holdings. For several successive winters the Feather River had overflowed its banks, inundating much of the farm and causing heavy damage to outbuildings, gardens, and fields. Meanwhile his old enemies, the squatters, emboldened by the Supreme Court decision setting aside the Sobrante grant, grew bolder in their raids on his property, slaughtering or driving off what remained of his livestock, destroying his crops, and cutting down his trees and selling them for lumber or firewood—all of which he was powerless to prevent.

The blow that finally decided the issue came on the morning of June 21, 1866, when fire—believed to have been set by an itinerant whom Sutter had punished for theft—swept through the big farmhouse, burning it to the ground. In its next issue the *Marysville Appeal* reported: "The house was completely destroyed—home, clothing, pictures, busts, curiosities that had been accumulating for the last forty years, except a few medals and his family portraits . . . There is no insurance."

Five months later the elderly couple boarded a steamer at San Francisco and sailed for the East Coast. California, which had been Sutter's home for more than a quarter century and where he had known both the heights of success and the depths of failure, was to see him no more.

4   WASHINGTON AND LITITZ

Sutter's destination was the national capital, where he had every expectation that the nation's lawmakers, once his case had been presented to them, would right the wrong he believed had been done him.

Before leaving California, Sutter had revived a long-standing custom; that is, he had provided himself with letters of introduction from prominent West Coast citizens, which he intended to present to members of the Senate and House and to other high officials. One of his letters was from California's Governor Low, which enumerated its bearer's valuable services to emigrant parties prior to the American occupation and urged that he be indemnified for the heavy losses he had suffered because of the gold discovery. The influence of his letters, together with the fact that he and his fort were already known by reputation to many of the legislators, assured him of a sympathetic hearing in both houses. Before he had been in Washington a month a petition asking compensation for his losses (the sum he originally sought was $125,000, though the amount was later scaled down) had been filed with the Senate and referred to the Committee on Claims.

Up to that point, Sutter's hopes for an early and liberal settlement were high. But he was not permitted to hold that belief for long. The Civil War had ended only a short time before he reached Washington, and the Thirty-Ninth Congress was too much occupied with matters growing out of that conflict to consider his relatively unimportant plea. The result was that, like hundreds of other claims, his petition never reached the floor of the Senate either during that session or at any time during the next half-dozen years.

Yet despite successive disappointments the aging petitioner stubbornly continued to press his campaign. He remained in Washington whenever Congress was in session, making daily trips to Capitol Hill, assiduously cultivating the friendship of members of both houses and repeating his well-rehearsed story to anyone who could be prevailed on to listen.

Not the least burdensome of his troubles during that period was the fact that he was perpetually short of funds, his only income being the $250 monthly pension the California legislature had voted him in 1864 and which was to run for five years. His frequent complaints prove that the need to practice economy in his personal life was galling to this product of the free-spending frontier—and this was particularly so because penny-pinching had never been a Sutter characteristic. "I have to be at the Capitol every day," he wrote in 1868, "where I must call upon the senators and members of the congress, etc., and you can imagine that I must be elegantly dressed and that costs money . . ."

During the greater part of the year he and his wife lived in small Washington hotels or boardinghouses. Then, after Congress had recessed for the summer, it was their custom to move to some quiet town in Pennsylvania or elsewhere to escape the hot climate of the capital. One spot to which they returned several times was Lititz, a picturesque town in south-eastern Pennsylvania that had been founded in the middle of the eighteenth century by members of the Moravian sect. Sutter found the atmosphere of the place, with its well-kept houses fronting on tree-lined streets and with the surrounding hills dotted with prosperous farmhouses and big stone barns, much to his liking. Besides, Lititz then enjoyed a considerable renown as a health resort and Sutter was convinced that the waters of its springs were beneficial in treating the rheumatic attacks from which he suffered during his later years. The result was that he at length decided to make the place his permanent home.

However, he continued to spend a major part of each year at Washington, still determined to get his bill before and through a Congress that had consistently turned a deaf ear to his pleas. When, in 1876, Hubert H. Bancroft visited him at his home in Lititz, the seventy-three-year-old veteran was still convinced that his claim would eventually be allowed, although by then he had drastically reduced the amount he was asking, "For eleven years I have been a petitioner before Congress pleading for justice," Bancroft quoted him as saying. "The *sobrante* grant at a dollar and twenty-five cents an acre, just what the government received for it, would amount to $122,000. This was the sum for which I was asking. The members of the committee were afraid to ask for the whole amount and proposed a recompense of $50,000. I am sure that I will receive this sum, though in order to get it, I have already spent $25,000 and owe my lawyers an additional $10,000."

Sharing with the elderly couple the house Sutter had built at

Lititz—it was a modest, two-story brick structure at one end of the town's main street—were a grandson and two granddaughters. They were children of John, Jr., who had become the United States Consul at Acapulco; following the breakup of his first marriage he had sent his offspring to their grandparents to be educated. At Lititz the eldest child, John Augustus, III, became a pupil at the John Beck School for Boys, and the two daughters, Anna Eliza and Maria del Carmen, were enrolled at Linden Hall, a girls' academy; both were Moravian schools.

From the mid-1870's onward, despite recurring rheumatic attacks and other infirmities of age, the indomitable old pioneer continued to press his campaign. Impeccably attired in frock coat and broad-brimmed hat and carrying a gold-headed cane, he became a familiar figure as he shuffled in and out of the offices and committee rooms of the Capitol.

5   THE CURTAIN FALLS

There were times when, despite his successive disappointments, his flagging spirits were buoyed up by reminders that his services to California and the nation had not been altogether forgotten. Sutter's name was still familiar to thousands who had been part of the gold rush. Moreover, with the passage of time, that episode had come to seem to them a singularly exciting and romantic adventure, and in various parts of the country groups of California pioneers were meeting annually—usually on September 9, the anniversary of the state's admission to the Union—to renew old acquaintance and listen to nostalgic speeches recalling "the days of gold."

One such organization, which bore the unwieldy title of Associated Pioneers of the Territorial Days of California, had its headquarters in New York. At the Association's annual meeting for 1877, held at the Ocean Hotel at Long Branch, New Jersey, Sutter was the guest of honor, and the lengthy program was given over entirely to praise of the old man's character and accomplishments. The two hundred guests—who were all former Forty-Niners and included a liberal sprinkling of politicians, Civil

War generals, and other celebrities—sat down to the banquet
table in the middle of the afternoon, listened to a long series
of speakers, drank an even longer series of toasts, and then, while
the band played "Hail to the Chief," settled back as the guest
of honor got unsteadily to his feet.

Samuel C. Upham, an ex-Californian who had earlier read
"The Song of the Argonauts," a poem he had composed for the
occasion, thus described what happened next:

> General Sutter rose in response to the hearty applause . . . ,
> and with a suppressed voice expressed his inability to respond
> adequately to the remarks which were so flattering to him, and
> which he so thoroughly appreciated. "It is not possible," he
> said—but there words failed him, and he sat down, and the
> assembled Argonauts rose up as one man, and waving their
> glasses in the air, gave three cheers that utterly drowned the
> music of the band.

At another meeting of that group, this one held in January,
1878, Sutter was further honored by being elected president of
the Association. At the same time the members commemorated
his seventy-sixth birthday by presenting him with a walking stick,
"wrought specially . . . of California gold and California redwood." On August 1 of the same year the Association tendered
a dinner at New York's Sturtevant Hotel to General Frémont,
who was soon to leave to assume his duties as Governor of Ari-
zona Territory. But President Sutter was suffering one of his rheumatic seizures and was obliged to remain at Lititz while another
presided over the meeting.

Nor was he present at the organization's annual banquet the
following January. The tone of the message he sent his fellow
members explaining his absence was that of a disillusioned and
frustrated old man.

"Sick at heart and body," he wrote, "in vain appealing to
Congress to do me justice and to return only part of what was
wrongly taken from me, and with little hope of success unless
you my friends by your influence will aid my cause, I could not

feel cheerful as your guest at table tonight, and did not want to mar your pleasure by my presence. Remember old times without me."

Stirred by that appeal, the Association members unanimously pledged themselves to use "all honorable means" to induce Congress to act favorably on Sutter's legislation—which by then had been pending for more than a decade and a half. It may be that their efforts had some effect on that slow-moving body. In any event, by the spring of that year bills granting the petitioner "up to $50,000" as compensation for his losses had been favorably passed on by committees of both the Senate and the House.

Sutter was greatly cheered and encouraged by these developments. His letters show that he regarded the passage of a compromise bill and its signing by the President as no more than formalities. Within a few weeks at the most he would, he confidently believed, be able to leave Washington, which had grown increasingly distasteful to him and, his last and longest battle won, spend his remaining days in peace and security at Lititz.

But although he failed to realize it at the time, his chances of success were much less bright than he imagined them to be. For 1880 was an election year; a President, congressmen, and other federal, state and local officials were to be chosen that fall, and members of both houses were anxious to wind up their affairs in time to attend the national conventions which were to be held in late June. The result was a last-minute rush to jam through essential legislation before Congress adjourned for the summer. And that in turn meant that scores of lesser bills would have to be put over until the lawmakers reassembled in the fall.

But through it all Sutter remained confident. Even as the hour of adjournment drew near he refused to doubt. He spent the final day in his room at the Mades' Hotel, preparing to leave for home the moment the good news reached him. Accordingly, when on the evening of June 16 he was told that the Forty-Sixth Congress had adjourned *sine die* without having taken action on his bill, the blow was a shattering one. He took to his bed and refused to be comforted. Two days later when Senator Daniel W. Voorhees of Indiana, one of the bill's sponsors, called at his hotel to assure him that the legislation would surely be taken up and passed early in the next session, he was too late. Sutter had died the previous afternoon.

The pioneer's body was taken to Lititz and, on the afternoon of June 24, buried in a corner of the community's picturesque little Moravian cemetery. A numerous group of townspeople and a number of distinguished guests joined the funeral procession. At the graveside one of the visitors, John C. Frémont—with whom in the past Sutter had often been at odds—delivered a brief eulogy paying tribute to the dead man's services to his adopted country and expressing regret that "a life so filled with kindly acts . . . should have met with so cruel neglect and such harsh injustice."

Sutter was seventy-seven. In commenting on his passing, newspaper writers from coast to coast echoed Frémont's sentiment; all shared the belief that his country had indeed been less than generous in its treatment of the courageous pioneer.

His widow survived him by less than a year. She was buried beside her husband, and their joint grave was covered with a marble slab surrounded by a granite coping. On the slab were engraved two simple inscriptions:

GENERAL JOHN A. SUTTER
Born, Feb. 28, 1803,
At Kandern, Baden
Died, June 18, 1880,
Requiescat in Pace

ANNA SUTTER (*nee Dubeld*)
Born Sept. 15, 1805,
Died January 19, 1881
At Lititz

EPILOGUE

When Sutter moved to Hock Farm early in 1849 and the ownership of the fort he had founded ten years earlier passed to others, the deterioration of the property—which he had always kept in good repair—was already far advanced.

As noted earlier, during the first months of the gold rush the space inside the walls was crowded with merchants, gamblers, innkeepers and others, most of whom kept their places of business open day and night. With the rise of Sacramento City, however, nearly all the fort's tenants had moved to more convenient quarters nearer the river, and the place gradually took on a forlorn and deserted appearance. Visitors to the fort in the early and middle 1850's told of weeds growing in the courtyard, of dilapidated walls and sagging roofs, and of debris littering the empty rooms.

During the next decade and a half the disintegrating process continued. By the mid-1860's Sutter's Fort had been all but obliterated; only the big central building with its thick adobe walls and hand-hewn timbers had withstood the years of vandalism and neglect. The sturdy old structure was then standing vacant, its doors and windows missing, and with the plaster peeling from its walls, exposing the earthen bricks beneath. Since Sutter's day it had been used successively as a trading post and gambling casino, a hospital, a storehouse, a residence, and finally a stable, a chicken house, and a pigpen.

But even during its years of neglect the building's historical significance had never been completely forgotten. At meetings of pioneers and in letters to Sacramento or San Francisco newspapers, demands were made that something be done to prevent the picturesque old relic from disappearing entirely. One of the earliest of the little band who urged the restoration of the building was Lucius Harwood Foote, a local poet of some renown. Foote put his plea in verse form:

Sutter's Fort

I stood by the old fort's crumbling wall,
    On the eastern edge of the town;
The sun through the clefts in the ruined hall
    Flecked with its light the rafters brown.

Charmed by the magic spell of the place,
    The present vanished, the past returned,
While rampart and fortress filled the space,
    And yonder the Indian camp-fires burned.

I heard the sentinels' measured tread,
    The challenge prompt, the quick reply,
I saw on the tower above my head
    The Mexican banner flaunt the sky.

Around me the waifs from every clime,
    Blown by the fickle winds of chance,
Knight errants, ready at any time
    For any cause, to couch a lance.

The staunch old Captain, with courtly grace,
    Owner of countless leagues of land,
Benignly governs the motley race,
    Dispensing favors with open hand.

Only a moment the vision came;
    Where tower and rampart stood before,
Where flushed the night with the camp's red flame,
    Dust and ashes and nothing more.

Proposals that the old building be preserved continued to be made from time to time, but it was not until the late 1880's that the first definite steps toward that end were taken. That came about because early in 1888 the Sacramento city trustees announced a plan to open a new street in the area—one that would pass through the center of the property and necessitate the wrecking of what remained of the old building.

It was this threat that belatedly stirred the historically minded citizens of the state to action. The leader of the campaign that followed was a Sacramento resident, General James G. Martine, who on June 4 published a letter in the local *Record-Union* addressed to "The Pioneers of the Pacific Coast." In it he pointed out that the quaint old landmark was in imminent peril of being destroyed, and proposed that a fund be raised by public subscription "to purchase the ground and repair the old fort."

Martine's letter was reprinted in a number of papers up and down the state, and the response was so encouraging that a movement was launched to raise the $20,000 needed to buy the site—which consisted of the two city blocks bounded by K, L, Twenty-Sixth, and Twenty-Eighth streets—and present it to the state. The success of the fund-raising campaign was assured when the family of railroad-builder Charles Crocker contributed $15,000 toward the sum, and Crocker's ex-partner, former Governor Leland Stanford, agreed to make up any deficiency.

In the fall of 1889, the full purchase price having been raised, the deal was consummated. Title to the property was transferred first to the Native Sons of the Golden West—a California fraternal organization that had taken an active part in the campaign—and, early the following year, to the state, the legislature having meanwhile agreed to provide funds to rebuild the fort and to maintain it afterwards.

The work of reconstruction began in 1891. The aim was to restore buildings and grounds as nearly as possible to their condition during the heyday of the fort; that is, the period just prior to the beginning of the gold rush. Guided by drawings and written descriptions of the spot as it was then, and after consultations with a number of Sutter's former close associates, including John

Bidwell, the task of reconstructing not only the battered central building but of the entire establishment, including the massive outer walls, got under way.

The methods and materials employed by the restorers were in most cases the same as those used by the original builders. An account of the reconstruction of the central building states: "The original adobe bricks were made by the Indians, who used their hands for molding them, and their finger marks were to be seen when they were used again." One incident of the rebuilding period that attracted wide attention took place when several workmen washed out a number of pans of earth they had scooped up near the east gate, and from them recovered a small quantity of gold dust; this was later cast into a medal and placed on exhibit at the fort. The theory is that the gold was part of sweepings from the floors of the fort's bars and gaming rooms, where it had been dropped by the improvident miners.

In general, the reconstructed fort closely follows the original plan, although later research has made clear that a number of miscalculations were made. For instance, it is now known that the walls once enclosed a larger area than they do today. The number and arrangement of rooms in the central building differed from what they were in Sutter's day, but have now been restored to their former condition. Another feature that until recently was in doubt is the precise location of many of the workshops, living quarters, offices, and other facilities that occupied the series of shedlike structures on the inner side of the walls.

Once the reconstruction of the buildings was completed, the surrounding grounds, where in the old days corrals, stables, and storehouses had stood, were transformed into a park-like area of trees, lawns, and flowerbeds, with two small lakes replacing the former unsightly slough on the north side. Meanwhile, it had been decided to convert the restored fort into a pioneer museum. In the beginning and for several decades thereafter, there was no fixed policy governing what type of material was to be displayed. The consequence was that buildings and grounds gradually filled up with a varied assortment of objects ranging from Indian artifacts to oxcarts, stagecoaches, miners' tools, pioneer costumes, and the like.

Then, in 1926, a new policy, one designed "to retain and impart the romantic atmosphere of the 'Days of Forty-Nine,'" was adopted. By it, the museum's field was narrowed to the thirty-year period from 1839, when the fort was founded, to the year of the completion of the transcontinental railroad, 1869—a date that had come to be regarded as the end of the pioneer era. Thereafter the objects displayed, whether tools, weapons, vehicles, household utensils, or printed or manuscript material, were all restricted to the 1839–69 period. Among the innovations of that time were several dioramas reproducing dramatic episodes in the history of the fort. One pictures the hospitable Sutter welcoming Frémont and Kit Carson on their arrival at the fort in 1844; another shows Marshall and Sutter in the latter's office on the night of January 28, 1846, with the Captain testing the historic metal particles, while his companion looks on with rapt interest.

The next step in the long story of the fort's restoration was taken in 1947 when buildings and grounds were put under the jurisdiction of the State Division of Beaches and Parks. Soon thereafter a further change of policy was adopted: that of making the spot not merely a depository for objects belonging to the 1839–69 period, but of attempting to restore both buildings and contents to the condition they were in in Sutter's day. This involved discarding many of the former exhibits and replacing them with others in keeping with the new concept. It also necessitated certain changes in the design and arrangement of the buildings themselves—changes that were based on newly uncovered documentary evidence and on an archeological examination of the site.

One source of information that has proved highly useful to those in charge of the "re-restoration" program—as it has been called—is an obscure publication that recently came to light. This is a forty-two-page pamphlet printed in Darmstadt, Germany, in 1848, the title of which reads in translation: "Upper

California, A Geological Description for the Purpose of German Emigration and Settlement . . . With a Map of the River Sacramento and a Ground Plan for the Fort New Helvetia." Where the author, one Heinrich Künzel, got the information on which the little work is based is not definitely known, but there is reason to believe that it was supplied by Sutter himself, who was then making persistent efforts to persuade Germans and other Europeans to migrate to California and settle on his land.

The pamphlet contains two illustrations. One is a map of the New Helvetia grant showing Sutter's holdings extending from a little distance below the fort to the group of rugged hills called Sutter's Buttes in the center of the valley, about forty-five miles farther north. The other is a ground plan of the fort itself. Of the two, the second is by far the most illuminating. For it is a carefully drawn and seemingly accurate representation of "Das Fort Neu Helvetien" as it appeared during the period just prior to the gold discovery. Its chief value lies in the fact that it not only shows the location and arrangement of all buildings and other objects in and about the fort but also indicates the uses to which each was put. This is important because while, as stated earlier, it had long been known that millers, weavers, wood and metalworkers and other artisans plied their trades there, in only a few instances had the location of their shops and workrooms been definitely established. Thus the Künzel plan has been extremely helpful to those in charge of the fort's re-reconstruction.

Present-day visitors to the fort find it hard to realize that only a little more than a century ago it was the sole outpost of civilization in California's interior valley—a tiny, isolated settlement separated by nearly a week's travel from its nearest neighbors. Today the spot is surrounded by a city of more than 200,000, and the city in turn is the capital of a commonwealth that has in excess of 18,000,000 inhabitants, making it the most populous state in the Union.

So complete a transformation in so brief a time is worthy of note, even in a region where changes that once required a century or more were frequently crowded into a single generation. Moreover, the extraordinary growth of the territory once served by the fort is evidence that Sutter used sound judgment when he came to choose a site for his colony. For the spot he selected was at the confluence of the Sacramento and its largest tributary, the American, and the fact that both were navigable for some distance upstream led him to believe that the place would one day become an important trading and transportation center.

The gold rush speedily proved that belief to be correct. Within a space of a few months the fort's former embarcadero had become a city of several thousands, its inhabitants busy supplying the needs of the many mining camps that had sprung up to the east and north and northwest. During the next several years, despite frequent destructive fires and damaging floods, Sacramento's rapid growth continued, reaching 6,000 in the spring of 1850 and an estimated 10,000 a year later.

By the mid-1850's, however, the richest of the placers had been stripped of their treasure and Sacramento's trade with the mining towns had slackened off. But that decline proved to be only temporary. The approaching end of the mining era saw a simultaneous rise of agriculture all over the northern part of the valley. Throughout the next two decades traffic on the river remained heavy as the product of huge wheat ranches from Sacramento north to Red Bluff was loaded on barges and floated down to the bay, there to be stowed in the holds of fast clipper ships and sent to markets around the world.

From its beginning, Sacramento drew its sustenance from the channels of trade. During the early years its prosperity and growth were almost entirely dependent on its water-borne commerce. Then, as traffic on the river began to thin out, the citizens turned their attention to the development of other modes of transportation. In 1856 the city became the terminus of the Sacramento Valley Railroad, the first to be built in California, which connected it with the town of Folsom, some twenty-two miles to the northeast. A few years later, in 1861, four Sacramento merchants successfully performed a more difficult feat of railroad building, that of constructing the western half of the first transcontinental line. When the Central Pacific was completed in 1869 and for some years afterward, Sacramento was its western termi-

nus; there through-passengers and freight were transferred to fast
river steamers for the balance of the journey to San Francisco.
Sacramento was the terminus, too, of the romantic but short-lived
Pony Express, the riders for which, traveling day and night and
changing horses every fifteen miles or so, carried the mail (at a
charge of $5 per half-ounce) from the Missouri River to Cali-
fornia in the fast time of nine and a half days. This service began
in the spring of 1860 and was discontinued when the line of the
overland telegraph was completed in the fall of the following
year.

In recent years a program of restoration has also been carried
on at Fort Ross, which the Russian-American Fur Company established in 1812 and which was sold to Sutter when the company withdrew from California thirty years later.

The rehabilitation of that north coast settlement has been a
much less complex undertaking than that of restoring New Helvetia. For unlike Sutter's Sacramento Valley headquarters, Fort
Ross has ever since remained a small, remote community, off the
main-traveled highways and far removed from the thickly populated centers. One consequence of its location is that instead of
having had its buildings, stockade, and other installations
dismantled for the lumber they contained, many remained virtually undisturbed from decade to decade, subject only to the
toll taken by neglect and by exposure to the weather. It was not
until the earthquake of 1906—which was felt with particular in-
tensity in that section of the coast—that what remained of the
old fort suffered major damage by having its picturesque little
Russian Orthodox chapel shaken to the ground.

Like Sutter's Fort, the former Russian colony had a succession
of owners before it was eventually acquired by the state, partially
restored to its original condition, and opened to the public as
a State Historical Monument.

In 1845 Governor Pico granted the 18,000-acre Muniz
Rancho—which included the site of the fort—to Manuel Torres,
a native of Peru, and the spot became the headquarters of a large

cattle ranch. During the next quarter century cattle and sheep-raising remained the chief industry of the area, although some redwood lumber was cut in the wooded canyons leading down to the sea. The needs of residents of the sparsely settled country-side were served by the small settlement that grew up about the fort. In 1877 a post office was established there; three years later the place had a grocery store, a hotel, a saloon, a blacksmith shop, and a meat market.

A visitor to the old fort in 1880 reported that by then the greater part of its massive wooden stockade had disappeared, that the bastions at the stockade's northwest and southeast corners were "tottering under the weight of years," and that the former chapel had become a stable. Thirteen years later, in 1891, another visitor stated that no trace of the stockade then remained, that the chapel had become a grain warehouse and hay barn, and that the northeast bastion was serving as a pigpen.

The fruit trees the Russians planted on a nearby hillside have withstood the ravages of time better than the fort itself. The small orchard, which consisted of about one hundred peach, pear, cherry, and apple trees was set out in 1820. The orchard contained the first Gravenstein apple trees to be planted in California; today hundreds of acres of that variety of apples are grown in the foothills of western Sonoma County a few miles southeast of the fort. A recent examination of the old orchard revealed that fifteen of the original trees were still standing: two Gravenstein and three Bellflower apples, four Russian pears, and six seedling cherries. Although the two Gravenstein trees were then close to a century and a half old they were described as "large vigorous trees, covered with moss and well laden with delicious fruit."

The story of the restoration of this picturesque north coast settlement closely parallels that of Sutter's Fort. As was the case with the latter, suggestions that steps be taken to preserve such buildings as remained before they fell to complete ruin were made from time to time. And again like New Helvetia, several decades passed before anything was done to bring that about. In its initial stages the Fort Ross restoration was the outgrowth of a campaign launched in the early 1900's by the San Francisco *Examiner* aimed at preserving buildings and other landmarks of historical importance at Monterey, Sonoma, and elsewhere. With funds raised in part by popular subscription and in part contributed by the paper's owner, W. R. Hearst, who was then at the outset of his spectacular career, the fort and a few acres immediately surrounding it were purchased early in 1906 and later that year deeded to the state, with the understanding that it would be rebuilt and made into a public park.

Never over-hasty in such matters, the state held title to the property for another ten years before the restoration commenced. First to be rebuilt was the quaint little ninety-year-old chapel of the Russian Orthodox Church, which was completed in 1917. Other features that have since been restored are the stockade with its two corner blockhouses, or bastions, and the Commander's House. The twelve-foot-high stockade, which encloses an area of about 275 by 310 feet, is made, as was the original, of eight-inch-thick slabs split from the logs of redwood trees that grow throughout the region. The blockhouses—one of which has seven sides, the other eight—are built of heavy, hand-hewn timbers laid horizontally, their upper stories pierced by cannon ports that once commanded the approaches to the fort by sea and land.

The Commander's House, which stands near the southeast corner of the enclosure, dates from 1812, the year the colony was founded. Like the chapel, the only other original building to survive, it offers ample evidence of the skill of its builders, whose only tools were the adze, axe, broadaxe, chisel, and plane. The interior is divided into seven small rooms, where a collection of pioneer relics pertaining to that coastal area are on display.

Future plans call for the reconstruction of several other buildings that once stood within the enclosure, including a storage warehouse and the soldiers' barracks. Also in the planning stage is a museum, which will be built outside the enclosure; in it will be assembled material designed to picture life at the fort as it was in the days when this was the most remote of Czarist Russia's outposts in the New World.

Two other locales that figured largely in the saga of Sutter's Fort and its founder are Coloma and Lititz, the first a quiet village in the California foothills where gold was discovered, and the second the Pennsylvania town in which the Captain spent his last years. Neither place has undergone very marked changes since Sutter's day. Coloma differs from a dozen other once lively towns of California's Mother Lode only in the fact that, because the initial discovery was made there, it attracts a greater number of visitors than its neighbors. Throughout the summer months crowds of tourists daily fill its winding, tree-lined streets, viewing such relics of gold rush days as still remain. Chief among these are two small stone buildings, their doors and windows protected by iron shutters. One was formerly the shop of a Chinese merchant, Wah Hop, the other served as the town jail; both date from the middle 1850's. The site of the mill where Marshall first noticed the shining particles of metal well over a century ago is marked by a stone monument at the edge of the river. On the hillside above stands a bronze statue of the discoverer, and nearby is the restored cabin where he lived.

Like Sutter's Fort and Fort Ross, Coloma is now part of the state park system and is administered by the State Division of Beaches and Parks. A museum of relics of pioneer days has recently been added to the attractions of the place, and plans are under way to build a replica of the historic old mill.

One consequence of Sutter's decision to settle at Lititz is that his career thereby completed a full cycle. For in many ways the pre-Revolutionary town in which he proposed to spend his declining years closely paralleled those he had known during his childhood and youth. Founded in 1757 by members of the Moravian sect who had crossed the Atlantic to escape persecution at home, its inhabitants had ever since clung stubbornly to their Old World customs. In Sutter's time German was universally spoken among the older residents, and the distinguishing characteristics of the people—their industry, their straitlaced piety combined with a love of music and a deep-seated respect for learning—all were reminiscent of Kandern, Burgdorf, and other towns of the German-Swiss border. It is not surprising that after having spent several summers in so familiar an environment Sutter decided to make the place his permanent home.

The house he built there still stands at 17–19 East Main Street. Originally it was an attractive, two-story building—"the only one besides the hotel which was built of brick"—with steep-pitched slate roof, green shutters on the windows and, in the rear, a brick-paved patio where in fine weather the proud owner liked to receive and entertain guests. After his death and that of his widow the property was sold and the building extensively remodeled; today a hardware store occupies its ground floor.

Sutter's name is still an honored one in this quiet Pennsylvania town. As recently as 1957, in which year Lititz celebrated the bicentennial of its founding, he was remembered by a local ancient as "a fine looking, courtly old gentleman" who because of his urbane and hospitable ways "was much esteemed and respected by the whole community." One evidence of that esteem and respect is the fact that the former Lititz Springs Hotel, where Sutter spent several summers and which has long been one of the town's best known landmarks, has been renamed in his honor and is now the General Sutter Hotel.

In 1939 a bronze tablet was unveiled at Lititz to commemorate the one-hundredth anniversary of the founding by its distinguished former resident of a fort on the far side of the continent. Its inscription reads:

JOHN A. SUTTER
1803–1880
Eminent Pioneer of California, who
founded Sacramento in 1839
and over whose lands poured
the Gold Rush of 1849,
lived his last nine years in
Lititz and is interred in an
honored corner of the nearby
Moravian Cemetery

BIBLIOGRAPHY

Sutter's Fort and its colorful founder played so conspicuous a part in California affairs during the most eventful decade of its history that both figure largely in the voluminous literature of the period. Sutter himself has been the subject of several book-length biographies as well as numerous shorter pieces in newspapers, magazines, and scholarly journals. References to the fort are even more abundant. They are to be found not only in formal histories of the period but in biographies, volumes of reminiscence, diaries, collections of letters and official records, as well as in manuscript and printed material of great bulk and variety dealing with the gold rush and its aftermath.

To attempt a complete listing of sources would require many pages and would serve no useful purpose. Here the aim has been to single out those works that throw revealing light on some aspect of life at Sutter's Fort, Fort Ross, and Sutter's Mill during their brief period of activity, and that in most instances are readily available to those who may wish to read further.

Bancroft, Hubert Howe. *History of California.* 7 volumes. San Francisco: The History Co., 1884–1890.

——. *Literary Industries.* New York: Harper & Brothers, 1891.

——. *Popular Tribunals.* San Francisco: The History Co., 1887.

Bidwell, General John. *Echoes of the Past About California.* Chicago: The Lakeside Press, 1928.

Borthwick, J. D. *Three Years in California.* Edinburgh: William Blackwood & Sons, 1857.

Browne, J. Ross. *Muleback to the Convention*. San Francisco: The Book Club of California, 1950.

Bruff, J. Goldsborough. *Gold Rush: The Journals, Drawings, and Other Papers of J. Goldsborough Bruff*. New York: Columbia University Press, 1944.

Bryant, Edwin. *What I Saw in California*. New York: D. Appleton & Co., 1848.

Caughey, John Walton. *California: A History*. New York: Prentice-Hall, Inc., 1940.

Chamisso, Adelbert von. *A Sojourn at San Francisco Bay in 1816*. San Francisco: The Book Club of California, 1936.

Colton, Walter. *Three Years in California*. New York: A. S. Barnes & Co., 1850.

Crosby, Elisha Oscar. *Memoirs*. San Marino, Cal.: The Huntington Library, 1945.

Cummins, Ella Sterling. *The Story of the Files*. San Francisco: World's Fair Commission, Columbian Exposition, 1893.

Davis, William Heath. *Seventy-Five Years in California*. San Francisco: John Howell, 1929.

DuFour, Clarence John. *The Russian Withdrawal from California*. San Francisco: California Historical Society *Quarterly*, Volume XII, Number 3, September 1933.

Essig, E. O. *The Russian Settlements at Ross*. San Francisco: California Historical Society *Quarterly*, Volume XII, Number 3, September 1933.

Frémont, John Charles. *Report of the Exploring Expedition to the Rocky Mountains in the Year 1842, and to Oregon and north California in the Years 1843–44*. Washington, D. C.: Gales & Seaton, Printers, 1845.

Gudde, Erwin G. *Sutter's Own Story*. New York: G. P. Putnam's Sons, 1936.

———. (editor) *Bigler's Chronicle of the West*. Berkeley: University of California Press, 1962.

Hall, Carroll D. *A Donner Miscellany*. San Francisco: The Book Club of California, 1947.

———. *Sutter's Fort: State Historical Monument*. (pamphlet) Sacramento: State of California, Division of Beaches and Parks, 1965.

———. *Heraldry of New Helvetia*. San Francisco: The Book Club of California, 1945.

Hammond, George P., editor. *The Larkin Papers.* 10 volumes. Berkeley: University of California Press, 1951–1964.

Hastings, Lansford W. *The Emigrant's Guide to California.* Cincinnati: George Conclin, 1845.

Hoover, Mildred Brooke; Rensch, Hero Eugene; and Rensch, Ethel Grace. *Historic Spots in California.* Stanford, Cal.: Stanford University Press, 1948.

Kantor, J. R. K. *Grimshaw's Narrative.* Sacramento: Sacramento Book Collectors Club, 1964.

Kemble, Edward Cleveland. *A Kemble Reader.* San Francisco: California Historical Society, 1963.

Künzel, Heinrich. *Obercalifornien. Eine geographische Schilderung für den Zweck deutscher Auswanderung und Ansiedlung . . . Mit einer Karte des Rio Sacramento und einem Grundriss des Forts New-Helvetien.* Darmstadt, Germany, 1848.

Landis, Jacob B. *The Life and Work of General John A. Sutter.* (pamphlet) Lancaster, Pa.: Lancaster County Historical Society, 1913.

Letts, J. M. *California Illustrated.* New York: R. T. Young, 1853.

Lienhard, Heinrich, *A Pioneer at Sutter's Fort, 1846–1850.* Los Angeles: The Calafía Society, 1941.

Lititz: 1756–1956. Lititz, Pa., 1956.

Lyman, George D. *John Marsh, Pioneer.* New York: Charles Scribner's Sons, 1930.

Massey, Ernest de. *A Frenchman in the Gold Rush.* San Francisco: California Historical Society, 1927.

McGlashan, Charles F. *History of the Donner Party.* Truckee, Cal.: The Truckee Republican, 1879.

Mofras, Eugène Duflot de. *Travels on the Pacific Coast.* Santa Ana, Cal.: Fine Arts Press, 1937.

Parsons, George Frederick. *The Life and Adventures of James W. Marshall.* Sacramento: James W. Marshall and W. Burke, 1870.

Phillips, Catherine Coffin. *Portsmouth Plaza.* San Francisco: John Henry Nash, 1932.

Pioneers of the Sacramento. San Francisco: The Book Club of California, 1953.

Revere, Joseph Warren. *A Tour of Duty in California.* New York: C. S. Francis & Co., 1849.

Rezanov, Nikolai Petrovich. *The Rezanov Voyage to Nueva California in 1806.* San Francisco: Thomas C. Russell, 1926.

Royce, Josiah. *California From the Conquest in 1846 to the Second Vigilance Committee in San Francisco.* Boston: Houghton Mifflin Co., 1886.

Sacramento Guide Book. Sacramento: *The Sacramento Bee,* 1939.

Sandels, G. M. Waseurtz de. *A Sojourn in California by the "King's Orphan."* San Francisco: The Book Club of California, 1945.

Schoonover, T. J. *The Life and Times of Gen. John A. Sutter.* Sacramento: D. Johnson & Co., Printers, 1895.

Shuck, Oscar T. *Representative Men of the Pacific.* San Francisco: Bacon & Co., 1870.

Soulé, Frank Gihon, John H.; and Nisbet, James. *The Annals of San Francisco.* New York: D. Appleton & Co., 1855.

Stewart, George R. *Ordeal by Hunger.* New York: Henry Holt & Co., 1936.

Sutter, John A. *The Diary of Johann August Sutter.* San Francisco: The Grabhorn Press, 1932.

——. *New Helvetia Diary.* San Francisco: Society of California Pioneers, 1939.

Sutter, John A., Jr. *Statement Regarding Early California Experiences.* Sacramento: Sacramento Book Collectors Club, 1943.

Taylor, Bayard. *El Dorado.* 2 volumes. London: Richard Bentley, 1850.

U. S. Congress, House of Representatives, 31st Congress, 1st Session. Executive Document Number 17: *California and New Mexico.* Washington, D. C.: Government Printing Office, 1850.

Upham, Samuel C. *Notes on a Voyage to California, Together with scenes in El Dorado.* Philadelphia: Published by the author, 1878.

Zollinger, James Peter. *Sutter: The Man and His Empire.* New York: Oxford University Press, 1939.

INDEX

217

222

ABOUT THE AUTHOR

Oscar Lewis was born in California and now lives in San Francisco, his native city. He is the author of more than twenty books, fiction and non-fiction, nearly all of them on Western themes. His first published stories were written while he was still a high school student at Berkeley, California. For the next several years he contributed stories and articles to a variety of young people's magazines, including the *Youth's Companion, St. Nicholas,* the *American Boy* and *Boys' Life.* During World War I he served with the U. S. Army Ambulance Corps in the United States and France, and on his return, resumed magazine writing. His work appeared in *Harper's, Scribner's,* the *Atlantic Monthly,* the *Saturday Review,* the *New Republic,* and many others.

In the mid-1930's he abandoned magazine work and devoted himself exclusively to writing books. Among these are *The Big Four,* the story of the builders of the first transcontinental railroad (which, after serialization in the *Atlantic Monthly,* was published in 1938), *Bonanza Inn,* written in collaboration with Carroll D. Hall, *Silver Kings* (like *The Big Four,* a group biography about the men who controlled the Nevada Comstock Lode), *High Sierra Country, Here Lived The Californians* and two novels *I Remember Christine* and *The Uncertain Journey.* He has also edited and written introductions for numerous books of Western history and literature.

Mr. Lewis lived for some years in the Sacramento Valley and it is because of his long-standing interest in the career of Captain John Sutter that he comes naturally to writing about him and the fort he founded there in 1839 which first opened the valley to settlement.

Typography and Binding Design

by

CARL A. KOENIG